MANAGING YOUR
ANXIETY

Please Read This Important Notice

A personal physician is an essential member of the support
network of anyone who seeks to overcome the problems of
psychological stress, panic or anxiety attacks, or agoraphobia.
This is especially true for those who receive medication for
such conditions as diabetes, high blood pressure, epilepsy, or
a thyroid condition; changes in nutrition and patterns of physical activity can have significant effects on bodily chemistry
and on the body's ability to utilize insulin and other medications. It is also especially important for those over 40 or who
have been inactive for a long time to consult a physician before
starting an exercise program; a medical doctor has the training
needed to detect signs of heart disease that might require a
cautious approach to exercise.

Many people suffering from anxiety-related problems find
that a professional psychotherapist who is able to provide
understanding, moral support, and encouragement is an equally
valuable member of their recovery network. If you feel des-
perate and are unable to cope with stressful events, we urge
you to seek help from a qualified therapist.

What we attempt to do in this book is share general information, to clarify general choices, and to describe an array of
available self-care tools. Because you have a unique personal
history, unique characteristics, and unique life circumstances,
no book can substitute for individual attention from a medical
doctor or professional psychotherapist.

MANAGING YOUR
ANXIETY

Regaining Control When You Feel Stressed, Helpless, and Alone

SELF-CARE PROGRAM INCLUDED

Christopher J. McCullough, Ph.D.
DIRECTOR, SAN FRANCISCO PHOBIA RECOVERY CENTER

and

Robert Woods Mann

JEREMY P. TARCHER, INC.
Los Angeles
Distributed by St. Martin's Press
New York

The authors would like to thank the following authors and publishers for their kind permission to reprint.

Material adapted by permission from Earl Mindell, *Earl Mindell's Vitamin Bible*, New York: Warner Books, 1979.
The "Social Readjustment Rating Scale" is reprinted with permission from the *Journal of Psychosomatic Research*, V. 11, T. H. Holmes and R. H. Rahe, Copyright 1967, Pergamon Press, Ltd.
Excerpt from *Supernutrition* by Richard A. Passwater. Copyright © 1975 by Richard A. Passwater. A Dial Press Book. Reprinted by permission of Doubleday & Company, Inc.
"Guidelines for Relaxed Travel" reprinted by permission of *American Way*, inflight magazine of American Airlines. Copyright 1984 by American Airlines.
Excerpt from *The Search for Existential Identity* by James F. Bugental. Copyright 1975. Published by Jossey-Bass, Inc., San Francisco.
Excerpt from "Calm Down in Six Seconds: How to Handle Stress with Fast Method." Courtesy *VOUGE*. Copyright © 1981 by The Condé Nast Publications, Inc.

In loving memory of my sister Sue.—C.J.M.

To my teachers and my family—and to Doni in gratitude for her kind and honest spirit.—R.W.M.

Library of Congress Cataloging in Publication Data

McCullough, Christopher J.
  Managing your anxiety.

  Bibliography; p. 293
  Includes index.
  1. Anxiety. 2. Stress (Psychology)
3. Helplessness (Psychology) 4. Loneliness.
5. Self-care, Health. I. Mann, Robert Woods.
II. Title.
BF575.A6M39   1985   152.4   85-9783
ISBN 0-87477-352-0

Jeremy P. Tarcher, Inc.
9110 Sunset Blvd.
Los Angeles, CA 90069

Design by Robert Ishi

Manufactured in the United States of America
S 10 9 8 7 6 5 4 3 2 1

First Edition

Contents

Preface

This book is the result of our intellectual friendship and partnership. Each author appreciates strengths of experience, education, and skill in the other that complement his own. We share equally the responsibility for attempting to fit together a new picture of the human experiences of chronic anxiety and self-defeating fear, a picture that treats their natural and spiritual dimensions as a meaningful unity.

We wish to thank Dr. McCullough's clients and to those who have used the self-care program *Outgrowing Agoraphobia* for their kind permission to quote from their letters and questionnaires. As they will recognize, the case histories in this book are generalized for the sake of exposition, although they are intended to portray real life accurately. Many of the quotations given are verbatim, although some have been edited for the sake of clarity and readability—without, we trust, changing their meaning or spirit. All names, locations, and other identifying information have been changed to protect the privacy of those whose experiences are being discussed.

We recognize that we have barely touched on the social origins and implications of anxiety-related problems, a vitally important subject that deserves more attention than it has received to date. However, we hope we have succeeded in our main purpose: showing those who suffer from such problems the path into the trap of anxiety and—at the same time—the path out.

We are not convinced that anxiety is a disease, and we question the wisdom of spending enormous amounts of money to find a pharmacological "cure," while—as Nobel Laureate Linus Pauling laments—very little money is spent to study the sources of optimum health and well-being. This is not to say that the psychoactive medications developed in the last three decades have not been a blessing to many people living through periods of extreme psychological stress. However, the fact that 5 billion Valium and Librium pills were consumed by Americans in one recent year (according to the authors of *The Tranquilizing of America*) is grounds for sober reflection by all American citizens. Something is wrong when a society erects a shield of psychoactive medications to protect people from their own feelings.

We believe that many of those in the health-care field are acutely aware of this problem and are open to re-examining the basic issues related to anxiety disorders in contemporary society. We hope that they will respond to the ideas put forward in this book.

Someone said of our earlier self-care program that what was novel about it was not any of the particular ideas or self-care techniques we described but rather the fact that we drew together ideas from many different fields into a unified program. We feel that this was a fair comment. We have strived not for novelty but for coherence.

We owe a debt to many people who have helped us to understand agoraphobia and related anxiety conditions. We are especially indebted to the published contributions of Marvin R. Cohen, Psy.D., Coordinator of the Centrum Clinic in Oak Park, Illinois; Robert L. Dupont, M.D., Director of the Phobia Program of Washington, Rockville, Maryland; Alan J. Goldstein, Ph.D., of the Department of Psychology, Temple University Medical School, Philadelphia, Pennsylvania; Thomas W. Uhde, M.D., Chief, Unit on Anxiety and Affective Disorders, Department of Health and Human Services, National Institute of Mental Health; Manuel D. Zane, M.D., Director of the Phobia Clinic at the White Plains Hospital Medical Center, White Plains, New York; and Charlotte Marker Zitrin, M.D., Director of the Phobia Clinic, Long Island Jewish-Hillside Medical Center, Glen Oaks, New York.

We also owe an intellectual debt to psychoanalysts Karen Horney and Margaret Mahler for their probing of the roots of neurotic anxiety; to psychotherapist Albert Ellis, a pioneer both of the self-care approach and of the cognitive approach to anxiety; to physician Edmund Jacobson, who scientifically studied habitual muscular contraction in anxious patients in the 1920's and developed the progressive-relaxation technique; to psychiatrist Ferris N. Pitts, Jr., for his pioneering work on the biochemistry of anxiety; to Joseph P. Wolpe, whose name is linked to virtually every therapeutic technique based on the principles of modern behaviorism; and, finally, to physician Claire Weekes, who listened carefully to her agoraphobic patients and has long held that they should be fully informed about the nature of their experiences.

Christopher J. McCullough thanks:

Peter Koestenbaum, my mentor, whose teaching and kind support made this book possible; Rollo May, whose authentic being and penetrating insights inspire and challenge me; Arthur B. Hardy, from whom I first learned about people with phobias; the Everett A. Gladman Memorial Hospital for having the courage to establish a unique in-patient program for the treatment of agoraphobia that is based on the ideas in this book; Bonnie Bell, for helping to sustain my energy during this difficult past year; Martha Culley-Spencer for being around with her "you can do it" view of life; my patients, who have challenged me over the years to understand their world so that I could help them learn to manage their anxiety; my parents who, unlike so many, gave room for me to be me.

Robert Woods Mann also thanks:

Louis Bloch, Kellogg Smith, and John S. Gildersleeve—skilled editors who taught me that clear writing is clear thinking; N. H. Pronko, who opened my eyes to the plasticity of human behavior and who will recognize his influence on this book; Howard Rachlin, for his friendship and for showing me the rich therapeutic potential of modern behaviorism;

Linus Pauling and V. G. Longo, who allowed me to glimpse
the spirit of science in the service of humanity; Rev. Shunryu
Suzuki, Rev. Hosokawa, and Rev. Ekai Korematsu, of the San
Francisco Soto Zen Mission, for kindly pointing to the unity
of body, breath, and mind; Mary Evelyn Woods Mann for
her unlimited kindness and generosity; my friends Joan, Al-
vin, Betty, Grace, Theresa, Tom, and Lloyd for their interest
and encouragement; my friend Robert Ishikawa, a gifted art-
ist, for the typographic design in this book; Myron the cat
for keeping me company during many late-night writing
sessions.

Both authors thank Jeremy P. Tarcher and the members
of his staff, including our editor Janice Gallagher, production
manager Derek Gallagher, copy editor Sheryl Strauss, com-
positor Publisher's Typography, and proofreader Vera
Trapnell.

To the Reader

This book has been written for those whose lives are limited by psychological stress, chronic worry, anxiety attacks, self-defeating fears, or agoraphobia—overwhelming fear associated with separation from familiar surroundings or people. It is an invitation to pause and step back from the experiences of anxiety and fear in order to see them whole.

If you have ever experienced episodes of acute anxiety or sudden, unexplained panic, the chances are that you have already made a number of unsuccessful attempts to find help in dealing with your problem. Here are some typical experiences:

> You have consulted your physician or even visited a hospital emergency room.
>
> You have been told that you are having an anxiety attack of some sort and that you shouldn't worry about it.
>
> You have been given a tranquilizer to calm you down.
>
> You have been referred to a psychiatrist, who utilized drug treatment in combination with psychotherapy.
>
> If drugs and psychotherapy failed to produce a full and satisfactory recovery, you or your physician may have requested further medical tests in the hope of finding a medical cause for your problem.
>
> Following medical testing, you were probably disappointed because, as many people put it, "They couldn't find anything wrong with me."
>
> You picked up a magazine or newspaper or turned on a radio or television set and came across a discussion of "panic attacks," "phobias," or "agoraphobia." If your

own symptoms matched those discussed, you probably
had a strong feeling, "This may be it!" or "That's what
I've got!"

You turned for help to someone specializing in treating these
disorders. Their treatment most likely included behavior
therapy (which attempts to directly modify fearful responses) and may have included group therapy and drug
therapy.

While you attribute some degree of relief to drug therapy,
psychotherapy, or behavior therapy, you may not have
achieved a sense of complete recovery from the problem
("I still don't feel like myself"). Something is missing.
You still want to get to the bottom of it.

OUR OBJECTIVES

Our main objective is to systematically dispel the mystery
that surrounds anxiety attacks, illogical fears, and their treatment. We intend to explain why various one-dimensional
approaches to treatment are not entirely satisfactory and often
do not succeed in producing complete and lasting recovery
from anxiety-related conditions. We intend to show what is
missing from these approaches. Above all, we intend to fit
what is known about chronic anxiety and illogical fear into
a meaningful whole that will be useful to those who suffer
from these conditions as well as to those who seek to help
alleviate this suffering in others.

If we imagine the pain, the suffering, and the energy lost
from lives affected by chronic anxiety, we can begin to see
an enormous drain on human happiness, creativity, and pro-
ductivity. We think of a woman from Georgia who said, after
years of suffering, "I feel like my whole life has passed me
by." Like her, millions of Americans have grown up—and
are growing up—believing that life is something that happens
to them, not something they themselves create through their
own choices and decisions.

We feel especially close to readers who suffer from severe agoraphobia and are housebound or who have extreme difficulty in traveling any distance to a treatment center. It was for them that in 1982 we originally developed the home-study self-care program *Outgrowing Agoraphobia,* on which *Managing Your Anxiety* is based. At that point, self-care did not seem to be an ideal approach to severe agoraphobia but simply the only possible approach for those unable to reach (or be reached by) appropriate treatment.

Today, more than 400 people have used the program, and most of them report significant improvement in their ability to go places without suffering panic attacks and a significant decrease in the time they spend worrying.

Letters and telephone calls from those who found in the program a catalyst for personal growth and change—and from members of their families—convinced us that the very idea of self-care and the act of taking responsibility for one's own recovery help to activate self-healing processes and have a positive effect on the life of the chronically anxious person.

The successful users of the program also helped us to see, as one put it, that "this program would be good for anyone." If anxiety were a great tree that invites us to climb its branches, common self-defeating fears like the fear of making telephone calls, of speaking to answering machines, of flying, or of speaking before groups of people would be down among its lower branches; simple phobias, chronic worry, and other anxiety-related problems would be among the middle branches; and agoraphobia would be up among its higher branches. We decided that if our program can help people retrace their steps and climb down from the higher branches, it should work as well to help them climb out of the lower ones. We also feel that the developmental and philosophical model we have developed to explain how people get into the trap of agoraphobia, and our interpretation of the nature of psychological stress, have broad relevance to other anxiety disorders, such as chronic worry, panic attacks, and the self-defeating fears that diminish lives.

Anxious people lack confidence in their ability to make choices, to be in charge of their lives, and to tell the world who they are. They habitually magnify and exaggerate the normal anxiety associated with uncertainty into chronic worry and illogical fear.

We intend to show that the only real antidote to anxiety is a strong sense of one's own human identity and human freedom. If one has not entirely outgrown helplessness and dependency in childhood, then one faces the task of outgrowing them in adulthood.

The central theme of this book—and of the Self-Care Program it includes—is that *someone who learns to be genuinely self-caring (and competent in self-care) cannot be a chronically anxious or fearful person.* Let us briefly sketch out the topics to be covered in Part 1 of this book and in Part 2, the Self-Care Program.

In Chapter 1, "What's Happening to Me?" we will look at the three dimensions of anxiety—physical, psychological, and cognitive—as well as at various forms anxiety can take, including panic attacks, phobias, chronic worry, and agoraphobia.

In Chapter 2, Growing Up Anxious, we will see how the illusions of our own helplessness and incompleteness can take root in emotional disruption in childhood and can remain continually present in our thinking and behavior as self-defeating beliefs and attitudes.

In Chapter 3, Freedom and Responsibility, we will examine our freedom to gain self-knowledge through self-honesty. We will consider the consequences of finding ourselves in our freedom rather than seeking our identity in the admiration and approval of other people.

In Chapter 4, Self-Expression, we will look at the habitual ways we communicate with others on the basis of our own assumed helplessness and incompleteness. We will see how assertiveness fits in as one of the most essential skills in overcoming phobias and anxiety.

Chapter 5, The Roots of the Self-Care Program, and Chapter 6, Using the Self-Care Program, explain the various self-training activities presented in the Self-Care Program. The program, outlined in detail in the table of contents, includes setting up a recovery network; keeping a daily journal; learning to cope with emotional distress; caring for your body's needs; recognizing your own self-diminishing behaviors, feelings, attitudes, beliefs, and assumptions; systematic desensitization training; assertiveness training; cultivating inner freedom through relaxation and meditation; and creating a realistic and positive self-image.

Please read this book in a truly self-caring manner. There is no need to force yourself to read any material you are not yet comfortable reading. Nor is there any need to force yourself to do anything you are not yet ready to do. Force and coercion contribute to anxiety. Gentle, persistent, self-caring effort produces recovery from anxiety-related problems.

Part 1

1

"What's Happening to Me?"

"I thought I was dying."
"I felt unreal."
"I felt doomed."
"I felt as though I were losing my mind."
"I was afraid of going out of control."
"I thought I was having a heart attack when I woke up at 3 A.M."

Those who are attempting to describe the intense emotional reactions that sometimes characterize a sudden, mysterious episode of acute anxiety often make such extreme statements.

Anxiety attacks are manifestations of psychological stress and thus are like warning signals that indicate a need to reduce both the external and internal sources of this stress. Let us look briefly at the way this experience is affecting the lives of six contemporary Americans, so that we may understand it better.

GEORGE K., ENTREPRENEUR

George K. is a 39-year-old businessman who is an electrical engineer by education. George spent most of his working life employed by a giant corporation that manufactures business machines. Seven months ago, he left his job in New England to start a business of his own in Colorado. He has contracted with two programmers he has known for some years to help him develop an integrated business software program that will run on personal computers. The program is his brain-child. George is convinced that he and the programmers are well on their way to producing a sophisticated, elegantly simple, and highly useful system. However, the project is taking longer to complete than he expected, and he recently mortgaged his house in Connecticut to obtain more money to put into his business. His wife was not enthusiastic about George's quitting his job in the first place, and now she is unable to conceal her skepticism about his new venture and her fears concerning their financial future.

On two occasions recently, George has awakened in a cold sweat at 3:00 or 4:00 A.M., feeling as though the bottom had dropped out of his world. He remembers having similar feelings just before he got married at the age of 21. He is ashamed of the feelings and troubled about what they may mean.

FRANK K., SALES REPRESENTATIVE

Frank K., a successful commercial real estate salesman in Portland, Oregon, is on his way to work, after an altercation with his wife concerning the family budget. Driving on a bridge across the Willamette River, Frank is caught in a traffic jam. His impatience turns to mild anxiety about being late for work. Suddenly, Frank's heart starts to race, his feet turn cold, a chill runs across his back. "What is happening to me?" he wonders. He fights a panicky urge to jump out of his car and start running. There is only one explanation he can think of—he must be on the verge of madness!

Later, arriving at work, he smiles wanly at the receptionist and wonders whether she can see the abject fear that must show in his eyes. He begins to worry about his 10:00 A.M. appointment with an important prospective customer. The thought arises: "What if it happens again—while I'm in there with the prospect?"

BETTY D., HOMEMAKER

Betty D., a 40-year-old homemaker who lives in Atlanta, Georgia, enters a supermarket at opening time. She deliberately arrives at an early hour, wishing to avoid the crowd of shoppers she had encountered on a recent afternoon.

Betty feels reasonably calm as she takes a shopping cart and starts toward the produce section. She is relieved that the strange feelings she experienced on her last visit to the store are not present. She's glad, too, that she hadn't told her husband, Stan, about them. He would have thought she was crazy!

Down at the end of the aisle, the produce manager calls out to someone before he disappears into the storeroom. Betty is all alone in the aisle. Suddenly, mysteriously, the myriad rows of canned goods look unreal to her. She gasps, her knees feel weak, her hands turn warm and moist, and the muscles of her back and neck begin to tremble as though something were pulling her world apart. "It's happening again!"

The most striking thing about these feelings is their intensity. They simply don't match up with anything in the supermarket environment—the bright fluorescent lights or the dazzling displays of merchandise. Betty begins to wonder whether she is losing her mind.

Abandoning her shopping cart, she walks toward the entrance, trying with all her might to conceal the terror that clutches her heart. She decides to go straight to the emergency room at a nearby hospital. After what seems like a long wait, an intern tells her she is just suffering from "nerves."

PAT M., PROGRAMMER

Pat M. is a 23-year-old programmer who works for a software publisher in Boston, Massachusetts. Pat enjoys her work and the recognition she receives for the long hours she spends translating procedures into a computer-readable code. She finds the job challenging and fascinating. While she is working, she generally feels safe and secure, except when she has "caffeine nerves" from the six to eight cups of coffee she drinks each day.

Away from her computer terminal, life is a different story. She has experienced a series of confidence-shattering emotional earthquakes over the past three months, starting with a lunchtime anxiety attack. One day in a restaurant, her own hands looked unreal to her, her heart began to pound, and she felt overwhelmed by fear. Now, she is filled with apprehension when she goes out for lunch.

A former mathematics major in college, Pat scorns psychology and psychotherapy. She is determined to overcome her problem on her own.

Her instinct to take responsibility for her problem is healthy; however, her problem is getting worse, not better. She does not understand why.

RON C., SHERIFF'S DEPUTY

Ron C. is a 30-year-old sheriff's deputy in a western state. Ron prides himself on being a conscientious and professional deputy. It's a difficult job in many ways, but it is the only one Ron has ever wanted.

While he is in uniform, Ron has few problems, but off duty. he finds himself increasingly wondering when and where his next anxiety attack will occur; he has experienced five in the last three weeks.

A divorced father of two children, Ron also finds himself increasingly visiting his parents' home in his off-duty hours. He feels safe there. In fact, he has gone there every time he has experienced the mysterious, overwhelming surge of fear. He has never told his parents about his problem.

Ron has begun to keep a diary to see if that would help him discover any pattern in the attacks. The diary vividly describes his painful uncertainty and suffering. One day he wrote:

> Now I'm worried about the superstitious things I am doing. I rechecked the stove this morning 3 *times* to make sure everything was off before I left home.
>
> I have had two "spells" of anxiety this week. In between the "spells," especially when I am off duty, I often find myself dreading the next one. I feel nervous, restless, and mentally confused at these times. Thoughts fire off in my mind faster than I can sort them out.
>
> I take a drink now and then (off duty) to settle my nerves, but I definitely don't want to become dependent on alcohol.

MARILYN M.

Marilyn M. is a 50-year-old widow who lives in a small downtown apartment. For most of the day, she sits in the gloom of her apartment watching television. After her husband died two decades ago, panic attacks gradually drove her to take refuge there. She sought help unsuccessfully from three different doctors. Relying on assistance from her sister and a neighbor, she has not set foot outside her front door for the past 18 years. She cannot remember the last time she had a panic attack or what they felt like. She has made avoiding them a way of life.

THE NATURE OF ANXIETY

Here we have six different people, five of whom are wondering "what is happening to me?" and one who long ago retreated from the world to escape this question.

To understand what is happening (or happened long ago) in their lives, we need to look at the nature of anxiety and to explore its three dimensions: (1) the physical, (2) the psychological, and (3) the cognitive, or philosophical.

Once we are familiar with these dimensions of anxiety, we will be able to understand how Marilyn M. became a housebound victim of agoraphobia. Understanding that, it will be relatively easy to understand various other anxiety symptoms, such as inappropriate phobic (fearful) reactions to situations, places, and things; other types of self-defeating fears; anxiety or panic attacks; and chronic worry.

We'll begin by taking a look at the general nature of anxiety.

"Anxiety" refers to that troubled state in which we find ourselves looking forward to an uncertain event with apprehension or fear. Anxiety can be sudden and acute, as when we hear a skid nearby and wait for the sound of a crash, or when our child doesn't get off a school bus as expected. Anxiety can also be chronic; for instance, when we worry daily about whether our new boss will treat us with respect or how much longer we will be able to keep our job.

The spectrum of anxious feelings and emotions ranges from uneasiness through agitation, dread, brooding fear, and panicky feelings, to outright terror and panic. The stronger emotions in this spectrum actually represent a temporary disruption of behavior that makes it hard for us to think clearly, to be aware of what is happening, and to find an appropriate response.

This disrupted or disorganized behavior occurs in at least three circumstances: when we perceive ourselves to be under attack or threatened and helpless to defend ourselves; when we perceive ourselves to be trapped and helpless to escape; and when we perceive incompatible choices that we are help-less to choose between. From the time of Ivan Pavlov on, experimenters have created emotional disruption in dogs and cats by systematically putting them into such situations. One of the effects of such coercive treatment is that the animals tend to become agitated, forgetful, and unable to pay close attention to their surroundings.

In order to understand anxiety and why it can take var-ious forms, we must first of all give up the idea that it is something that "happens to us." _Anxiety is the way we have learned, based on our past experiences, to respond to situa-tions in which we perceive ourselves to be helpless_. It is some-thing we do. Even though we do not wish to be anxious and do not understand why we are anxious, the exaggerated anx-ious feelings and emotions we feel are almost always the result of choices we have made in the past. In Chapter 2, Growing Up Anxious, we will look at the crucial role played in anxiety conditions by the idea of our own helplessness.

Before we do that, we need to consider the three dimen-sions in which anxiety operates.

THE PHYSICAL DIMENSION

Physiological Arousal

People who say that "anxiety is all in your head" simply are not very observant. Anyone who has experienced severe anx-iety knows it can involve virtually the entire body. Here are just a few of the potential physical sensations that can signify acute anxiety in a given person at a given time:

Prickling or tingling sensations of the skin.

A jumping or jerking movement.

A chill on the surface of the skin.

Shortness of breath.

Dizziness, vertigo, or unsteadiness.

Cold feet or hands.

Shivering, trembling, or shaking.

Chest pain or discomfort.

Choking or smothering sensations.

Sweating.

Stomach discomfort or diarrhea.

Weakness in the legs.

In his book *The Psychology of Fear and Stress,* psychologist Jeffrey Gray explains the "emergency reaction," which was first fully described by physiologist Walter B. Cannon: "The emergency reaction, as described by Cannon, is due to the sympathetic nervous system acting in conjunction with the hormones secreted by the adrenal medulla (known as 'adrenaline' and 'noradrenaline' in England, but as 'epinephrine' and 'norepinephrine' in America)."

According to Gray, Cannon believed that the emergency reaction serves a vital role in protecting us from harm:

> Its function is to mobilize the body's resources for swift action—"fight or flight"—that may be needed. There is an increase in the rate and strength of the heart beat, allowing oxygen to be pumped round more rapidly; contraction of the spleen, releasing stored red blood cells to carry this oxygen; release of stored sugar from the liver for the use of the muscles; redistribution of the blood supply from the skin and viscera to the muscles and brain; deepening of respiration and dilation of the bronchi, to take in more oxygen; dilation of the pupils, perhaps to improve visual efficiency; an increase in the blood's ability

to seal wounds by coagulating; and a rise in the supply of the special blood cells known as "lymphocytes," whose function is to help repair damage to the tissues. All this takes place in a matter of seconds or minutes.

Thus we can see that cold feet, for example, are not a fatal symptom but simply a natural consequence of the movement of blood away from the skin and visceral organs to the brain and muscles where it may be needed to help us meet the "emergency" that we confront.

Gray notes that the emergency reaction is often out of synchrony with the conditions of modern life: "Under modern conditions, it is often too late and in any case unnecessary, as the danger probably calls for neither fight nor flight. You have almost certainly experienced this if you have narrowly missed an accident while driving and your heart starts pounding several seconds after you have steered to safety."

Even making the assumption that some of us, like certain strains of laboratory-bred animals, may be genetically somewhat more "reactive" than others, there is no reason to believe that we are destined at birth to live habitually at the upper end of the anxiety spectrum while others are not at all at risk. We all need to cope with emergency reactions that are often inappropriate for "modern conditions" of life. Nor is there any reason to believe that higher-than-average reactivity would necessarily be a bad or maladaptive trait to have; it may marginally increase our ability to respond to emergencies. There is nothing wrong with emergency reactions as such; the problem lies in inappropriate emergency reactions that lead to transient disruptions in our behavior.

One more point about acute anxiety: it cannot last indefinitely. Our body cannot sustain the emergency reaction for a very long time, and acute anxiety seldom lasts much longer than a few minutes. Our body will always insist, sooner or later, on returning to a more relaxed and balanced condition. As we shall see in the Self-Care Program, there are many things we can learn to do to help this process along as well as to minimize the number of inappropriate emergency reactions we experience.

The Biochemistry of Anxiety

Some medical researchers seek to find the basis of anxiety attacks in their study of biology and biochemistry. They are looking for evidence that a genetic trait or abnormality directly causes anxiety attacks.

Much of the discussion of the possible existence of a genetic problem centers on the role of unusually high blood-lactate levels in triggering physical feelings like shakiness, dizziness, and numbness and tingling of the skin.

Lactate is a normal byproduct of the conversion of the sugar glycogen to energy by muscle cells. The more work our muscles do, the more lactate they will discharge into the bloodstream. A very large amount of lactate in the blood is thought to increase nervous reactivity by binding with calcium molecules and thus interfering with the normal functioning of calcium in the transmission of nerve impulses from nerve fiber to nerve fiber in the central nervous system.

Dr. Ferris N. Pitts, Jr., found that injections of extra lactate into the bloodstream produced paresthesia, "a numbness and tingling of the skin that is usually caused by a low level of calcium in the tissues," in all 24 subjects of a study he described in 1969 in an article in *Scientific American* entitled "The Biochemistry of Anxiety." In addition, the injections produced reports of a wide array of feelings (including tremor, shakiness, dizziness, palpitation, cold, nervousness, nervous chill, and weakness) from the 14 anxiety patients and, to a lesser degree, from the 10 "normal" controls in the study. During the injection of the lactate, which took 20 minutes, 13 of the anxiety patients and 2 of the control subjects had "typical acute anxiety attacks." When calcium was added to the lactate solution, fewer symptoms were reported and "there was no significant difference in the extent to which each symptom was reported by the two groups."

Pitts and his colleague James N. McClure, Jr., concluded that "a high concentration of lactate ion can produce some anxiety symptoms in almost anyone, that it regularly produces anxiety attacks in patients but not in controls, and that calcium ion largely prevents the symptoms in both patients and controls."

Pitts observed no difference between the anxiety patients and the control subjects in their ability to clear lactate from the blood: "In all our subjects the excess lactate from the infusions was removed normally by the liver in 60 to 90 minutes."

In a recent book called *The Anxiety Disease,* psychiatrist David V. Sheehan contends that anxiety disorders stem from "a biological and probably a biochemical disorder." To support the idea that there is a possible "genetic weakness" in anxious people, Sheehan cites a 1966 study by Pitts, which he describes as follows:

> In 1966 . . . Pitts found that giving an intravenous infusion of sodium lactate to victims of this disease brought on spells of panic just like their original symptoms. It is possible to turn the condition on simply by injecting this substance, which is produced in everyone's body in response to exercise. If you give sodium lactate to normal individuals, nothing happens; with anxiety disease victims, turning off the lactate infusions stops the symptoms.

The conclusion Sheehan draws from this 1966 study does not seem to accord with that offered by Pitts himself in the 1969 article, in which he said that something *does* happen when you give sodium lactate to normal individuals. All of his subjects experienced numbness and tingling of the skin, and many of them experienced other "anxiety symptoms."

Pitts and McClure's findings are consistent with a differ-

ent interpretation: People who suffer anxiety attacks are simply normal people under prolonged stress. Their bodies are
overproducing adrenaline (epinephrine) and, as a consequence, the muscles in their bodies continuously contract.
The tendency of anxious people to keep their muscles contracted (which was scientifically documented in 1929 by Dr.
Edmund Jacobson, the creator of the progressive-relaxation
technique) produces the excess lactate that is believed to deplete the amount of calcium available at nerve synapses, leading to overreactivity—especially when additional lactate is
injected into the bloodstream.

This view is bolstered somewhat by a finding reported by
cardiologist Herbert Benson in the *Relaxation Response:*

> If increased lactate is instrumental in producing regular at-
> tacks of anxiety, the finding of low levels of lactate in meditators
> is consistent with their reports of significantly more relaxed,
> less anxious feelings. Blood-lactate levels fall rapidly within the
> first ten minutes of meditation, and remain at extremely low
> levels during meditation. Though the reason for decreased lac-
> tate is uncertain, it is consistent with decreased activity of the
> sympathetic nervous system.

There may be another biochemical link between psychological stress and the sudden, unexplained experience of acute
anxiety. Anxious people typically tend to hold their breath
for a few seconds at a time or to overbreathe (hyperventilate)
at least slightly when they are distressed and, particularly,
when they are startled. These habits disrupt the natural rhythm
of breathing and, if strong enough, play havoc with the body's
ability to maintain optimum levels of oxygen and carbon
dioxide in the blood. The resulting series of chemical changes
in the brain and body may trigger the heightened feelings of
physiological distress that constitute anxiety symptoms.

The balanced, relaxed posture and rhythmical abdominal
breathing that characterize meditation (1) may reduce the
blood-lactate level by reducing overall muscular tension, and

(2) may help maintain optimum levels of oxygen and carbon dioxide in the blood by eliminating jerky, arrhythmical breathing.

THE PSYCHOLOGICAL DIMENSION

Psychological Stress

Hans Selye, the great pathfinder in the field of physiological stress, has described "the general adaptation syndrome," which includes not only the immediate emergency reaction but also the long-term strategies of the body to resist prolonged adverse or noxious conditions. Jeffrey Gray explains this strategy:

> Under prolonged stress . . . there is a massive shutdown of those bodily activities which are directed towards growth, reproduction, and even resistance to existing infection, in favor of mechanisms which promote readiness for immediate high-energy action. And this pattern—like the pattern observed in the immediate emergency reaction—is seen no matter what kind of stress is applied, whether it be physiological (surgery, injection of foreign protein, anaesthesia), environmental (extreme cold) or psychological (a threatening predator, intense competition among members of the same species, prolonged conflict, learning how to avoid an electric shock).

Psychological stressors not only produce the bodily feelings called "anxiety symptoms" but can also, if they are severe or prolonged enough, affect our physical health. According to Kenneth Pelletier, author of *Mind as Healer, Mind as Slayer,* medical textbooks estimate that psychological stress plays a role in as much as 50 to 80 percent of recorded illnesses.

As we shall see, the current generally accepted explanation of physiological stress of psychological origin (or "psychological stress") is confusing and is thus of little practical use to us in attempting to liberate ourselves from severe and pervasive anxiety. We shall offer a simpler interpretation of psychological stress, one that ties it directly to anxiety. First, however, let us consider stress as it is generally viewed today. We will start with the widely published Holmes-Rahe "social readjustment scale" shown in abridged form in Table 1–1.

Here is how Dr. Benson has explained the way the scale is conventionally interpreted: "Drs. Thomas H. Holmes and Richard H. Rahe, psychiatrists at the University of Washington Medical School, have devised a scale of stressful events. . . . According to the doctors, change whether for good or bad causes stress to a human being, leaving him more susceptible to disease."

Based on this reasoning, some theorists go so far as to classify such events as those listed on the Holmes-Rahe scale as "good" stressors (eu-stressors) or "bad" stressors. However, if virtually *every* significant event in our life is either a good or bad stressor, it is difficult to see how the concept of psychological stress adds anything to our understanding of the cause of human suffering. It does not tell us why some people suffer from stress-related diseases and disorders—like anxiety attacks—and others do not. If *everything*—whether enjoyable or painful—is a stressor, then perhaps some people simply thrive on stress and others do not. This implies that there is something fundamentally wrong with people who suffer from such stress-related problems as anxiety.

But there is no evidence for this assumption. Those who suffer may simply be people who have learned to perceive particular types of changes to be threatening.

Stress, as Selye pointed out, occurs *within* us. And it results from an interaction between us and our environment. The character of this interaction is principally determined not by some intrinsic quality in an event like marriage, retirement, pregnancy, or outstanding personal achievement, nor by how reactive we are to our environment in general, but rather by the *meaning* that we choose to place on the particular event.

Table 1–1
The Holmes-Rahe Social Readjustment Scale (Abridged)

Events	*Scale of Impact*
Death of spouse	100
Divorce	73
. . .	. . .
Marriage	50
Fired at work	47
Marital reconciliation	45
Retirement	45
Change in health of family member	44
Pregnancy	40
Sex difficulties	39
Gain of new family member	39
. . .	. . .
Change to different line of work	36
. . .	. . .
Change in responsibilities at work	29
Son or daughter leaving home	29
Trouble with in-laws	29
Outstanding personal achievement	28
Wife begins or stops work	26
Begin or end school	26
. . .	. . .
Change in work hours or conditions	20
Change in residence	20
. . .	. . .
Vacation	13
Christmas	12
Minor violations of the law	11

Source: Holmes, T. H., and Rahe, R. H. "The Social Readjustment Rating Scale." *Journal of Psychosomatic Research 11* (1967) :213.

If we marry, retire, have a child, or succeed in some pursuit wholeheartedly and without misgivings, none of these events will threaten us. On the other hand, as psychoanalyst Karen Horney explained some years ago, at a deeper level, people may feel themselves to be put at risk by such apparently unambiguously happy events as marriage. If you think about it, you can see that marriage may be highly threatening to an unprepared and ambivalent bride or groom.

For years, people pointed to air traffic controllers as an example of an occupational specialty subject to more than its share of stress-related disorders like chronic anxiety and alcoholism. The generally accepted reason for this stress was the heavy responsibility for the safety of human lives borne by the controllers. This reasoning overlooked the fact that commercial airline pilots, with a high rate of job satisfaction and a low rate of stress disorders, are responsible for the safety of the very same lives. More recent studies have shown the source of the controllers' stress to be strained labor-management relations and strained relations with the Federal Aviation Administration (FAA). Over the years, the controllers felt that their recommendations regarding safety measures (especially backup computer systems) were not given due consideration by their employers or the FAA. Naturally, feeling that their recommendations on the important issue of safety had not been listened to, the controllers developed mixed feelings about their jobs. It is probable that those who suffered from anxiety and other stress-related problems were among the most capable and conscientious controllers—and it is extremely doubtful that there was something "fundamentally wrong" with them.

Fortunately, since the mass firing of controllers three years ago, during a bitter strike, stress-reducing measures have been implemented to allow controllers to have greater input into air safety policies.

Where does psychological stress come from, then, if it does not stem from a genetic disorder or from an inability to handle responsibility or to cope with significant changes?

Psychological stress occurs in any situation in which *we perceive ourselves to be in danger of losing our freedom and moving toward helplessness.* In other words, it is nothing more nor less than the physiological manifestation of anxiety. This is why any of the experiences on the Holmes-Rahe scale can be highly stressful to particular individuals at particular times, no matter how "good" they look to an outsider; it is also why any of them can cause little stress or anxiety to a particular individual at a particular time, no matter how "bad" they look to the outsider.

The freedom to interpret events and to assign meanings to experience makes all the difference in whether we experience anxiety and stress in a given set of circumstances. It is when we rightly or wrongly perceive ourselves to be threatened, and then *misinterpret* our own physical reactions to the perceived threat as in themselves threatening, that we experience the disrupted emergency reactions we call anxiety or panic attacks.

The Subjective Threshold of Danger

On a bright, sunny day, when brown-eyed people are showing no signs of discomfort, we may notice a fair-skinned, red-haired baby in her stroller covering her green eyes with her tiny hands to block the intolerable glare of the sun. Like our reflexive defenses against pain—such as shielding our eyes from bright light—our reflexive defenses against danger are triggered when the intensity of stimulation rises above a subjective perceptual threshold; it is this mechanism within us that signals "danger!" when we smell smoke or notice a reckless driver approaching.

Like other psychological thresholds, this danger threshold varies from person to person. The threshold is affected by fatigue, malnutrition, and other bodily states, as well as by our emotional state. When we believe that we live in a hostile environment, our danger threshold is lowered and we scan the world for threats and enemies. When we have friends, feel loved, and find satisfaction in our work, our danger threshold rises and we are less likely to perceive insults and injuries in our daily experiences.

To a great extent, the danger threshold is influenced by past experience. Fifteen to 20 years after they survived naval battles in the Second World War, U.S. Navy veterans still showed a significantly strong galvanic skin response (an indication of physiological arousal) to the Navy "Battle Stations" signal. Their response was compared to that of Army veterans of the same war by Allan E. Edwards and Loren E. Acker in a study published in the journal *Psychosomatic Medicine.* In the parlance of experimental psychology, Navy combat veterans were more or less permanently "sensitized" to the Battle Stations signal.

Like the Navy veterans, those who suffer from phobic reactions to single stimuli—dogs, insects, or tall buildings, for example—were sensitized by specific past experiences. In relation to other forms of chronic or acute anxiety, as we shall see in the next chapter, sensitization appears to be more generalized: the more that we felt endangered by abandonment or withdrawal of love in early childhood, the greater the probability that our danger threshold will tend to be maintained at a low, ever-vigilant setting for years to come. We will go through life finding more than our share of threatening situations unless (1) we have the good fortune to be continuously protected from danger by friendship, love, or rewarding work, or (2) our danger threshold is reset through intensive retraining and significant new experiences. It is the second alternative that we will address in the Self-Care Program.

Sensitization

In the field of psychology, "sensitization" means becoming reactive to an object or situation through the action of conditioned learning. It is the process that lowers our danger threshold in relation to specific stimuli in the presence of which we have felt threatened and unable to defend ourselves.

Sensitization is a process we all experience. We can be grateful that as children we were sensitized to hot stoves, traffic in the streets, and other dangerous "conditioned stimuli." A similar process occurs in relation to such pleasant stimuli as the aroma of bread baking. The next time you walk past a deliciously fragrant bakery, you will probably find your mouth watering. You will be responding to a *conditioned stimulus* (the mouth-watering odor of fresh-baked bread) to which you are sensitized. By the way, if you are salivating right now (as we are), you have just proved that a *thought*— as well as an object or a situation—can serve as a conditioned stimulus.

This is very important to those who suffer from severe anxiety, because it is often thoughts that trigger the disrupted emergency reactions associated with acute anxiety.

Furthermore, not only can we become sensitized to thoughts but also to the bodily feelings produced by emergency reactions. It is obvious that the inner conflict produced by such maladaptive sensitization can create emotional disruption and can in itself become an internal source of ongoing psychological stress. This process becomes especially clear in agoraphobia, in which the fear of having an anxiety attack in public becomes the main subject for ongoing and sometimes obsessive worry.

Fortunately, sensitization is a reversible process, as the experimental study of animal behavior has shown. What this means to us humans is that any particular phobic reaction or self-defeating fear in our repertoire of behaviors *can be unlearned.*

The reverse of sensitization is called "extinction." Extinction, like sensitization, can occur in everyday life. This explains how phobic reactions sometimes wane over a period of time as people simply get used to previously feared stimuli.

People who wish to free themselves from any kind of self-defeating fear—whether from a fear of leaving home or from such relatively minor fears as that of speaking to an answering machine—should be grateful to Joseph Wolpe, A.A. Lazarus, and the other behavioral scientists who pioneered the technique of systematic desensitization, which we will explain in step-by-step detail in the Self-Care Program.

Behaviorists quite rightly insist that organisms (including humans) are always doing *something,* even when they look as though they are doing nothing. For this reason, the goal of systematic desensitization is not simply to eliminate an undesirable behavior, it is to replace the undesirable behavior with another, incompatible behavior. Since physical relaxation (and smooth abdominal breathing) is incompatible with physiological arousal, systematic desensitization gradually substitutes relaxation for physiological arousal in the presence of a feared stimulus.

The incompatibility of relaxation and arousal means that anything that helps us improve our ability to relax physically can be helpful in eliminating unwanted physiological arousal from our lives.

In view of what we know about desensitization, it is clear that anyone using a myorelaxant (muscle-relaxing) medication like Valium to control anxiety would be well advised, in the long run, to use the opportunity to learn how it feels to relax rather than to passively rely on the medication to banish anxiety. A pill's effects are temporary; learning is more permanent.

THE COGNITIVE, OR PHILOSOPHICAL, DIMENSION

There is a tantalizing similarity between descriptions of the "out of the blue" fear that affects the lives of millions of stress-ridden modern people and descriptions of *satori,* the sudden experience of enlightenment associated with the Rinzai school of Zen Buddhism. It almost seems as though the former is a kind of mirror image of the latter, seen through the reversing and distorting lenses of helplessness. Both experiences have been described as a "loss of self," though one carries with it a deeper and more secure sense of self and the other the terror of being isolated and helpless in a hostile environment.

Whereas enlightenment is rooted in wholehearted compassion for oneself and others, acute anxiety is what happens when people give up too much of themselves for the sake of ingratiating themselves to others. This will be explained in the next chapter, Growing Up Anxious.

The loss of self in meditation suggests a craftsman losing (finding) himself in his work, a musician losing (finding) herself in her music, or a traveler losing (finding) himself in a beautiful sunset. This loss of self implies a harmonious unity of personal and universal existence. By contrast, an anxiety attack involves the weakening of the self under stress and a regression to an early stage of development and to the feelings of a helpless and dependent being. No wonder that the person living through such an episode of emotional upheaval feels threatened and fearful for a few moments that seem to pass all too slowly.

Descriptions of an anxiety attack make it abundantly clear that it is perceived as *life-threatening* and that it elicits physiologically based reactions that are appropriate to a life-threatening situation in which the source of danger is unknown: *intense fear, dread, terror, horror, a sense of doom.* Feelings of separation and isolation may be present, linking this experience to the normal separation-anxiety reaction of the very young child.

Although it may seem hard to accept at first, the experience of out-of-the-blue fear is almost certainly the reenactment, under stress, of similar experiences that occurred in early childhood. It is as though the experience was rehearsed in early childhood and is being acted out and reexperienced in adulthood. It is likely that the victim of an anxiety attack never fully claimed his or her psychological center of balance during childhood and has thus maintained an exaggerated emotional dependence on others.

As unsettling and painful as the experience of an anxiety attack is, it does invite its victim to examine the assumptions and beliefs on which his or her life, at least to some extent, has been based. It is at this point that the person asks, "What is happening to me?"

A better question would be: "What have I done to create the conditions in which this is happening?" If you are able to see that what is happening to you is fundamentally a way you have learned to exist in the world, you dispel much of the mystery surrounding the experience.

THE FORMS OF ANXIETY

Panic Attacks

Naturally, people are greatly troubled when, for no clear or logical reason they are aware of, they suddenly experience dizziness, cold hands or feet, shaky legs, a dry mouth, a rapid or heavy heartbeat, tingling skin, difficulty in breathing, or any of a large number of other alarming physical sensations.

Millions of American adults have experienced so-called panic attacks that seemed to come from out of the blue. Such experiences typically occur in everyday situations, such as shopping, driving, crossing bridges, walking down a crowded street, going to restaurants, and attending public performances.

We have used the term "so-called panic attacks" to call attention to the fact that panic does not really *attack* us but is actually a disrupted defensive reaction to a perceived grave, life-threatening attack. The particular symptoms we feel are not the core of the problem. The question that really faces us after such an experience is not why we are trembling, have cold feet, diarrhea, or a pounding heart, but *why we are acting as though we are gravely threatened* when we can find no source of danger in our immediate environment.

We now face a very important choice: whether to start climbing up the tree of anxiety or down. The path up the tree leads through avoidance, denial, and concealment. The path down leads through acceptance, self-honesty, and openness.

Phobias

A phobia is an irrational fear related to an object or situation. The person who feels fearful and can find a definite object or situation causing the fear—no matter how illogical it might be—is in a sense fortunate. The presence of such an object or situation makes our fear understandable, sets a limit to it, and clearly links the experience to sensitization resulting from an episode of emotional disruption in the past. A woman with a morbid fear of cats recalled that as a little girl she had watched her father drown a litter of kittens in a tub of water.

As you may well suspect, such an experience in itself does not automatically create a phobia. The little girl had to perceive the incident as *threatening and harmful* and herself as *helpless* in order for long-term emotional effects to be left. This is why unexplained experiences of panic can create subsequent phobic reactions if we perceive them to mean we are helpless victims of life-threatening attacks.

Conceivably, if the child had been wholeheartedly convinced—rightly or wrongly—of the necessity of cat "population control" and had seen the drowning as a way of preventing suffering for uncared-for and unfed animals, she would not have experienced such an intense emotional reaction.

A 1984 study sponsored by the NIMH found the rates of incidence of simple phobias in men and women in three American cities indicated in Table 1–2.

Table 1–2
Incidence of Simple Phobias in Three American Cities

	New Haven, Conn.	Baltimore, Md.	St. Louis, Mo.
Women	1 in 11	1 in 4	1 in 11
Men	1 in 27	1 in 7	1 in 25

Source: Robins, L. N., et al. "Lifetime Prevalence of Specific Psychiatric Disorders in Three Sites." *Archives of General Psychiatry* 41 (October 1984).

Other Self-Defeating Fears

Any time we have a problem making a simple decision or refrain from doing something we truly want to do or need to do because we are afraid, we are in the realm of self-defeating fears.

In a sense, the person who feels he just cannot pick up the telephone to make a business call because of his anxiety is, for a moment at least, in the same trap as Marilyn M., who feels she cannot take the first step outside her own door. In either case, self-diminishing beliefs based on an unworkable philosophy of life are exerting their influence.

A great many people have reason to be interested in the subject of such self-defeating and illogical fears. Approximately one in five Americans (45 million people) will not get on an airplane that is not firmly bolted to the floor of an aviation museum. These people will find that many of the issues in the Self-Care Program are relevant to their fear. Perhaps twice as many people will do anything—including inventing a family emergency, faking an attack of laryngitis, or hiding in the restroom—to avoid speaking to a group. These people especially need to examine the issue of assertiveness, which is covered in the Self-Care Program.

Chronic Worry

As we have already suggested, we can become sensitized to our own thoughts. Obsessive patterns of thoughts can result from a vicious cycle of sensitization, pain, and sensitization, as we struggle to escape from painful thoughts. In the Self-Care Program, we will consider the idea that we can learn to calmly accept each thought that arises *as a thought*—no matter how painful, grotesque, or humiliating it may seem—and can thus liberate ourselves from this self-defeating, time-consuming activity.

Agoraphobia

For many decades, agoraphobia was defined as "the morbid fear of public places or open spaces" because the initial episodes of fear often do occur in such locations. It turns out that not only are those suffering from agoraphobia often afraid in certain public places and open spaces, but they are also often afraid in private places (like strangers' homes) and closed spaces (like elevators). The situations and locations in which they are most apt to become afraid are those in which they feel trapped—and denied access to a source of emotional support. It is for this reason that they are less likely to become afraid in familiar surroundings, like home. In fact, the territorial limitations of agoraphobia can become so severe in extreme cases that the sufferer will not set foot outside his or her home—or even outside a particular room.

Child-development specialist John Bowlby, in his study of childhood fears, *Separation, Anxiety, and Anger,* suggests that agoraphobia is not a true phobia at all, in that it is less a fear of something specific and identifiable (like dogs, snakes, high places, or escalators) than it is the fear of the absence or loss of an "attachment figure" (mother, husband, wife, child—anyone depended upon for emotional protection). Most experts agree that agoraphobia has less to do with fear of particular locations or situations than it does with anxious anticipation that the unexplained fear they have experienced in the past will recur and that they may—in the absence of emotional support—lose control of themselves and harm or humiliate themselves or put themselves in jeopardy.

Agoraphobia was long thought to be a relatively rare disorder, with an incidence of only 6 in 1,000 in the general population; however, the NIMH study published in 1984 suggests that 1 in 20 Americans suffers from this condition. The ratio is higher for women than for men. The prevalence of agoraphobia reported among women in New Haven, Connecticut; Baltimore, Maryland; and St. Louis, Missouri, was, respectively: 1 in 19, 1 in 8, and 1 in 16. We think that the dramatic increase in the reported incidence may reflect improved research techniques as well as a healthy openness among people of the 1980s to the investigation of such long-concealed problems. It is not easy to confront such problems; in fact, it is painful and disturbing to do so. However, the only way we succeed in controlling them is by informing ourselves about them and dealing with them with honesty and realism.

The tendency of agoraphobic people to hide their problem is reinforced by health-care professionals who fail to grasp the subjective life-and-death severity of the more severe anxiety attacks from their patients' guarded reports and thus tend to minimize or trivialize the problem.

Since agoraphobia is essentially a seductive but unworkable strategy for dealing with anxiety, it contains lessons for anyone who confronts anxiety. As we have seen, it is an anxiety condition that is based on a self-diminishing philosophy of life—a philosophy that many of us, including nonphobic people, share to some degree, or at least encounter quite often. To the extent that you suffer from any kind of illogical, self-defeating fears, you could be said to have adopted this agoraphobic philosophy of life. Nowhere does the nature and meaning of illogical fear become more clear than in the lifestyle adopted by an agoraphobic person facing this problem.

If you have agoraphobia, and your world has become hemmed in on all sides by illogical fears, consider the old Chinese proverb, "Suffering is a divine favor in disguise." Those who recover from agoraphobia do not simply get over the symptoms; they emerge from a process of personal growth and development with more energy, concentration, relaxation, and enjoyment in their lives than they have ever known— possibly more than most people have ever known. Those who have recovered from agoraphobia feel that they have completed a great journey, have solved a great riddle, and have reached a new stage of maturity and wisdom. Most would agree with the woman who said, "I don't feel as good as I ever did. I feel better than I have ever felt in my entire life."

recovery (handwritten margin note)

Other Problems Related to Anxiety

The philosophy of helplessness does not lead only in the direction of agoraphobia. There are many other problems in the upper branches of the tree of anxiety. These include compulsive eating and smoking, alcoholism, and drug abuse and drug dependency.

It is beyond the scope of this book to consider these complex issues in detail. However, one thing is clear about them: Rather than involving dependency on *people,* they involve dependency on *substances* (like alcohol, caffeine, and sugar). We know several things about these substances. They can (1) displace essential vitamins and minerals in the diet; (2) deplete them in the body; and (3) create a false sense of well-being, which, in turn, can mask the harmful effects of suboptimum nutrition and vitamin and mineral deficiencies; and (4) tune out the body's signals that it is time for self-caring action.

Ironically, much of the pleasure of smoking may come

from the opportunity to inhale deeply that it offers to the smoker—simulating in exaggerated form the natural deep, abdominal breathing of meditation.

In regard to alcoholism, Ferris Pitts cited a study made by Dr. Paul Dudley White and his colleagues at Harvard some years ago that indicated that "alcoholism may often be symptomatic of anxiety neurosis in men, and when it is, the alcoholism makes it difficult to diagnose anxiety neurosis." This probably explains why so many more women than men report phobic or agoraphobic symptoms. Almost one in five American men have a problem with alcohol abuse or dependency in their lifetimes, a much higher rate than that for women.

THE FUNDAMENTAL PARADOX OF ANXIETY

We have established that the question that faces the anxious person is not "What is happening to me?" but "What am I doing and why am I doing it?" It is a lack of awareness and understanding of our own physiology, our own psychology, and our own essential nature that leads us up the tree of anxiety, not some external, unpredictable force. It is only by outgrowing this ignorance that we can find a feeling of *completeness and wholeness.*

We will conclude this chapter by describing an experiment you can perform if you wish. (You can skip it if you are feeling tense.) First, point your index fingers at each other and hold them about three inches apart. Now imagine that they are stuck inside either end of a woven straw cylinder— a Chinese finger trap. If you try to pull them out of the cylinder, it tightens and traps them. The harder you struggle to pull your fingers out, the more tightly they are held. Yawn; feel your abdomen push out gently and your shoulders and chest walls remain still. Now imagine that you are pulling your fingers apart for a few seconds. You may actually be able to feel the muscles in your arms vibrate with tension as you try to pull your fingers apart. Be aware of how this feels. Continue breathing normally as you stop trying to pull your fingers apart. Be aware of how it feels to stop struggling and to allow your shoulders and arms to relax. Yawn again. Gently push your fingers into the woven-straw cylinder, letting them move with it as it expands. You have now released your fingers from its grip. Remove one at a time from the trap. Be aware of any sensations in your arms—these sensations are the natural aftereffect of exertion. Wiggle your fingers. Give your arms and shoulders a good stretch and a gentle shake-out if they need it. Yawn once or twice. Any residual tension in your muscles will gradually disappear and will be replaced by a pleasant sensation of warmth.

Our simple experiment has illustrated the paradoxical nature of anxiety: anxiety is a trap in which we can snare ourselves and from which we can release ourselves. If we struggle helplessly against anxiety, we are very likely to find ourselves feeling trapped and overwhelmed. If we relax, alertly examine and investigate our anxiety, and become aware of its message, we will find ourselves released from its grip. To some extent, it may be helpful to allow ourselves to *be moved* by anxiety, just as we allowed our fingers to *move with* the finger trap—to go ahead and observe our uneasy or worried feelings instead of feeling uneasy about our uneasiness or worried about our worry.

It is very important to remember that the lower levels of anxiety are virtually built into our sympathetic nervous system, or at least are established there very early in life. Attending and orienting reactions and various gradations of the startle reaction (including the full-blown emergency fight-or-flight reaction) are nature's way of preparing us to respond to danger.

When we resist or ignore these lower levels of anxiety, we are, in effect, fighting against our own survival-linked behaviors: we are attempting to remain perfectly calm and cool while our body is preparing to run, jump, yell, or scream. In other words, we, as integrated organisms, are trying to do two incompatible things at the same time. It is seldom appropriate in modern life to run, jump, yell, or scream; these behaviors are frowned upon in supermarket checkout lines. But it is often possible to compromise with our sympathetic nervous systems and to do some abdominal breathing, to move a bit, stretch, walk, or do some other gentle exercise. This may help our bodies use up the internally generated muscle-activator, epinephrine, that is released during defensive physical reactions.

Chronically and acutely anxious people need not accept emotional disruption as a permanent part of their lives, but they do need to learn to recognize and accept the normal feelings of anxiety at the lower end of the spectrum. As they learn to be more aware of (and more expressive of) their feelings, they will also be learning how to turn off the warning signals of anxiety. Ignoring these signals only sets off more and more of them and thus moves the already anxious person up the spectrum of anxiety toward full-scale physiological arousal and emotional disruption.

By fighting their feelings, George, Betty, Pat, Frank, and Ron, whom we met earlier in this chapter, have reached the point where they are startled by their own startle reactions, seek to fight against or flee from their own emergency fight-or-flight reactions, and are afraid of their own fear. In order to learn how to live *without* such severe anxiety, they need to find a way to be mindful and relaxed while they live *with* some anxiety at the lower end of the anxiety spectrum. This is not an impossible quest. Many people who were formerly subject to pervasive and severe anxiety have been able to do this by using the ideas presented in the Self-Care Program at the end of this book.

2

Growing Up Anxious

"What is believed to be essential for mental health is that the infant and young child should experience a warm, intimate and continuous relationship with his mother (or permanent mother substitute) in which both find satisfaction and enjoyment. "

—Developmental psychologist John Bowlby

"Home is not a place, it is an idea."

—Anonymous

Thirty-two years ago, a child was born in a town not unlike the town where you were born. Her name was Elizabeth. She was born totally honest, without any pretense or concealment in her behavior.

During the second year of the child's life, her father's business was failing. He worried about his family and himself and his ability to make a living. He was depressed, moody, and critical. Sometimes he became very angry.

The child's mother was pregnant. Her own fears caused her to cling to her little girl and to worry excessively about her. It was easier for Elizabeth's mother to express anxiety about her child's welfare than the anxiety she felt about herself and her own life. Sometimes she cried as she held the little girl.

During this critical period of Elizabeth's life, as she struggled to assert her own identity in the world, she continually experienced her mother's anxiety, fear, and overprotectiveness. Whenever she showed an adventurous or independent spirit, her mother became fearful and upset.

There was much wrong with Elizabeth's world, but the false lesson she learned was that there was somehow something wrong with her. As she grew up in a home filled with fear, worry, and criticism, she continued to believe in her heart that not only was there something wrong with her but that it was something almost beyond repair. Elizabeth felt inadequate and weak. She felt as though she lacked a solid center and clear boundaries—that she would easily lose herself away from familiar faces and surroundings. In a sense, she learned to rely on her mother and her home to tell her who she was.

Secretly, Elizabeth longed to be adventurous and independent. But her daring spirit was held in check by the part of her that still believed she was little and weak and that the world was a big and dangerous place.

On the outside, she put up a brave front and prided herself on appearing to others as "very mature" and "very polite" —the kind of person others would not criticize. Although Elizabeth was always a good student and eventually a responsible manager for a business firm, her inner feelings of inadequacy led her to depend on familiar surroundings and on her mother and later her husband to reassure her that she was really there.

She was extremely sensitive to the smallest criticism and lived in fear that others would discover she was a flawed, fearful person. For many years she hid from this inner conflict and from the clear signs that it limited her life.

In any kind of confrontation, Elizabeth felt close to tears and became apologetic. When she spoke up, she found that her voice sounded strained and she said things she "didn't really mean." She described herself as a worrier. She was apprehensive about meeting strangers and making business calls. She was afraid to assert herself at work or to tell her husband about small things he did that displeased her. She was fearful of losing control if she let herself get angry.

Eventually, during a period of psychological stress at work brought about by her reaction to an overbearing and critical manager, Elizabeth began to experience anxiety attacks and episodes of outright panic. She was 30 years old.

In quick succession, she became afraid to drive on freeways, afraid to ride in elevators, and afraid to sit in the middle of crowded restaurants. In short, she exhibited some of the classic symptoms of agoraphobia.

THE ROOTS OF ANXIETY

This chapter tells the story of the development of one relatively severe anxiety disorder—agoraphobia—from its roots in childhood experiences through its culmination in a philosophy of life that is based on the idea of helplessness.

Suppose you have a simple phobia, like a fear of insects or high places. Or suppose you do not experience phobic reactions but rather, like Elizabeth's mother, are living through a period of heavy psychological stress and find anxious worry displacing relaxation and enjoyment in your life. Suppose you wake up at 3:00 A.M. worried sick about your cash flow, or your grades, or your spouse's health. Understanding agoraphobia can help you deal with such anxieties because the issues that are implicit in them in ambiguous form are crystal clear in agoraphobia. All anxious people will recognize many of the elements in the story of agoraphobia even though they are not present in their own lives to the same degree they are in the life of an agoraphobic person.

In a sense, agoraphobia is the end point of a very logical but unworkable approach to life. Each of us, as we go about daily life, is continually faced with choices between this unworkable approach and an alternative approach, rooted in personal freedom, that emphasizes self-care and self-assertion.

Full-blown agoraphobic behavior develops in adult life as a reaction to one or more episodes of panicky feelings that seem to come from nowhere. Of course, agoraphobia does not arise out of thin air; it arises out of perceptions, attitudes, beliefs, and assumptions that have their roots in early childhood development. The following description of the way people get into the trap of agoraphobia is based on what we call a "developmental-philosophical model" to emphasize both the historical dimension of the problem and the system of beliefs on which agoraphobic behavior is based.

Life as a Totally Helpless Being

We humans are born as physically and psychologically underdeveloped beings who, in order to live and to survive, must bond with our mothers (or primary caretakers) and depend on them for continuous care for a prolonged time. Only after a normal period of development and the coming together of our own self-awareness and personal identity are we ready to begin a process of physical and psychological separation from our mothers and start an independent life.

Even though we are helpless at birth, we already possess a full complement of built-in reactions as part of our biological endowment. Serving our body's basic needs, these reactions include the cry of distress, which serves to elicit help or reassurance, the startle reaction, which will eventually help us get out of the way of danger, and the visual avoidance of high places.

Eleanor Gibson and Richard D. Walk's well-known "visual cliff" experiments showed that human babies, like chicks, lambs, kids, pigs, kittens, and other baby animals, balked at the edge of a "visual cliff"; however, unlike other animals, human infants also tended to back out over the apparent drop without looking, underscoring their total helplessness and dependence on continuous care during their early development.

Those who study the behavior of human infants have identified regular stages of development as infants gain cognitive and motor skills, learn to manipulate objects with their hands, to move about on all fours, and eventually to stand erect and walk.

The world of the infant is expansive, and during the second year of life, the natural direction of the infant is away from the nestlike security of the maternal relationship. The infant seeks to leave *here*, represented by the mother, and to explore *there*, the bigger world.

Frequently, during the infant's early explorations, when it is, in a sense, "between here and there," it will orient itself in relation to its mother by looking around to establish visual contact. This behavior, like the avoidance of high places, has strong survival value for a being unable to feed or protect itself. Like many other manifestations of physiological arousal, this defensive reaction is naturally accompanied by a transient feeling of uncertainty or anxiety. Let us emphasize that the "separation anxiety" experienced by the helpless infant on its first ventures away from its mother is normal and healthy.

By the age of two, the developing child will begin to test its own psychological boundaries by asserting its desire to make its own choices, thus bringing it into conflict with its parents and others. This assertiveness is also healthy and is a necessary part of establishing a sense of personal identity and freedom, although it is often perceived in our culture as "bad" behavior by the child.

Ideally, the toddler will experience a genuinely "warm, intimate, and continuous relationship" with its mother (to use John Bowlby's words) as it moves out into the bigger world. Psychoanalyst Margaret Mahler, who specializes in the study of child development, has described the type of help the child needs from its parents. The mother, she says, is "ready to share some of the toddler's activities, while at the same time, able to let go and give a gentle push to encourage further independence." The father will provide "vital support against the backward pull of the symbiotic relationship." The relaxed and caring mother will keep an eye on her child and will provide a center of safety and security to which it can return to seek reassurance. She will not aggressively seek to stop the child's explorations or its self-assertion. The loving encouragement the infant receives from its parents and the other significant people in its life will allow the child to explore its own independence in safety.

A distinctly agoraphobic reaction to an anxiety attack is to retreat impulsively toward a familiar person or familiar surroundings, just as a young child at the stage of separation anxiety moves close to its mother if it perceives a threat. This tendency indicates that emotionally disruptive events at the separation stage of development have special significance in agoraphobic behavior.

Arguably, a similar pattern of events could occur later in a child's life (and, certainly, traumatic events in later life can be important). However, the life-or-death intensity of the agoraphobic experience suggests that its roots go all the way back to the time when a tiny, helpless infant was totally dependent on its primary caretaker for its very existence and survival.

More than likely, Elizabeth was completely shielded by her mother from normal separation anxiety in infancy so that, eventually, when initial separations from mother, home, and family did occur, they were experienced as emotionally overwhelming and severely punishing. Such traumatic separations can occur, for example, the first time the child is left in the care of a stranger or on the first day of school. Elizabeth later recalled her first day at kindergarten:

> It was a grey day. A black limousine arrived carrying two or three other children. The woman driver looked like a witch to me. My mother was acting tense and artificially cheerful. As my mother guided me toward the limousine door, I started to

sob. The driver angrily told me that cry babies could not ride in her limousine, so I sat petrified and sobbing silently in the back seat until my chest ached. We drove several miles across town through the rain.

As we crossed a bridge across a broad grey river, I realized that I could never find my way home on my own. Now that I look back on it, I'm sure the words "dread" and "doom" surely apply to my feelings at the time. I was so scared that the kindergarten teacher held me in her lap part of the morning. I felt safe when she held me, but I was also terribly ashamed and humiliated to be so frightened in front of so many children. On my first day of school, I felt like a complete failure as a human being.

Notice how the wracking pain of prolonged silent sobbing came to be an integral part of the emotional disruption produced by the impossible conflict between Elizabeth's natural impulse to cry and the need she saw to protect her right to exist by not crying. Her halting breath and overbreathing undoubtedly heightened and prolonged the panic she experienced that day.

The Psychological Birth of the Human Infant

If all goes well, the child's earliest experiences of its own freedom will be nurtured within the security of its family circle. Later the circle will expand to include adult and child friends and will allow an even greater independence of action.

Successful habituation to life as a separate and unique being culminates at around the age of 30 months in what Margaret Mahler calls "the psychological birth of the human infant." At this point, the child begins its own psychological life with a sense of its own separate identity ("identity" in the fundamental sense of *existence*). Of course, many more years of development and growth are required before the child will be ready to function in a truly independent manner, yet, ideally, the foundation has been laid for a balanced and healthy life.

If a child has a clear sense of its own identity, the self it shows to the world will be firmly rooted in its own honest self-concept. It will be free to tell the world who it is, what it feels, what it wants, and what it likes or dislikes.

In real life, of course, it is hard to imagine a child arriving at the age of 30 months without some physical or emotional scars. In fact, the emotional disruption of early childhood development is very common in the United States today. Mahler and her colleagues have found in their empirical observations of mothers and infants "innumerable degrees and forms of partial failure of the separation-individuation process." In other words, many children in the first 30 months of life have been able to achieve only a weak grasp on their own identity and freedom.

Various forms of emotional disruption can lead us toward a philosophy of life based on helplessness. (In the following list, we have emphasized the mother's role in emotional disruption simply because she is typically the primary source of emotional support in the life of the totally helpless infant, not because the father's role or the role of siblings are without significance in shaping the child's world.)

1. Suppose our mother is a fearful person. Our helplessness and anxiety bring up unhappy memories from her own childhood, to which she reacts by feeling helpless and anxious herself. She then treats us with exaggerated anxiety and concern, thwarting our efforts to venture out into a world she perceives to be dangerous.

2. Suppose our mother is so depressed or self-engrossed that she ignores our need for reassurance as we seek to venture out into the world. She has no concern with "being there" for us when we return from our initial forays into the world.

3. Suppose our mother believes that by our anxious or exploratory behavior we are willfully seeking to cause her discomfort. She may perceive in us an anxious and tyrannical parent remembered from her own childhood—and therefore aggressively seek to put a stop to our "unacceptable" behavior (which might be

something as simple as spitting out a new food with an unfamiliar texture).

4. Suppose our mother is alcoholic or otherwise subject to drastic shifts in mood so that her reactions are unpredictable. Sometimes she offers reassurance, sometimes she ignores us, sometimes she shows exaggerated concern.

5. Suppose our father or other family members are indifferent, critical, or hostile toward us, thus failing to support our efforts to expand the realm of our freedom or actually driving us back into the domain of helplessness and dependence on our mother.

The Role of Punishment

As newborn infants, we are able to recognize and react to two fundamentally different conditions in our world; one in which we feel *safe*, and one in which we feel *threatened*. The "threatened" condition (which can be produced by the withdrawal of love and protection) triggers built-in defensive reactions in our hormonal, nervous, and respiratory systems. These reactions will help us cope with danger or avoid it after we have outgrown the helplessness of early infancy, but now they serve only to create feelings of excitement and distress— and to trigger cries for help that may be in some way punished. Because of its dramatic physiological effects and the unpleasant feelings that ensue, the "threatened" condition has the power to limit and restrict our behavior as we grow toward psychological birth.

Just as the "safe" condition can gradually teach us confidence in our ability to move out into the world and to meet life's challenges, the disruptive "threatened" condition reinforces our helplessness by *punishing* any and all of the feelings and behaviors that happen to precede it. "There is no question that punishment works," as behaviorist Howard Rachlin points out, "the trouble with punishment may be not that it works but that it works too well."

Rachlin explains that intense punishment may produce

harmful and long-lasting effects. For example, a single intense electric shock to a pigeon can permanently suppress a specific behavior (like pecking on a key to obtain food) that immediately preceded the punishing shock. Thus, suggests Rachlin, "If we severely punish a child for 'being fresh' we must ask ourselves whether we want to suppress his outspokenness completely and permanently." (In these cases, the effects are "permanent" unless a systematic effort is made to reverse them.)

Rachlin makes clear the disruptive effects of random punishment: "Consider the mother who is constantly spanking, shaking, or slapping her child for reasons that are only tenuously related to his specific acts. She will never understand why he is so naughty despite her constant attempts at discipline."

Rachlin also raises the issue of the appropriateness of punishment. According to him, "The classic example of an inappropriate punishment is spanking a child for crying. The spanking generates still more crying, which in turn is punished by still more spanking, and so on, until the child or the parent becomes exhausted."

There are obvious forms of punishment and there are subtle forms. Whether or not there is a deliberate attempt to control or punish our behavior, if we perceive our survival to be threatened, we will suppress those behaviors that seem to evoke the "threatening" condition. This tendency is in the nature of all living organisms.

Punishment, whether intentional or inadvertent, of such built-in defensive behaviors as separation anxiety or cries of distress is especially harmful. It creates an impossible conflict for us as psychologically underdeveloped beings: to avoid the "threatening" condition, we are forced to fight against our own nature and to attempt to suppress virtually automatic behaviors whose very function is to ensure our safety. An almost equally impossible conflict is created later on if we feel unloved and therefore unsafe when we express our own feelings, needs, or desires. In this case, we will learn to smother ourselves, to keep quiet, and to split apart the way we act from the way we really are in order to remain lovable—and safe.

False Assumptions

When we, as an infant (and later as a child), are left with a life centered in the avoidance of the "threatening" condition, with a dissatisfied craving for loving care, and with an impoverished sense of our own identity, we are led to some assumptions about ourselves and the world we live in that are logical for a helpless being but false for an autonomous being. If we carry them forward with us into adulthood, they give rise to beliefs, attitudes, and perceptions that add up to a way of life based on helplessness.

The Avoidance of Risk. If, as infants, we are exposed to "threatening" conditions before we are equipped to deal with them, we will tend to assume that (1) the world is essentially a threatening place, and (2) we are not capable of surviving for very long without extraordinary effort.

These assumptions lead to the belief that we must always be on the lookout for trouble so we can avoid it. One problem with this belief, of course, is that if we are continuously looking for trouble, we will find it. If we assume it is there, we will find it even if we need to put the worst possible interpretation on events and to magnify small problems in order to do so.

Our vigilance for signs of trouble translates directly into an avoidance of taking chances. We attempt to evaluate carefully every potential action or potential interpretation of events in terms of the ways it might get us into trouble.

The Craving for Love. If, as infants, we have been overwhelmed by fear during the periodic loss of maternal love, we will assume that (1) our safety and survival depend on being loved, (2) love can be turned on and off by our behavior, and (3) we must act in a lovable way in order to keep love turned on so we can survive. Our concept of acting "in a lovable way" will be shaped largely by punishment— we will tend to stop doing anything that seems to produce the punishing "threatening" condition. Since we are psychologically incomplete beings, we will be unable to distinguish clearly the boundary between our actions and our thoughts and feelings. Thus, in addition to acting in an acceptable and loving way, we will attempt the impossible: to experience nothing but the thoughts and feelings that we believe *someone else* wants us to think and feel.

We will come to believe that certain thoughts and feelings are dangerous because other people won't like them. We will believe that we have a problem whenever an "unacceptable" thought or feeling arises. Of course, the harder we try to ignore an unacceptable thought or feeling, the more persistently it will seek our attention—like a hungry cat or dog at dinnertime. Our problem will then become concealing our unacceptable thoughts or feelings from other people. Obviously, in this situation, we can't afford to let down our guard or relax too much, because if we did, someone might discover us having an unacceptable feeling.

Who Am I?

Personal identity seems a simple and obvious concept, yet it bears a closer look from anyone who suffers from chronic worry, inappropriate fears, or agoraphobia. When we say that we have acquired a strong sense of our identity by the time of our psychological birth, we don't mean that we merely recognize our own face in a mirror; what we mean is that we grasp our own ability to define ourselves through our freedom in the present moment—our freedom to choose among possible courses of action and possible interpretations of events. After all, at a fundamental level, our identity is the way we choose to exist in the world.

If the disruption of our early development has left us with a weakened and impaired sense of our identity, we assume that we need the world to define us continually, to tell us who we are, *so that we may continue to exist.* This assumption leads us to believe that our safety and survival depend on conforming to the expectations of other people. In effect, we make an implicit, one-sided bargain with others: "I'll give up my unacceptable behaviors, thoughts, and feelings, if you will continue to allow me to exist."

The idealized self is thus an imaginary image of ourselves that is tailored to meet the expectations of other people and is stripped of all "unlovable" or unacceptable traits. In the short run, the idealized self is a clever, even a brilliant, defensive strategy we adopt to ensure our survival. Behind it is a human being who perceives himself or herself to be helpless and incomplete.

A client once told therapist Manuel Zane, "If you don't talk to me, it feels like I'm not here." During an anxiety attack, the fact that you really aren't sure who you are becomes painfully clear as you experience feelings of dread, doom, or unreality. You may perceive these feelings as signaling the end of your world, whereas if you truly knew who you are, you would know that life goes on and that such feelings are transitory.

James Bugental, an existential psychotherapist, describes this insight into the personality of a patient who suffered from panic attacks:

> After Laurence leaves, I walk to the window and look out at the gray day, thinking of this competent machine which is so unaware it is a man. He doesn't value, hardly even knows there is a life going on within himself. Those panics. Wait! Those panics just might be the only real touch he has right now with his inner aliveness. The panics are the frantic signals of his lost subjective center.

The patient is a man who acquired his sense of identity almost totally in terms of his social roles, which were created as a product of how others saw him. Without a strong inner sense of identity, and in the face of stressful life conditions, he began having panic attacks, especially when he was not in the presence of those people and things that mirrored and validated his idealized self. Bugental states: "The crucial thing that Larry learned was that his achievements, his image in others' eyes, and his self-observation were insufficient to give him a solid feeling of his own being."

Larry had been so preoccupied by how others saw him that he had lost touch with his inner feelings.

Larry's recovery came as "he began to listen to his fear and anger, rather than pushing them aside until they grew so strong they broke through his control."

When he recognized and gave room to his feelings, Larry gradually began to experience his inner freedom (the source of his true identity). Since his early development had not encouraged or supported the exercise of that freedom, he had an underdeveloped sense of who he was. Learning to feel free was the unfinished business he had to deal with in order to be able to free himself from chronic anxiety.

Larry had discovered an important truth: Who you are is not a given within yourself, nor is it a product of how others see you—it is the act and process of *honestly being yourself.*

Everyone's life story is unique, yet people with agoraphobia share certain negative assumptions about themselves that almost everyone can recognize in himself or herself to some degree. Here is what has happened to Elizabeth and to the millions of Americans who have experienced an agoraphobic identity crisis in adult life:

Since, from their point of view, the world into which they were born did not accept them, and they were treated as though they should be someone else, they set out to become the person the world wanted them to be. In a sense, they succeeded. The task of building an "idealized self" was so urgent that they abandoned the process of self-discovery and instead clung to the imaginary idealized self:

> They renounced their right to tell others what they wanted or needed.

They renounced their right to express displeasure or anger.

They renounced their right to express anxiety.

They accepted the right of others to tell them who they were and how they should act.

They strived to always be a perfect little lady or gentleman or a "mature adult."

In other words, they believed themselves to be unfree—the helpless victim of circumstances they could not control—and they acted accordingly. In order to survive, they built themselves a life raft out of lovable and acceptable traits.

In 1983 and 1984, we surveyed 186 people with agoraphobic symptoms who were using our original Self-Care Program, *Outgrowing Agoraphobia*. We asked them to what extent they agreed with a number of self-descriptive statements. Table 2–1 shows the results for the 12 most highly rated statements.

The table clearly shows us the attitudes that result from the false assumptions and beliefs that are left over from an emotionally disrupted childhood.

Almost all of those we surveyed expressed moderate to strong agreement with the statement that they "hate" hurting other people's feelings. It is probably closer to the truth to say that they are afraid of being jumped on or ridiculed if they say something someone else doesn't like. This can be a problem when one needs to be honest—for example, in negotiating with someone, recommending against something, refusing a request, or otherwise dealing with others on the basis of equality.

People with agoraphobia grew up believing that acting *nice*—in spite of impatience or frustration—is better than being *honest* about opinions and feelings.

The need to look good in the eyes of other people naturally leads to problems:

"I know that I have spent a great deal of my life doing what other people wanted me to do."

Table 2–1
How Those Who Suffer from Agoraphobia See Themselves

Statement	Number Reporting Moderate to Strong Agreement (Total = 186)	Percent
I hate to hurt the feelings of others.*	178	96
I am unusually polite and considerate.	177	95
I am a worrier.	176	95
Sometimes I am afraid to tell people how I feel.	169	91
I am too sensitive to criticism.	166	89
I usually know what to do in an emergency.	166	89
Sometimes I am confused about my own feelings.	160	86
I have a problem dealing with anger.	155	83
I have never felt entirely free from anxiety.	144	77
Sometimes I am full of self-contempt.	138	74
Sometimes I ridicule myself.	137	74
People often underestimate my abilities.	128	69

*A better survey statement would have been, "I often sacrifice my own feelings to avoid hurting the feelings of others."

> "I'm always helping or 'being there' for everyone else but
> myself. Also, I've always felt I've had to be strong
> all the time, even if I didn't want to be or felt I
> couldn't be."

> "I tried all my life to suit everybody but myself. I was San-
> dra the wife, Sandra the mother, but where the hell was
> Sandra?"

There is, of course, nothing wrong with being a polite, considerate, nice person. However, there is something terribly wrong with struggling to be someone other than who you are. In the first place, it is impossible. In the second place, the effort makes you unhappy. You can never be good enough to satisfy the demands set by your parents' insecurities and limitations. You will always be running to catch up. You will always be worried and anxious. You will always believe, "I can be relaxed and happy just as soon as everything is perfect, but I can't be relaxed and happy right now."

When we also asked those people using the Self-Care Program to indicate the kinds of problems concerning their parents that they remember from their childhoods, we obtained the results shown in Tables 2–2 and 2–3.

Almost all of the respondents checked one of the first five categories on each table. Naturally, we did not expect people to remember events from their first 30 months of life, but we did believe that we could extrapolate backwards from their childhood memories to the time of their early infancy.

From the scores, we infer that agoraphobic people tend to grow up in families in which they experience intolerance and criticism along with anxious overprotection.

The Crisis

You naturally wonder what is happening to you if you suddenly experience emotional disruption for no obvious reason—as 30-year-old Elizabeth did one day while driving home from work.

Thirty is a significant age to many people. Among those we surveyed, it is the average age at which the onset of panic attacks occurred. (Significantly, the single most frequent age of onset reported in the survey is 21, the symbolic threshold

Table 2–2
Childhood Problems Concerning Mother Reported by 186
Agoraphobic People

Problem	Number	Percent
Nervous or Anxious Behavior	97	52
Overprotective Behavior	92	49
Argumentative	89	48
Overly Worried About Safety	75	40
Did Not Touch or Hug Children	74	40
Highly Critical	70	38
Excessive Emotional Clinging	60	32
Played Favorites	57	31
Excessively Close Supervision	57	31
Financial Problems	53	28
Used Ridicule	49	26
Displayed Extreme Anger	46	25
Major Illness	46	25
Hospitalization	45	24
Passive	40	22
Indifferent	39	21
Excessive Praise	27	15
Aggressive/Threatening Behavior	24	13
Alcoholism	22	12
Death	16	9

of adulthood.) But age is not the only stressful factor. If we look carefully at the period just preceding an episode of out-of-the-blue fear, we will probably be able to identify other sources of significant psychological stress, such as illness, a financial or career setback (like Elizabeth's new boss), an accident, or a death in the family.

Quite often, episodes of emotional disruption follow life events that would be psychologically stressful for anyone:

Table 2–3
Childhood Problems Concerning Father Reported by 186
Agoraphobic People

Problem	Number	Percent
Did Not Touch or Hug Children	99	53
Argumentative	86	46
Indifferent	69	37
Displayed Extreme Anger	67	36
Financial Problems	59	32
Highly Critical	57	31
Used Ridicule	55	30
Passive	49	26
Employment Problems	46	25
Played Favorites	40	22
Overprotective Behavior	37	20
Aggressive/Threatening Behavior	35	19
Alcoholism	33	18
Nervous or Anxious Behavior	26	14
Death	25	13
Overly Worried About Safety	24	13
Major Illness	19	10
Excessively Close Supervision	18	10

"My wife left me. A good friend was killed in an auto accident. I lost all my possessions. . . . All this happened within a three-month period."

"I had a sudden onset of responsibilities I thought I was ready for but wasn't."

"I almost died several times from severe drug allergies. I am frightened by the finality and physical pain and suffering associated with life and death. I feel such a lack of control."

"I lost my belongings in a fire, lost a good friend, developed
functional hypoglycemia, and had problems with my future in-laws."

The body's resources are strained by such events, and the
threshold of perceived danger may drop lower and lower.
Self-honesty, enjoyment, relaxation, and good self-care habits
(including optimum nutrition and exercise) may start to disappear from one's life. Everything else being equal, the agoraphobic person will tend to experience more and more
psychological stress. He or she will feel increasingly threatened by other people's actions and by events.

In these circumstances, people become ripe to have an
anxiety attack in any situation in which they are forced by
circumstances to confront the condition of their life and their
feelings.

Claire Weekes, a physician who specializes in the treatment of agoraphobia, has suggested that subsequent anxiety
attacks can arise in this manner: "In a sensitized person, the
connection between merely slightly anxious thought and intense panic may be so close that its victim may be unaware
of the thought and may believe that panic has struck them
from out-of-the-blue."

By now it is clear that those who suffer from agoraphobia
are repeating, or regressing to, an early stage of development.
Their fear comes from their old, deeply felt—though con-
cealed—belief that they need to be validated and "made real"
by familiar people or surroundings. For a number of years,
perhaps, they may have dodged this humiliating belief and
successfully avoided feelings of intense fear. From their point
of view, they have perhaps seemed to be "very mature" because of the energy they have used to counter this persisting
childhood belief, and yet they acknowledge that they have
never really felt free from lingering anxiety.

The fear that seems to come from nowhere dislodges this
unstable balance. First of all, the person immediately seeks
to return to home, office, or other familiar surroundings and
to get in touch with husband, wife, mother, or another sig-

nificant familiar person, thus acting on an old belief in one's inadequacy and dependency. Second, the thought occurs, "If it happened once, it can happen again."

Following such an experience, one woman said, *"My whole world has changed. I am afraid to exist."*

After people have experienced a number of such episodes of acute anxiety, they may be able to list many objects and situations to which their fear has become attached. Yet somehow they realize that the fear is driven more by their inner anxiety than by real threats in the external world. They are aware that they are actually more afraid of *becoming afraid* and *being overwhelmed by their own fear* in supermarkets or on bridges, for example, than they are afraid of supermarkets or bridges themselves.

If we consider anxiety attacks and panic attacks to be the primary result of a philosophy of life based on helplessness, then what follows from that experience might be termed its secondary effects:

As the sensitivity of those suffering from agoraphobia is generalized to places and situations that are similar to those in which the experiences occurred, they begin to avoid any place where they might feel trapped (unable to exit instantaneously), such as buses, airplanes, and elevators.

They begin to feel anxiety whenever they anticipate an episode of intense fear, remember an episode of intense fear, or are reminded of a place or situation where intense fear occurred.

They begin to focus their activities on concealing their condition and preventing episodes of intense fear. (They may get to be quite good at this—at a high cost to themselves and those around them.)

They begin to adopt habitual ways of thinking and acting (such as making up excuses) that are aimed at avoiding episodes of intense fear.

They begin to feel anxiety when they anticipate the humiliation and embarrassment of experiencing intense fear in front of other people.

They may begin to adopt little rituals or compulsive actions (such as checking the stove repeatedly before leaving home) to defend themselves against danger.

They may tend to become obsessed with lining up emotional care and support from other people so they won't have to be alone.

All of these tendencies add up to a regressive, agoraphobic lifestyle.

HOW WE BECOME TRAPPED IN THOUGHT

Let us begin by summarizing what we already know: if we assume that we are unsafe because we are basically helpless and unfree, then we may attempt to reach security by becoming (or by seeming to be) someone other than who we are. We will perceive that anything that threatens to expose this deception exposes us to *life-threatening* punishment (the withdrawal or loss of love, approval, and acceptance). Our concern with threats can lead us into a variety of negative, distorted ways of thinking.

In our everyday experience, we will search for supposed threats to our survival with a large magnifying lens called "either-or" thinking. We will attempt to see threats in the future with a powerful telescope called "what if" thinking. When we feel forced by circumstances into acting or choosing, we will do so only after we don our opaque "have to" sunglasses. When we tire of wrestling with the largely imaginary threats that we are able to find, we may try to see ourselves and our situation in the distorting mirror of "if only" thinking.

Needless to say, when our mind is filled with these distorting lenses and mirrors, we will seldom find time to stop and admire the scenery with our own eyes. We are too busy searching for threats (near at hand or on the horizon) or looking for someone or something to blame for our chronic anxiety and suffering.

Either-Or Thinking

The assumption that we need to be ever-vigilant to prevent our emotional support from being turned off leads us into a logical error that can pervade our thinking. This well-known error is called the black-or-white fallacy, or either-or thinking. For example:

> "Is my work excellent or is it terribly bad?"
> "Am I a perfect housekeeper or am I a terrible slob?"
> "Do I win or do I lose?"
> "Is my day perfectly free from anxiety or is it another rotten day?"
> "Do you agree with me or are you angry with me?"
> "Is my feeling good or bad?"
> "Am I a heroic figure or a helpless victim?"

These unbalanced either-or questions recognize only one extreme condition or another. They leave no room for intermediate conditions ("Am I a reasonably good housekeeper?") or alternative conditions ("My feeling is simply a feeling—it is neither good nor bad in itself").

The either-or mind demands unrealistic, inhuman perfection. What it is really asking is: "Is my idealized self intact or isn't it?" In other words, "Am I safe or am I threatened?" The slightest deviation from perfection—the slightest sign of disinterest, disapproval, or anger from another person—can be interpreted as a danger signal.

It is easy to see that the either-or mind tends to see other people either as sources of emotional support or enemies and leaves little room for other people's points of view. The either-or mind creates a win-lose approach to interpersonal dealings. For example, it does not entertain the possibility that both parties to a negotiation might win, or that we might enjoy working with co-workers even if they are not our personal friends.

Also, it is the alarmist either-or mind that decides we are threatened whenever we encounter the slightest anxiety or have any kind of unpleasant experience. Either-or thinking limits our ability to interpret our experience and thus limits our understanding of the world and our ability to respond spontaneously and naturally to events.

What-If Thinking

Negativism, pessimism, and worry are the hallmarks of hypothetical what-if thinking:

> "What if the phone company representative gets sarcastic with me when I call up to complain about my bill?"
>
> "What if the car has a flat tire while we are driving through the mountains?"
>
> "What if Grandmother talks George into going up on the roof to fix the television antenna and he falls off?"
>
> "What if the theater catches on fire and everyone panics?"
>
> "What if I start to cry at the meeting?"

There is nothing inherently good or bad about any of these thoughts. They are simply thoughts that could arise in anyone's mind. We could simply accept such thoughts, freely decide whether they are worth examining further, and if so, think through the consequences of available responses to the possibilities raised in the thoughts. The anxious person, on the other hand, is not alert to the difference between thoughts and events. He or she reacts to such thoughts as though they were in themselves harmful events—or at least as though they represent almost unavoidable danger and harm.

Furthermore, the anxious mind believes that if things are bad, they are bound to get worse. The anxious wife will (mentally) be furious with Grandmother for killing her husband, while the alert and relaxed wife will simply plan to share her concerns with her husband and perhaps suggest he take along some safe work shoes when they visit Grandmother. Likewise, the anxious person will (mentally) be trudging along a dangerous mountain road at night, while the alert and relaxed person is simply deciding to have the tires checked. The anxious person will (mentally) be telling off the phone company representative, while the alert and relaxed person has decided that possible sarcasm is not worth worrying about—"If someone's sarcastic with me, I'll simply be very clear and assertive with him." While the anxious person is (mentally) being crushed in a theater panic, the alert and relaxed person has simply told himself or herself, "That's very unlikely, but if I'm really uncomfortable, I can sit next to an exit." While the anxious person is (mentally) crying at the business meeting, the relaxed person is asking, "Why would I cry? Why would I feel so frustrated and sad that I would cry?"

To the anxious mind trapped in what-if thinking, any kind of commitment looks more like an opportunity for loss or failure than an opportunity for progress.

Those suffering from agoraphobia are typically afraid that they may behave in such a manner that they will be humiliated or embarrassed if they experience an episode of sudden acute anxiety in a public place. This is one of the fears that spring from their strong tendency to engage in what-if thinking.

By focusing our attention on the future, what-if thinking distracts us from the present moment and the present action. It causes us to be less than fully aware of what we're doing.

A natural consequence of such thinking leads us to avoid the hypothetical risks we have conjured up. The fear of having a panic attack in the presence of other people is especially debilitating, since our defenses would be down, and others could see us clearly (we presume) as helpless beings. Social or business invitations place agoraphobic people in a painful predicament if they require venturing out of "safe territory" into a seemingly dangerous situation. Rather than admit their difficulty, phobic persons attempt to convince others—and perhaps themselves as well—that there is a plausible reason (or, typically, several plausible reasons) why they cannot accept the invitation. Instead of saying, "I can't fly to London to give a talk to a group of people because I'm scared to death of both flying and public speaking," the phobic person will say something like this: "I can't go because I am so busy getting ready for X, and besides, Y is about to happen, and anyway, I have to be here in case my cousin decides to get married." Or, "I can't go because I have to be here for a series of meetings with A, and B can't get his work done unless I'm available to advise him, and anyway, we think Freddie may be having his tonsils out about then."

Have-To Thinking

Rather than seeing decisions as opportunities for the exercise of freedom, anxious people see them as traps. They may, for example, act on the purchase of a home or car only when they feel trapped by circumstances into doing so ("I have to buy a car so I can commute to work").

Decisions affecting important personal relationships may seem especially threatening. For years, one agoraphobic woman blamed her husband for "forcing" her to marry him and to forsake a promising career to do so. She did not see that she had a right not to get married in the first place, and later she did not accept responsibility for her decision to marry. This led to years of misery for both husband and wife.

Have-to thinking is an expression of the idealized self's need to obey the wishes or conform to the expectations of others:

> "I have to go to this college because my father wants me to."
>
> "I have to go camping because my husband wants me to."
>
> "I have to remain in the restaurant because I ordered a sandwich."
>
> "I have to accept the new job because it pays more money."
>
> "I have to finish reading this chapter before I read the next chapter."

Have-to thinking cuts us off from the reality of our freedom and responsibility. It places control over our lives outside ourselves and creates a constant source of frustration and resentment.

If-Only Thinking

In attempting to look back through time, the regretful phrase "if only" takes the place of the anxious phrase what-if that is applied to the future:

"If only I had not been so shy and self-conscious."

"If only I had been able to look people straight in the eye and tell them what I was thinking."

"If only I had been as strong and brave as other children."

"If only I had been raised in a different family."

"If only my parents had not been so punitive and critical."

"If only my parents had allowed me to learn how to be independent."

If we feel an emotional reaction of anger, frustration, regret, sorrow, or shame when an if-only thought arises, the reaction is real and has meaning for us. Indeed, it may be beneficial to look closely at the painful memory and even— as an act of imagination—to talk honestly to ourselves and the other participants about our pain. Yet we must recognize that any attempt to go back to the past to ask others to treat us better is impossible and bound to make us unhappy. If-only thinking is yet another way the chronically anxious person makes the impossible attempt to become someone other than himself or herself.

WHO IS TO BLAME?

Before we examine the issues of our own freedom and responsibility, we need to consider the issue of parental responsibility. Many people are blocked from looking honestly at the childhood origins of their anxiety-related problems because they wish to protect themselves from the pain of remembering past suffering or because they wish to protect their now-aging parents from the child's feelings of resentment. In this section, we will point out a healthy alternative both to stirring up old feelings of resentment and to concealing the reality of the past. In other words, we do not have to choose between being angry at our parents and being dishonest with ourselves.

It is entirely possible both to feel love and gratitude toward our parents and to speak objectively—even bluntly—about their shortcomings.

It is also quite natural for feelings of displeasure and anger to arise when we remember painful conditions. At the same time, the temptation to blame our parents or primary caretaker for being demanding, critical, or overprotective is a path that leads away from the issue of embracing our freedom and taking responsibility for who we are in the here and now.

We can only guess at the nature of the psychological stress experienced by the parents of phobic persons, but we can be almost certain that the parents were doing the best they could. If they were being domineering and setting unrealistically high standards of performance for their infant, chances are they were following a pattern that had been established in their own childhoods.

It is healthy and honest to be able to say, "My parents did the best they could, though they did badly sometimes (or in certain respects)"; or, "Sometimes my mother (or father) did things that hurt me"; or even to say, "I remember a time when my mother (or father) was intentionally cruel to me."

On the other hand, if we say, "My mother wrecked my life," or, "My father is to blame for the way I am today," we are stating the case in such a way as to trap ourselves in a hopeless situation. The manifold roots of anxiety extend far wider and deeper into our family's and our society's history than merely to our parents' fearfulness, criticalness, or argumentativeness. Many people could be blamed for our fears, but in our hearts we know there is really only one person who can overcome them.

It is true that we might not be in the trap of anxiety and worry today if only our parents had been relaxed, nonjudgmental, not alcoholic, not worried about money, or not self-engrossed. But there is a more important truth than this: our anxiety today stems from the way we see the world today. To attach ourselves to our parents' behavior of 20, 30, 40, or more years ago by blaming them—or, for that matter, by covering up their shortcomings—is to remain in the trap. In a sense, such attachment to the past *is the trap*. We can think about going back in time to ask our parents to change their behavior—indeed, we can think about it for years—but we cannot really go back in time. Rather than blaming or excusing our parents, we need to get a clearer idea of why we perceive ourselves and our world the way we do. Of course, it is not easy to change the way we see the world—but to do so is to find the way out of the trap.

In addition to the issue of blaming our parents, there is the issue of blaming ourselves. Self-blame, like self-ridicule and self-contempt, is a self-diminishing behavior.

The pain (and, in a sense, the blessing) of an anxiety or panic attack comes from an acute awareness of the high price we pay for striving to please others at all costs—we are forced to recognize that it costs us our ability to relax, to communicate easily, to enjoy life, to be true to ourselves.

While the guilt we may feel over this waste of time is an honest and real feeling, it does not require us to waste more time and to miss more opportunities by engaging in self-recriminations. We have a choice as to how we respond to such guilt. We can choose to use it as a catalyst—to help start us on the path to recovery.

OUR VIEW OF THE RECOVERY PROCESS

"Recovery" is a perfectly good word, and we will use it in this book. However, it can be misleading in that it seems to suggest that it is your task, as an anxious, phobic, or agoraphobic person, somehow to go back and recover something you have lost. By now it is clear that the exaggerated "maturity" and "niceness" of the idealized self are illusions in which people wrap themselves like a chrysalis. They are not qualities that need to be recovered.

When a chrysalis opens up in the sunlight, perhaps the butterfly within has an anxiety attack. The task of the butterfly is not to crawl back in. Its task is to *grow*—to unfold its wings and fly. The task of someone who has experienced an anxiety attack is not to struggle to recover anything but rather to free and unfold his or her latent abilities to be more aware, honest, self-caring, and compassionate—and to look on life not as a trap but as an adventure.

3

The Key Issues:
Freedom and Responsibility

*"Our self-feeling in this world depends entirely
on what we* back *ourselves to be and to do."*

—William James, *The Principles of Psychology*

*"When we are anxious, we experience the truth. But
when we are anxious about being anxious, we are
sick and needlessly limit our potential for enjoying
life—and we do not experience the truth."*

—Peter Koestenbaum, *The New Image of the Person*

If children are granted their birthright of continuous, unconditional love in infancy and early childhood and are not de-
ceived about their own nature and the nature of the world,
they will grow up psychologically uninjured and secure. They
will be able to love and be loved. They will be competent to
meet the challenges of life, to know life's pleasures and joys,
to accept the pain, suffering, and loss that are equally part
of the fabric of life. They will eschew self-deception. They
will be free of the self-diminishing false assumptions that lead
to chronic anxiety and phobias. They will laugh when they
are happy and cry when they are sad. They will know who
they are.

But what about the rest of us?

If our childhood was less than perfect, must we always

remain helpless and incomplete in our own minds? Are we permanently condemned to live out our lives with an insatiable craving for safety, security, and love—without ever really knowing who we are?

THE FEAR OF FREEDOM

As we saw in Chapter 2, agoraphobia and other forms of self-defeating fear are a natural consequence of being afraid of our own freedom to exist as a unique being or separate person. One person suffering from agoraphobia wrote, "The thing I fear most is standing naked before my own freedom." Another said, "Most people are afraid to die. Agoraphobics are afraid to live."

The fear of freedom can lead to a passive, nonassertive approach to life. After all, if we are not even sure of our right to exist, how can we with any confidence ask others for good and fair treatment? And how can we be certain at any given moment that someone won't notice that we don't really have the right to be here?

In short, if we give up our freedom, we give up our right to protest. We give up our right to tell people what we don't like (hinting or going behind their back is not the same thing). We give up our right to tell others what we like, want, or need. And we give up our right to expect others to give our suggestions or ideas serious consideration. The enormous shyness many of us have experienced as children or teenagers is a pure example of what the absence of freedom feels like.

The natural consequences of giving up so much freedom are frustration and displeasure, which, in their most intense form, become anger. And yet, if we're not sure of our right to exist, we can hardly grant ourselves the right to show any signs of frustration, displeasure, or anger to others. If we "lost control" and got angry, people might notice us and remark, "Hey you! You don't have any right to be here!"

So we attempt to stifle our cravings and aversions and put on a mask of perpetual niceness and exaggerated maturity. We may say to ourselves, "I can't lose my temper. I'm too mature a person for that." As one woman using the Self-Care Program wrote, "When I was younger, I turned all of my feelings like sadness, jealousy, hurt, and loneliness into inner anger and hatred. I always felt that showing you care about someone or that you really need someone was a sign of weakness. I felt I had to be strong and not show my real feelings. I guess I acted as if I really didn't care, when I was really hurting the whole time." In a vicious circle, anxiety leads to shame, and the chronically anxious person tries all the harder to conceal the problem behind the mask.

In this chapter, we intend to show that there is a way out of the trap of anxiety and fear. No matter how bad things were in the long-distant past—or two weeks ago, or even five minutes ago—there is always a safe place we can reach in the present moment if we are quiet and alert enough to see it. But first we must examine the distorted sense of responsibility of the anxious person, which is a major obstacle to the relaxed and alert condition in which freedom flourishes.

A CONFUSED SENSE OF RESPONSIBILITY

Chronically anxious people tend to confuse logical responsibility—responsibility for the results of their own choices—with being accountable for the feelings and actions of other people. Their magnified sense of responsibility may cause them to become almost paralyzed by guilt, worry, and obsessive concern about the possible results of their own expressed feelings or actions. For example, they might suddenly start to worry about what someone might read into in a letter they have just mailed.

In one sense, chronically anxious people appear to be extremely responsible in their sometimes obsessive efforts to avoid harming or disturbing other people, but this is not entirely true responsibility. Often they are actually more afraid of disapproval, rejection, and emotional abandonment than they are concerned with the good or harm they might do.

Indeed, their fear-driven self-centeredness and lack of careful attention to others can cause them to inconvenience others inadvertently in their striving to look good—for example, when they insist on doing someone a favor that is not wanted or needed. As we have seen, anxiously overprotective parents may be so concerned with being "good parents" that they interfere with their children's psychological growth toward competence and independence.

Anxious people confuse worrying a lot with being responsible. They like to think that their problem is that they are "too responsible" or "too conscientious." It is hard for them to accept the fact that they are not acting in a truly responsible way.

If we are a truly responsible person, we see clearly that we are accountable only for *the foreseeable results of our own choices and actions*—not for what other people feel, think, or do. Thus, we take the time to do things properly, to express ourselves clearly and compassionately, to be aware of the likely consequences of our actions. Then we can express ourselves, pick up the telephone, drop letters into the mailbox, accept the consequences—and not worry about it at all.

Those who suffer from a confused sense of responsibility need to learn that the only defense we need against the awesomeness of freedom is an adequate answer to the question "Who am I?" This is a question that can only be answered by accepting ourselves honestly, just as we are, in the here and now—and by presenting ourselves to others in this same spirit. With a clear sense of ourselves, we can still care about others' feelings and needs without taking unwarranted responsibility for them, and without looking for total rejection or disapproval in every chance remark.

GAINSAYING TWO MYTHS ABOUT FREEDOM

We have observed that there are two common myths about freedom: First, that it doesn't exist. Second, that it does and is a problem.

Chronically anxious and agoraphobic people usually believe one of these myths. If we believe either of them, we diminish our lives and our chances for happiness. If we truly understand and use our freedom, as we will see in the Self-Care Program, we can use it in any given situation to liberate ourselves from the anxiety that arises from our painful attachment to the past.

Does Freedom Exist?

The immediate source of freedom is, of course, our human consciousness. Freedom consists of being able to choose deliberately, in the present moment, whether or how to respond to an event, to choose among possible interpretations of events, and to choose among possible courses of action or nonaction. If they represent deliberate choices, nonactions (like "not smoking," "not worrying," and "not holding my breath") count for as much as actions do.

Through the ages, ultralogical thinkers have concluded that human freedom cannot possibly exist because its source, human consciousness, or the mind, cannot be located, observed, or measured. They follow the dictum, "If it cannot be measured, it does not exist." There is really no answer to this insistence that the existence of all things under the sun is assured only by someone's ability to measure them. The Indian teacher Krishnamurti has pointed out the derivation of the word "meditate" from a Sanskrit word meaning "to measure." According to Krishnamurti, meditation, at a more profound level, has more to do with cultivating the act of observing reality—an act that logically precedes measuring (judging, evaluating, interpreting, etc.). The anxious person usually puts the cart (measuring) before the horse (observing). Those who meditate attempt to put the two processes in their proper order by refraining from measuring things, just observing them as they allow their minds to be quiet and alert.

Freedom (and control) ultimately resides in simple awareness, through which we can bring precision and clarity to our actions, not in the coercive manipulation of ideas, events, ourselves, or other people. Many creative and innovative people have discovered their own ways of cultivating the non-judgmental inner stillness of meditation, in which one can observe thoughts arise and depart in the present moment without reacting to them mechanically in terms of past conditions. Thomas Edison, for one, evidently practiced a kind of quiet sitting from time to time in the midst of his inventive labors.

We are obviously not acting as free human beings when we feel compelled to evaluate and categorize rapidly every thought that arises, in an effort to avoid danger—to keep everything under control. In this frame of mind, every thought must be labeled "safe," "unsafe," "acceptable," "unacceptable," etc.

When, in the present moment, we are able to relax physically and allow ourselves to experience our consciousness when it is almost empty of thoughts—a state similar to but not quite the same as those in which we are at one with our work or with a piece of music—everything becomes quiet and balanced, and we are free to measure or not to measure, to interpret or not to interpret, to judge or not to judge, to react or not to react. This is when we directly experience our freedom.

Is Freedom a Problem?

Psychologist Albert Ellis once described phobic people as those who "demand certainty in a world where there are no absolutes or certainties for any of us." This unrealistic demand for certainty stems from a fundamental sense of insecurity. To the extent that we have adapted to the idea that we are helpless and unfree, we devote our lives to concealing our weakness and avoiding risks at all costs.

If we live in such a trap, freedom may seem limitless and threatening. For example, some agoraphobic people wonder, "If I were truly free, what would keep me from going out of control? What would stop me from acting on some fearful or hostile impulse and injuring myself or someone else?" The answer is, of course, that we don't need anything outside ourselves to keep us under control. Self-preservation is part of our nature. We will be protected by the same powerful survival instinct that led us as helpless beings to put such great energy into constructing an idealized self. We need to see that we can place our trust in our own nature and in the control that lies in simple, relaxed awareness. As we go deeper into ourselves, we find that our self-regard is not separate from our compassion for other living beings.

The real problem is that the idealized self is such a drain on our energy that we are used to working very hard to maintain a sense of balance and security. We attempt to arrange our lives (and sometimes the lives of those close to us) to avoid "unsafe" conditions. As we gradually begin to relax and to stop working so hard at control, and as we sense the serene openness and spaciousness of freedom, we may miss the anxiety that tells us we are on guard. Since we have believed for so long that hard work is required to keep our world under control, we may find it difficult to believe that the simple mindfulness and alertness that freedom gives us will keep us balanced and protect us from harm.

Agoraphobic people may actually forget what it feels like to be relaxed. One morning, a client called Christopher and said, "I had the strangest feeling last night. It scared me. I think I was feeling relaxed."

The fear of going out of control confuses freedom with helplessness. The more we grow into our freedom and out of our helplessness and suffering, the greater will be our sense of inner security and safety. Freedom is a path not to danger but to self-awareness, wisdom, and compassion for ourselves and others.

To an agoraphobic person, freedom seems to require great effort. In one sense, this is correct. It does require a willingness to challenge old assumptions, as well as a willingness to learn from experiences—to learn new skills and practices. In another sense, freedom is effortless. We can see both the effort and the effortlessness of freedom in mastery of any activity, from playing the piano to driving an automobile.

Only the well-informed are truly free. In other words, only they are aware of all the available choices in a given situation. Before they can be free to make choices, anxious people need to learn to see the choices available to them. It is also helpful for them to understand the choices available to others. Many people with phobias say that simply learning how bridges, airplanes, or elevators are designed and constructed makes it easier to deal with these feared objects. It may help, for example, to understand the design considerations that led engineers to space the towers of a suspension bridge a certain distance apart.

There is a day-care center in Berkeley, California, where parents must donate a certain number of hours of volunteer labor. On her first day at the center, a young mother, who was also a skilled watercolorist, noticed a youngster dipping her brush into a series of pots of tempera paint of various hues. "Wait a minute," she said to the tiny painter. "If you rinse your brush out each time you change colors, the colors will be brighter. You're going to get muddy colors if you don't rinse your brush out." The young woman found herself pulled gently but firmly aside by a member of the staff, who told her, "We have a strict policy here of *never* interfering with the children's explorations."

Like the children at this care center, we may keep painting muddy pictures until the day we discover for ourselves that we can pause and rinse our brushes out in clean, clear water now and then and paint our days in bright, pure colors if we choose to do so.

THE THREE REALMS OF FREEDOM

Looking Outward

Our freedom in relation to the outer world is always limited. If we don't speak French, we may have trouble asking directions from a Parisian. If we are unemployed, we cannot spend our money freely. If we are extremely agoraphobic, we may feel unable to leave our town or even our house. Many of the conditions of our lives are outside the realm of personal choice and cannot be changed; others, like anxiety and self-defeating fear, can be changed over time, with enough awareness, understanding, and dedication.

A prayer attributed to Francis of Assisi pertains to the wise use of external freedom: "Lord, help me to change that which I can change, to accept that which I cannot change, and to tell the difference between the two." The great gift of *awareness* is, in a sense, an answer to this prayer. The more we cultivate the ability to pause and see things clearly, the less our lives are restricted by the distorting lenses and mirrors of what-if thinking, have-to thinking, if-only thinking, and so on—and the greater are the chances that our actions can be effective and productive. For example, if we discover that we have locked our keys in our car's trunk when we return from a hike in the woods, we can either rail at the fates (and engage in if-only thinking) or we can start considering possible courses of action.

Looking Inward

In contrast to external freedom, our inner freedom is virtually absolute. Our inner world can be spacious and filled with a feeling of warmth, light, and confidence, or it can be a dark, cramped place reverberating with nervous whispers and chatterbox worries. As psychiatrist Viktor Frankl has shown in his inspiring accounts of concentration-camp survivors, inner freedom can exist in a real prison as well as in a prison of the mind.

We always have a fundamental choice between remaining "trapped in thought" or granting ourselves freedom.

Phobic people who are on the road to recovery have discovered the most important and awesome freedom they possess: the freedom to be honest with themselves rather than to change or "fix" themselves. Growth often begins just at the point when we begin to feel trapped by a life that seems unworkable. It is at this point that the logic of the situation virtually forces us to discard the pretense that we have everything under control.

Sadly, in extreme cases, people refuse to pick up this great weapon—this "knife for cutting through illusions," as the Tibetans call our freedom to be honest with ourselves. People may spend months or years in a kind of unhealthy equilibrium, hiding from their own freedom and, as a natural consequence, living in fear.

Let's turn briefly to a remarkable book, *Human Behavior: An Inventory of Scientific Finding,* written over 20 years ago by Bernard Berelson and Gary A. Steiner. In their concluding chapter, the authors contend that the scientific study of human behavior shows that human beings "make their own reality" in two ways: first, through adaptive behavior; second, through self-deception. Of the latter, the authors write:

> Man is not just a seeker of truth, but of deceptions, of himself as well as others. . . . When man can come to grips with his needs by actually changing the environment, he does so. But when he cannot achieve such "realistic" satisfaction, he tends to take the other path: to modify what he sees to be the case, what he thinks he wants, what he thinks others want. . . .

We must agree with Berelson and Steiner's contention that human beings commonly "make their own reality" through self-deception. The idealized self is such a deception. However, self-deception is only part of the story, since there can be no deception without at least a glimmering awareness of truth—after all, "deception" means "concealing the truth in order to mislead." Without at least a dim awareness of truth, one can be ignorant but not self-deceiving. Thus, human consciousness not only makes self-deception possible but also leaves the door open to self-honesty and self-understanding.

If we go through this door and decide simply and honestly to observe the thoughts that continually arise in our consciousness, we will recognize them to be largely reflections of the past external conditions of our lives. Recognizing this, we can see there is no logical need for us to react blindly or automatically to particular thoughts in the present moment. If an unhappy thought arises—such as "My father never expressed love for me"—we can learn simply to observe it without reacting to it as though it were a sad event to be endlessly relived. When we learn to distinguish between thoughts and ourselves as observers of thoughts, we have cut through the illusion that thoughts control us and somehow require us to react to them emotionally.

If we observe our thoughts objectively instead of reacting to them blindly, we make our own reality through self-awareness rather than through self-deception. Such objectivity is not an escape from feelings and emotions. Indeed, when we give up concealment and avoidance as the major themes of our life, in favor of objective awareness, we may find ourselves crying more easily when we are sad, laughing more easily when we are happy, and in general being more relaxed and spontaneous in our behavior.

The Point at Which Inward and Outward Meet

If we pause, take a slow, complete breath, and ask ourselves who it is that looks inward and outward or who it is that breathes in and breathes out, we may remember something important that we have really always known: *who we are.*

This is something that cannot be put into words very well, because words are inherently metaphors for reality and thus—to some extent—distance us from it; who we are *is* reality.

One way to say it is that we are our freedom or that we exist in our freedom. Existential philosophy tells us that we are continually expressing who we are in the choices we make. Of course, our freedom to make these choices exists in finite moments, although we often have to live with the consequences of our choices for periods of time. Thus, if in one moment we choose to fly to Australia, we must live with our decision during the day-long flight to Sydney and during the return trip. The same principle applies when we cross a bridge, go across town on a bus, take a test, order a sandwich, or start a new job.

Another way of looking at it is that our external freedom to choose among possible courses of action varies considerably from moment to moment. This is one of the real limitations of freedom. It is the reason that planning and organizing are important skills to develop.

However, even while we are living with the consequences of a relatively important decision like flying to Australia, we still have a great deal of freedom of action, and we have virtually unlimited internal freedom to interpret our experiences, our thoughts, and our feelings from moment to moment on our flight. For example, we could spend our airborne time being anxious, conversing, sleeping, reading, relaxing or meditating, watching in-flight movies, or looking at the clouds.

In regard to every feeling (or thought) that arises within, our freedom always permits us at least two alternatives: to interpret the feeling as a threat to our very existence, or to accept the feeling and observe it carefully as it comes and goes.

At this juncture, we can see how our old habitual beliefs and ideas (such as "I must please others in order to survive" and "I must seek help now") can actually become our friends and guides on the road to personal growth and recovery. Whenever they arise and invite us to torment ourselves, we know that we are at a point of choice.

Instead of accepting their invitation, magnifying whatever physiological arousal exists at that moment, and leaping blindly into a fight or struggle with an invisible enemy, we can choose to take a slow, complete breath, relax, and exercise our human freedom. (In Rollo May's words, we can choose to choose rather than choosing *not* to choose.) The next step is to decide on our next action (or nonaction).

WHAT IT MEANS TO ACCEPT FREEDOM

Accepting freedom can be as simple as an act of self-care, like choosing to breathe naturally, from the abdomen, to calm us on our way to or from work. Many such small, self-caring actions can overcome our inertia and move us in the direction of wholehearted living. As two of Christopher's patients found out, freedom sometimes requires us to accept risks and to confront our anxieties.

Sarah

As a child, Sarah traded away her freedom for a false idea of security. Her anxiety was severe and pervasive.

When Sarah first came to Christopher for treatment, she was 29 years old. She had been virtually housebound since the age of 13. Her first panic attack occurred at school. She subsequently stopped attending school and was tutored at home.

Sarah lived with her parents in an apartment above their grocery in a small suburban town in Southern California. She would walk no more than a few steps outside the store with her dog. She was pale and thin and had developed a habit of twitching and clearing her throat almost continuously.

Sarah did the bookkeeping for the store and cooked lunch for her parents. She had an older sister who had had a "touch" of anxiety herself before getting married.

Her parents planned to retire, sell the grocery store, and move to Phoenix, Arizona. Sarah knew that if she went with them, she would live out the rest of her life as a socially isolated person—that she would never truly live her own life. The thought of her parents' deaths filled her not only with sadness but with fear. It would be terrifying to lose her psychological center of balance, which she placed in her parents' home rather than within her own heart.

It was clear that Sarah needed to distance herself from her parents. After several months, a small apartment became available two doors away from the family store. Although it was nearby, moving into it was a big step and the beginning of the road to independence.

Progress was slow. Sarah was brave, yet the anxiety and panicky feelings persisted even though she could now walk a few blocks and go into a small store down the street. When her parents put their store up for sale and purchased a home in Phoenix, both Sarah and Christopher felt pressure for her to achieve the degree of autonomy that would make it possible for her to stay and let her parents go. There wasn't enough time, however, at the pace recovery was going. Christopher advised Sarah that she should "go for it" and admit herself into a residential program at the hospital just a few blocks away.

(Few people with agoraphobia and other anxiety disorders actually require hospitalization. Most have a support network of friends and family who, with the proper understanding, can provide the kind of unconditional and uncritical emotional support needed during the challenging period of personal growth that leads to independent functioning. Sarah's agoraphobia was unusually severe, and circumstances indicated that the neutral "safe place" provided by the residential program was the best choice for her at a crucial time in her life.)

Here is the rest of Sarah's story, as told by Christopher:

She was terrified at the idea of hospitalization. I told her to think about it and reassured her that I would be available to her on a 24-hour basis in the beginning. She met me the next week with a small bag packed, telling me she knew she had to at least try. She wanted me to promise that I would not make her stay if she didn't want to.

The trip from the hospital parking lot into the hospital took nearly two hours, with many retreats and relaxation exercises. Sarah and I still joke about how she grabbed onto me so hard that my arm still has the scars. Through sheer determination we made it to the third floor and were met by a psychiatric social worker who offered a kind and reassuring welcome. Sarah was literally shaking all over and there was terror in her eyes. I stayed close to her and held her hand. She kept asking me, "You won't let them keep me, will you?" I told her that I had made her that promise, that we were just here to check things out and that she could leave anytime she wanted, but if she wanted to look around while she was here and talk to the social workers, it was OK. She did stay long enough to see that the people did not reject her even though she was displaying severe anxiety.

Leaving the hospital took about one minute. As she came out the doors, she took in a deep breath of cool air. She said she felt weak, yet I knew she had achieved a major triumph. She giggled on the way home and chatted about the experience as if she wanted to reinforce the fact that it had really happened.

The following session, Sarah again met me with her overnight bag as we had arranged. "Dr. McCullough, this time I'm going to stay," she announced quietly.

I called her that evening after leaving her at the hospital, just to let her know I had confidence in her ability to stick it out. It was important that I not give her the message that I was worried about her. I encouraged her and told her how strongly I felt that she was doing the right thing and was going to be OK.

She stayed in the residential program for several weeks, receiving group therapy and individual psychotherapy as well as doing field work (outings). Her parents initially did not like the idea of their neighbors learning about Sarah's condition through her hospitalization, but they became supportive as they saw her make progress. They did finally move to Phoenix, and without Sarah.

Four years have passed. Today Sarah has her own apartment, a car, a part-time job, friends—and a boyfriend. She has traveled some. She is still working on her anxieties, and when life stresses occur, it sometimes throws her off-balance for a while. However, she has learned to see such experiences not as failures but as opportunities for growth. She is truly living a fuller life than she ever dreamed possible. Of all my clients, including those with more dramatic success stories, Sarah still stands out in my mind as a great example of the power of freedom. Her courage in accepting responsibility for a difficult choice led her to a real victory.

Douglas

There are two things that people who have accepted their freedom and recovered from chronic anxiety and phobias often like to do: to take trips and to take classes. As they begin to conquer their most troublesome symptoms, they gain the courage to challenge various self-diminishing beliefs and behaviors. When they accept their freedom, they give up their attachment to the false assumption that they are helpless.

Douglas was a man in his early 50s when he enrolled in a class given by Christopher. Douglas avoided many public places, including theaters and banks. He had not ridden on a city bus for 30 years. He had experienced a panic attack on one when he was a young soldier returning home from the Pacific at the end of the Second World War.

After some field work on buses with a "support person" and several solo rides of several miles, Douglas decided to do something else he had feared and hadn't thought of doing for 30 years: he went back to school. He took a course in carpentry, to learn a skill he had always wanted to have, and one in English, because he decided it was time to stop being embarrassed by a few recurrent mistakes in his English.

Douglas's experience was typical of those on the road to recovery. Most people discover that their self-defeating fears are simply the most pressing and visible of their self-diminishing behaviors. This is one of the reasons such fears are a blessing in disguise: they raise the issue of freedom versus helplessness. Once this issue is confronted, people find themselves using their newfound freedom to expand their knowledge and skills as well as their "safe territory."

4

Self-Expression:
Telling the World Who You Are

"Taking a new step, uttering a new word, is what people fear most."

—Dostoyevski

"To be free to love other persons requires self-affirmation and, paradoxically, the assertion of oneself."

—Rollo May, *Freedom and Destiny*

A friend looked at the subtitle of this chapter and asked Robert, "Why is it necessary for me to tell the world who I am?" Our answer is that if you don't, the world will tell you who you are. For example, anyone can start feeling a bit overwhelmed and "unreal" in the midst of a throng of Christmas shoppers. At such a time, you need to speak back to the hustle and bustle, perhaps simply by taking a few slow, complete breaths and cultivating an attitude of patience and serenity within your own private "bubble." Christopher likes to call this attitude "living from the inside out instead of from the outside in." (In Yoga, this is called "creating an aura.")

"But why are you including a chapter on assertiveness?" the same friend asked. In the late '70s there were dozens of books published on the subject, and we cite three excellent ones in the list of suggested readings. The point of this chapter is to underscore that assertive self-expression is a great antidote to anxiety. People who are suffering from continual worry and anxiety, anxiety attacks, or panic attacks do not experientially understand the value of assertiveness, even if they have read books on the subject.

As we have seen, if we suffer from chronic anxiety, we may actually *not know how* to disagree with others, to express displeasure, to ask for something directly, or simply to say no without experiencing psychological stress—in other words, without feeling threatened. This is frustrating.

By learning how to express ourselves in a healthy, self-assertive manner, we can eliminate the self-generated psychological stress that comes from fighting such feelings as frustration, dissatisfaction, displeasure, or anger. This frees energy and makes it easier for us to be more natural and spontaneous in our behavior—and less frustrated and angry.

We are not saying that it is necessary to share intimate feelings with strangers or to express every thought or feeling at the expense of someone else's feelings. We are saying that it is vital to be able to express ourselves voluntarily when and where we choose to do so—when it is important to us. In particular, we need to be able to deal with people whose behavior we find to be coercive or hostile, in ways that leave us feeling all right about ourselves.

THE SELF-CENSORSHIP ISSUE

A great deal of the internally generated psychological stress that manifests itself as anxiety arises from self-censorship. Self-censorship reaches a pervasive extreme in agoraphobia, but the issue can come up for any of us, even in such small, everyday experiences as ordering meals in restaurants, asking someone to pass the salt, telling a salesperson it is our turn to be waited on, or asking someone to please move aside so that we can get by. If you experience the slightest doubt as to whether it is all right for you to request a normal service or customary favor, or if you are not relaxed and spontaneous when you do so, then the issue of self-censorship is relevant to your life.

The Third Annual National Phobia Conference was held in San Francisco during the summer of 1982. A number of sophisticated research reports had been delivered to the assembled psychologists, psychiatrists, and other health-care professionals. A white-haired general practitioner made his way to the front of the hall. Ignoring the microphone, he said words to this effect, "People with agoraphobia need to get their anger out. That's what it is. If they can just get their anger out, they'll be all right. That's what I think."

In our view, this was one of the shrewdest observations made at the conference, in spite of its simplicity.

Most agoraphobic people recognize that they have a problem dealing with and expressing displeasure or anger, which contributes to their anxiety. Not only are unacceptable feelings censored from transmission to the outer world, they come to be suppressed within the agoraphobics' own minds and hidden even from themselves.

When extremely anxious people do speak up for themselves, they are apt to choke with emotion as though they are expecting a severe rebuke—which gives us some idea of their feelings of dependence on what others think or do. As children, they learned that their very existence was only conditionally acceptable to other people. Such familiar messages as these may have played a role:

> "Mother doesn't like it when you cry."
> "Always keep a smile on your face."
> "Never contradict your father."
> "You shouldn't feel that way."
> "If you can't say anything nice, don't say anything at all."

Let's look more closely at these unacceptable feelings. They include pain or suffering; frustration, displeasure, or anger; anxiety; and any other feelings that tend to violate the unique rules of the idealized self—feelings that someone else might disapprove of.

There is a logical interrelationship between these feelings and out-of-the-blue fear: having unmet needs or wishes is experienced as pain or suffering. Suppressing pain can create anger. Suppressing anger can create anxiety or depression. Suppressing anxiety can create increased anxiety, up to panic levels. Therefore, habitually denying or fighting against these feelings can lead eventually to acute anxiety and emotional disruption.

It becomes clear that the idealized self created so long ago as a defense against the loss of life-sustaining support is actually a major source of anxiety in itself, and that we feed anxiety when we seek to affirm and validate the idealized self and to deny our true feelings.

We cannot successfully hide from anxiety, avoid it, conceal it, or fight it. The only way to cope with anxiety is to observe it, understand it, and allow it to disappear after we have acknowledged receipt of its message. This is easily illustrated by the experiences of Janet, a woman who is recovering from agoraphobia. We'll let her describe this process in her own words:

> I had a pretty good week until two days ago—I had another panic attack. I felt discouraged and felt like I wasn't making any progress. Then I started looking at what was going on with me emotionally rather than just worrying about the anxiety. I pulled out the Self-Care Checklist [see the Self-Care Program] and began to think about what might have happened that upset me. It hit me like a bolt of lightning.
>
> Our friends had called and invited us to a play—they had purchased the tickets and assumed we would jump at the chance to go. I felt that I couldn't say no even though it was the kind of play I wouldn't like—I can't stand depressing dramas. I just said something on the phone like, "Oh, that's great," and they came over for dinner before the play. I *really* didn't want to go, so I began to hint that I just didn't feel up to it. Finally I

told them that I was afraid I might have anxiety and it would ruin everyone's evening. My girl friend said not to worry; she would help me and we could leave if I needed to—no problem! Finally my husband, Bill, picked up on my not wanting to go and said that he didn't think he would go either. At the door I saw my friend's husband gesture sympathetically to Bill, and Bill just put his hands out and shrugged. I felt betrayed, I cried, and then I attacked Bill for not standing up for me.

Then I suddenly realized that I had not had enough nerve to speak up and be honest about not wanting to go because I didn't enjoy that kind of play. I made Bill the bad guy, but it was I who had betrayed myself. I thought about how passive I had been and how I had not said anything on the phone, then tried to use the agoraphobia as a way out, and then hoped Bill would speak for me and blamed him when he didn't.

I feel badly about what happened, but at the same time I'm excited for having seen the whole thing so clearly. It was a real "Aha!" experience. I began to ask myself why I didn't want to tell them how I really felt and came up with three reasons:

1. I wanted them to be happy, and I didn't want to spoil their excitement.
2. After all, how could I refuse a gift?
3. I wanted them to see me as someone who pleased them.

Janet took a huge step forward by just being able to recognize how she had betrayed her real feelings to protect herself from rejection. She will take another step forward the next time a similar situation arises if she says something like this: "You are so thoughtful for thinking of us by getting the tickets. Bill may want to go, but I just don't enjoy that kind of play, so I'll pass. Even if Bill doesn't go, would you like to come by for dinner before you go?"

Part of the problem is that Janet is so accustomed to not stating her feelings directly that it seldom occurs to her that she is free to speak up.

Her second insight was seeing how this self-betrayal—not recognizing and acting on her true feelings—translated itself into anxiety—in this case, a panic attack. By not saying how she felt directly, she created a feeling of being trapped. If Janet had freely expressed her desires and at the same time freely expressed her caring feelings toward her friends, she could have felt relaxed and good about herself. She would, in short, have felt in charge of her own life.

There is an enormous difference between feeling good about yourself because others don't reject you and feeling good about yourself because you value your own feelings and respect others enough to communicate directly and honestly.

There is some confusion in our television-saturated culture between "acting" and "being." Anxiety is often nature's way of telling us that we are choosing *acting* nice or *acting* mature over *being* authentic and honest.

In light of the above, let's consider some common agoraphobic attitudes and self-descriptions that are shared to a degree by many nonagoraphobic people:

"Sometimes I am confused about my own feelings."

"I hate to hurt other people's feelings."

"I don't want to sink to the level of those who display anger."

"They'll hold it against me if I tell them how I really feel."

"Sometimes I Am Confused About My Own Feelings"

People who are chronically anxious or experience anxiety attacks are often very confused about their own feelings; they find it difficult to differentiate between themselves and their feelings. If they have learned that anger, displeasure, or irritation is bad, they conclude that they themselves must be bad whenever these feelings arise. Agoraphobic people make the mistake of struggling not to *be* angry or not to *be* envious, when all they really need to do is acknowledge that an angry or envious thought has arisen.

"I Hate to Hurt Other People's Feelings"

Almost all agoraphobic people will acknowledge that they truly *hate* to hurt other people's feelings. This great concern with hurting others is not simple compassion. It is a defense related to certain unrealistic attitudes, or (in the jargon of psychoanalysis) "neurotic trends." Psychoanalyst Karen Horney identifies these trends as the need for affection and approval, the need for personal admiration, and the need for perfection and unassailability. As Horney notes, not all of these needs are necessarily unrealistic. What makes the need for affection unrealistic, for example, is that it is "devoid of the value of reciprocity." In other words, "For the neurotic person, his own feelings of affection count as little as they would if he were surrounded by strange and dangerous animals. To be accurate, he does not really want the others' affection, but is merely concerned, keenly and strenuously, that they make no aggressive move against him." This is the basis of the passive posture adopted by many agoraphobic people.

If we are keenly and strenuously trying to ward off an attack, we are not going to be communicating in a direct manner. More likely, we'll just be going through the motions and keeping an eye out for any sudden moves (literally or figuratively) on the part of the person we're dealing with.

We have discussed in Chapter 1 the factors that influence the subjective threshold of perceived danger. Communication is not possible when this threshold is very low and our attention is riveted on potential threats. Those recovering from agoraphobia and other anxiety conditions learn that it is all right to put much less energy into vigilance and more into communication.

"I Don't Want to Sink to That Level"

Agoraphobic people tend to have an intense dislike of ugly or ludicrous displays of anger. They say, quite honestly, that they don't like to sink to the level of angry people who rave, rant, and heap ridicule and abuse on the heads of their adversaries. At a deeper level, agoraphobics are afraid of feeling swept away by this threatening emotion. It is relevant that many agoraphobic people report that as children they had to endure displays of extreme anger and ridicule in their families.

Anger can indeed take a destructive and aggressive form, so in one sense this distaste for anger is understandable. The mistake some people make is to carry this aversion too far. They are too easily threatened by other people's anger, and they give up the right to express their own anger even in a constructive form. Worse, they give up their right to be clearly aware of their own angry feelings.

A self-caring person knows that the expression of anger is not necessarily good or bad; that it is not always necessary to tell another person about the angry feeling we may be experiencing; that it is not always necessary to conceal it, either. In other words, anger—in all its forms, from frustration to fury—lies within the realm of our freedom. There is no rule book that tells us whether we should express it in any given circumstances. If an order clerk ignores us while chatting on the phone with a friend, what should we do? No one can tell us exactly what to do, but it is obvious that if we communicate our needs simply and clearly, we will leave the situation feeling better about ourselves than if we say nothing.

The expression of displeasure or anger does not have to be ugly or ludicrous. We don't have to raise our voice or act petulant. We don't need to ridicule the other person or be abusive. We don't even have to get excited. All we really have to do is speak from the heart—to trust another human being enough to tell him or her about our inner experience.

"They'll Hold It Against Me"

Often, when people begin to see the value of being more open and honest about their inner world, they are concerned with what others will do with the information they provide. This is a legitimate concern. We may choose *not* to entrust our personal and private feelings to those who are hostile or who lack discretion and judgment. On the other hand, it is appropriate to share some of our feelings with those we work with and those who are close to us. And the ability to share our feelings openly with someone we love helps to bring relaxation and joy into life.

There are indeed a few people in this world who are hostile. Some people are greedy. Some talk behind others' backs. Some make up malicious lies. Such people are driven by an inner sense of emotional impoverishment. They are not trustworthy while they are in this state. On the other hand, there are many people who don't have these characteristics. They may not always have the gift of great understanding or wisdom, but they are able to trust and be trusted.

How do you tell the trustworthy from the untrustworthy?

The anxious person tends to avoid this question by entrusting as little information as possible to as few people as possible. People who trust themselves, however, will act on their experience and intuition and accept the risks involved in trusting others. Now and then, they will be disappointed, but they will usually be rewarded with a more open and workable relationship.

AGGRESSIVENESS, PASSIVITY, AND ASSERTIVENESS

One of the most powerful—and widely misunderstood—ideas in popular psychology is the value of self-expression and self-assertiveness in keeping people mentally healthy.

Assertiveness simply means claiming or owning one's feelings, thoughts, or actions. It is not a one-way, goal-oriented technique for controlling other people and coercing them into doing what you want. Assertiveness is a way of being honest, first with yourself, then with others. Being assertive means being open enough to be responsive to others. Since it improves communication, assertiveness no doubt increases the chances that others will decide to do what we want them to do, but it also increases the chances that we will decide to do what they want us to do.

Many people confuse assertiveness with aggressiveness. Let's consider the difference between the two and also consider a third communications strategy that is closely related to aggressiveness: passivity.

The basic stance of aggressiveness is to be on the attack. Aggressive verbal behavior is intended to control or dominate other people. The implicit message is, "I'm invincible. Watch out." Aggressive verbal behavior tends to be indiscriminate and hostile. For example: "Oh, shut up." "You're *exactly* like your mother." "You *always* do that." "You didn't come by. You *never* come by to lend a hand."

In a sense, passivity and aggressiveness are two sides of the same coin. The basic premise of the self-defense technique called aikido is that at the instant someone moves forward aggressively, he or she is off-balance and vulnerable to someone who is relaxed and alert. The basic posture of passivity is also off-balance—it is one of defensiveness and supplication. The implicit message of passivity is, "I'm helpless and incomplete. Don't hurt me."

Passive verbal behavior tends to be indirect, vague, self-justifying, and guilt-inspiring. Self-pity and easily injured feelings are typical passive responses. For example: "It seems like I'm *always* the one who's disappointed." "We were looking for you. We *thought* you *might* come down to lend a hand, but I guess you were busy."

By contrast, the clear message of assertiveness is, "We're two adults. Let's talk." The basic stance of self-assertiveness is one of strength and balance. Assertive behavior is direct, open, accepting, and nonthreatening. It lets people know where you stand as well as acknowledging your understanding of their thoughts and feelings. For example: "Can you come by on Wednesday? I know you're busy. At the same time, I really need some help."

A common statement made by people who are attempting to be more assertive is, "I couldn't be assertive. I was too angry." Being assertive is always appropriate. Anger is just as appropriately expressed assertively as is any other feeling. For example:

> *Aggressive reaction:* "You have ruined my whole evening. You *always* think only of yourself."

> *Passive reaction:* "I shouldn't get upset about such small things. It really doesn't matter."

> *Assertive response:* "I really feel terrible about this—I'm angry right now."

In the aggressive example, the speaker is blaming the other person; in the passive example, the speaker is blaming himself or herself; in the assertive example, the speaker is directly reporting inner feelings. The assertive statement is just as forceful as the aggressive one, but it is not threatening.

Do you remember the last time you came away from a minor disagreement or argument feeling relaxed and good about yourself? The chances are that you were neither aggressive nor passive, but assertive.

The Art of Active Listening

After we completely grasp the principles of assertiveness, we can begin to encourage others to be more assertive in their communications with us by using the technique psychologist Thomas Gordon calls "active listening," sometimes called "mirroring" or "reflecting."

When we first try this technique, we may sound like a human echo. The idea is not to repeat literally every word we hear, but to paraphrase important remarks briefly so that the speaker will know *what we think he or she has said*. Like any behavior, active listening can be artificial and manipulating or it can be genuine and honest. Over the past decade, some people have given assertiveness a bad name by attempting to use active listening as a means of control rather than a means of communication. At first the words may sound strange and artificial, but when we integrate the principle into our way of communicating, the practice can be an expression of our honesty.

Active listening is simply a direct way of telling the speaker that we have heard and understand what he has said. It does not mean we agree or disagree. Let's consider an example: The man behind you at a regular checkout stand in the supermarket says, "Oh, no!" and presses close to you when you start to write out a check. Here are some possible responses:

Aggressive: "How rude!"

Passive: "I'm trying to hurry—sorry I'm taking so long."

Active listening: "Waiting in line gets tiresome, doesn't it?" Or perhaps, "Sounds like you're in a hurry."

If we can step back and not take responsibility for the other person's feelings, then we can easily use the active listening response.

If we are already experiencing feelings of irritation, anger, or defensiveness, we might choose to express our feelings further with an assertive message (for example, "I understand it's tiresome to wait in line—I get uncomfortable when you stand so close").

One kind of active listening is a clear and direct reflection of what the other person has verbalized. For example:

The other person: "You frustrate me so much."

Active listening response: "How is that?"

The important issue is not that *I* am a frustrating person, it's that *the other person* feels frustration.

A second kind of active listening has to do with responding to someone who is expressing himself or herself to us using an *indirect* rather than a *direct* message. The example above is quite direct, "You frustrate me so much." It is aggressive—that is, blaming another person rather than owning one's feelings—but it is direct. Here is an example of an indirect message and an active listening response:

> *Indirect message:* "I wish someone would *do* something about this!"
>
> *Active listening response:* "You sound pretty upset. Do you want *me* to do something?"

The Assertive Message

What are the basic characteristics of an assertive message?

First, you use language that best describes how you feel. Therefore, the subject of an assertive sentence is the personal pronoun "I" rather than "you." Since I am the one who is experiencing the feelings, it is healthy and appropriate that what I say reflects that reality. For example, "I'm feeling hurt right now" is a clear expression of my experience, which at the same time gives direct information to the person I'm speaking to.

Using "I" in a sentence doesn't automatically make it an assertive expression. The difference has to do with the issue of blame. (Aggressive: "I feel that you hurt my feelings on purpose." Assertive: "I feel hurt when you speak to me that way." Passive: "I feel that I always let myself get hurt.")

Second, it is not important that you be "right" in order to have feelings or to express them. Assertiveness is important for its own sake, not for the sake of winning an argument or for proving that you are right and others wrong. Saying directly to another human being how you feel or what you think right now can be, in itself, an honest and a virtuous act. It is an exercise of your freedom as a human being.

Third, it is not important to be clear about your feelings before you say something. When we hold on to them for too long, feelings become magnified. A feeling of mild irritation can change into intense anger. If you don't have your feelings sorted out, you can simply say, "I feel confused right now— a bit sad and somewhat angry."

Here are some more examples of healthy and direct assertiveness regarding negative feelings:

"I feel frustrated right now."

"I really appreciate a call before someone comes to visit. Will that be OK with you next time?"

"I really feel irritated when someone calls me that."

"I feel angry when someone steps in front of me in line."

"Well, it's important to me to tell you how I feel."

"Now I feel confused. I don't really know why you are angry."

"That doesn't feel good."

Here are some positive feelings expressed assertively:

"I like you."

"I'm sorry you thought I was putting pressure on you."

"I admire the way you handled that."

"I'm glad we talked about it."

"I like it when you hold me like that."

Agoraphobic people are not the only ones who find it difficult to think fast enough to be assertive in a given situation. The mistake we all tend to make is to try in a hurry to design a "proper" or "correct" response instead of simply reflecting on how we feel.

If someone reports, "I was so surprised, I didn't know

what to say, so I just smiled," then, in a way, he has answered his own question. Instead of smiling, he could simply have paused, taken a deep breath, and reflected before he spoke. Then he might have said, "I'm so surprised, I don't know what to say." This is a fine example of a simple assertion, of a direct expression of feelings. (By the time he made that statement, he might have been clearer on what other feelings he had and what further assertions he may have wished to make.)

In order to get in touch with a feeling, we need to pause and reflect for an instant on the question, "What am I feeling right now?" Many people discover that when they pause, focus on their feelings, and then respond, others seem to pay more attention to what they say than when they react automatically.

LEARNING TO BE MORE ASSERTIVE

The idea of approaching assertiveness as a skill that can be studied and learned systematically has been in vogue since the pioneering work of behaviorists Andrew Salter and Joseph Wolpe over thirty years ago.

Two of our favorite books on the subject are Thomas Gordon's *Parent Effectiveness Training* and Pamela E. Butler's *Self-Assertiveness for Women*. We have drawn on both of these books in preparing the communications section in our Self-Care Program.

As Butler explains, there are four major areas in which people typically experience problems expressing themselves:

Many people, men especially, find it difficult to share *positive feelings* of warmth, affection, or appreciation with others. The failure to share positive feelings creates distance between people and stifles true intimacy.

Many find it difficult to express such *negative feelings* as, "I feel uncomfortable," "I feel annoyed," "I feel irritated," and so on, up to "I feel furious." This suppression of displeasure and anger leads to anxiety.

Many are unable to set *clear limits* on their willingness to accommodate others, especially in regard to time. This inability leads to mindless self-sacrificing behavior and consequent feelings of resentment toward others.

Many, women especially, hold back their ideas and opinions out of reluctance to *take the initiative* in a conversation when it is appropriate to do so. This lack of initiative leads to being underestimated and misunderstood by others.

Butler lists the main obstacles to self-expression in these areas as:

1. A lack of awareness that we have the freedom to respond assertively if we choose to so do.
2. Anxiety concerning what might happen if we were assertive.
3. Negative beliefs about ourselves—"Negative self-talk," as Butler calls it.
4. The lack of verbal skills.
5. The inappropriate use of gestures, facial expressions, tone of voice, etc.—for example, smiling when we are displeased.

In the Self-Care Program, our focus will be on overcoming these obstacles to assertiveness and on cultivating the ability to recognize and express negative feelings.

What to Expect from Assertiveness

It is very important that we reserve the right to tell others, especially those close to us, how we really feel. The fact that we are feeling displeasure is not really a threat to us or to anyone else. It is simply a fact that is worth noting and may be worth expressing.

The forthright expression of displeasure concerning something someone else has done can actually be a loving act, a way of giving some important information about ourselves to someone close to us. If we have been silent on the subject in the past, people may need some extra reassurance the first time we tell them about something they have done that triggers our displeasure. It is important to recognize that they, too, may believe erroneously that the expression of displeasure or anger indicates the absence of love.

As one agoraphobic woman said, "I think my husband likes me this way." It is easy to empathize with her husband if we stop to consider that from his point of view, his wife seldom reports feeling frustrated, upset, or irritated, as long as she remains agoraphobic. Unless his wife tells him why she is starting to express her feelings, any attempt at greater openness on her part may look to him like a change for the worse.

Also, if we are not used to talking about our feelings of displeasure or anger, we may go a bit overboard the first few times we try out our right to express such feelings. Bear in mind that when we speak up for the first time, we may surprise the person we are talking to. To avoid the Dr.-Jeckyll-and-Mr.-Hyde syndrome, we might first simply tell the other person that we need to be more open and honest in sharing our feelings—both negative and positive ones.

We shouldn't be surprised if we encounter skepticism and doubt with our initial attempts. The best course is to be simple and direct about our feelings without making lengthy explanations. Many people who are not used to talking about their feelings immediately retract them or invalidate them somehow, especially if they attempt long explanations.

We should be assertive and firm on one point: letting the other person know that what we are doing is for the sake of our own happiness. For example, we might say, "Many of my old habits have not made me very happy. I may sound artificial to you now, but that is how I'm learning to allow myself to act more naturally." Then we should drop the subject and not try to score a conversational victory for assertiveness.

If you are willing to take the risk of expressing yourself honestly and caringly, the other person may eventually respond in kind; in which case, the quality of your relationship will have been improved and the chances for good communications in the future increased.

We offer some practical guidelines on these issues in the Self-Care Program.

CHOOSING TO REVEAL OUR PHOBIAS TO OTHERS

People who experience phobic reactions sometimes hide their problem from others for years. Even those who have finally told their family often do not dare tell their friends for fear of being thought crazy. We may, of course, never choose to reveal our innermost feelings to strangers, but we pay a high price for concealing our feelings from those we care about and who care about us.

How and what we tell our children deserves special consideration. Telling them nothing when they notice our problem may leave them confused. The best course is to answer their questions matter-of-factly, to make clear that the problem is ours and not theirs, and to avoid magnifying the problem or leaning on them for emotional support.

As long as we try to hide our fears, family members may think we just like staying home, and friends may begin to think we don't like them anymore because we do not venture out to spend time with them. Meanwhile, because of our exaggerated concern over how others will react to our problem, we will remain painfully alone and isolated from what we need most from others—understanding and moral support.

We must realize that some family members and friends will, of course, not understand our problem. Some people will respond in discouraging ways, such as, "That's silly, just go out to the store and shop. There's nothing wrong with you."

Sometimes, it actually seems to matter less whom you tell than how you tell them. The people who get positive, supportive responses tend to be the ones who understand and accept their fears as fairly common and treatable stress-related problems. Others, who feel there is something fundamentally wrong with them because of their anxieties, may often tell people about them in shamefaced and self-effacing ways, which produces less desirable results.

If you have not made sure that your friends are aware of your problem and supportive of your efforts to deal with it, you add to your fears the fear that your friends will notice your anxiety at some point and think your behavior is "crazy." This effort to conceal fear creates the fear of fear commonly experienced by agoraphobic people; this secondary fear disappears when they stop trying so hard to conceal their problem from everyone else.

A valuable contribution to recovery from phobic reactions can be made by a compassionate and wise friend or therapist who is willing to act as your sounding board. It is helpful to talk out your problems as you investigate the ways old ideas shape your current behavior. The role of the friend or therapist is not to tell you what to do but simply to take you seriously, to listen actively, to ask good questions, and above all, to respect you and be honest with you.

Of course, talking about your problems is not enough. You need to experience new ways of dealing with them. However, talking can help you clarify and fit together for yourself what it means to be a truly self-caring person.

5

The Roots of the Self-Care Program

As we explained in Chapter 1, we originally designed the Self-Care Program presented at the end of this book for use by people suffering from agoraphobia, before we realized that it could be helpful to anyone who wishes to come to terms with anxiety. Our primary concern was to offer help to people who are so anxiety-ridden that they are unable to reach treatment centers or even to leave home. We had another concern as well.

In our view, current approaches to treatment have not proven to be wholly satisfactory or effective, for one or more of the following reasons: (1) they do not recognize the complex, multidimensional nature of agoraphobia, (2) they tend to ignore the unworkable philosophy of life that leads in the direction of agoraphobia and to ignore the conditions of life in which that philosophy arises, (3) they do not take into account the psychological individuality and unique needs of each person. In developing our program, as well as in writing this book, we have attempted to take these issues into account:

1. In order to respond to the complex nature of the problem, we include self-training activities that address several relevant dimensions of self-care—including such basic concerns as nutrition and exercise as well as specialized skills like desensitization and assertiveness training.

2. We aim at helping people confront and examine the pervasive philosophy of helplessness.

3. We have designed a flexible program that is self-directed, self-paced, and open-ended, rather than one that follows an arbitrary scenario or timetable.

Before we explain the program itself and how to use it, we need to clarify how we have selected and fit together relevant ideas from other current approaches to the treatment of agoraphobia; most of what is said here applies to other anxiety conditions as well. We will also briefly discuss Buddhist meditative psychology, which offers an interesting perspective on how human beings understand reality.

CURRENT APPROACHES TO TREATING AGORAPHOBIA

Claire Weekes's Self-Care Approach

For more than 30 years, physician Claire Weekes has pioneered the idea of giving self-care tools to those who suffer from agoraphobia. Her books, which show great understanding and empathy for those suffering from agoraphobia, have brought hope and help to hundreds of thousands of readers in Great Britain, Australia, and the United States. She describes her treatment in the following way:

My treatment is based on first, adequate explanation to the patient of sensitization and nervous symptoms and secondly, on teaching the importance of the four concepts—*facing, accepting, floating, letting time pass*—and finally, on full explanation of the obstacles met during all stages of recovery and warning of the probable occurrence of setbacks and their treatment. Working this way, many patients need little or no drug therapy. . . . Recovery lies, not in the abolition of nervous sensations and feelings (as so many patients believe), but . . . in their reduction to normal intensity. The four concepts in more detail are:

face—do not run away;

accept—do not fight;

float—do not tense;

let time pass—do not be impatient with time.

We agree entirely with Weekes's position on nervous sensations and feelings and with the importance she places on keeping her patients fully informed about the obstacles and setbacks that are part of the recovery process. We see her four concepts as constituting a useful self-care technique for coping with the experience of panic and anxiety, and one that would tend to establish conditions in which desensitization can occur.

The first concept outlined by Weekes, *facing*, is a skill that may take some time to acquire. Of course, as Weekes makes clear, what you really learn to face are arising thoughts and feelings, not locations or situations themselves. Should you retreat from a feared situation instead of facing it, it is important to see your behavior in terms of *learning a new skill*, not in terms of a life-and-death struggle. If you were learning to ride a bicycle and fell off, it would be reasonable to say, "whoops!" or whatever; it would not be reasonable to say, "Oh, what a terrible person I am! I will never learn how to ride a _____ bicycle!" Another way of looking at it is that even the greatest generals have made strategic withdrawals in order to regroup and replenish their supplies. So our advice is: face if you can, withdraw temporarily if you must—and don't feel guilty about it.

We think that full and complete recovery from agoraphobia can best be ensured by fitting together a self-directed treatment program that is both systematic and comprehensive. One major difference between our approach and Weekes's is our emphasis on the importance of understanding the philosophy of helplessness and how it arises in the first place. Another is our conviction that the agoraphobic person, like any chronically anxious person, needs to become aware of a number of habitual self-defeating ideas and behaviors that lead to poor performance, frustration, resentment, anger, and anxiety.

In any case, we include Weekes's "four concepts" in our program and recordings by Weekes in our listing of Suggested Cassette Tapes. Her wisdom and warmth have undoubtedly helped many people learn to cope with anxiety attacks.

The Value and Limits of Other Current Approaches

Attempts to treat phobic conditions have in general taken rather narrowly focused and often one-dimensional approaches. These approaches have tended to reflect the established methodologies of various health-care specialties more than they have addressed the complexity of the problem.

> Behavioral therapists employ systematic desensitization techniques that make use of relaxation training, mental imagery, and training based on the principles of conditioned learning.
>
> Advocates of nutritional therapy have recommended optimum nutrition as a means of altering the body's chemistry and thereby increasing the body's resistance to the effects of psychological stress.
>
> Clinical psychologists and psychiatrists have adopted a variety of techniques for helping agoraphobic people learn how to discover and resolve internal emotional conflicts.
>
> Some medical researchers have attempted to find psychoactive substances that can be introduced into the body to chemically block fear and anxiety.

Behavior Therapy

Systematic Desensitization.   Developed by behavioral psychologist Joseph Wolpe and other behaviorists in the 1960s, systematic desensitization is a therapy that seeks to remove the effects of phobic sensitization through the systematic application of the principles of conditioned learning. The goal of systematic desensitization is to gradually habituate the phobic person to a feared object or situation so that relaxation will eventually replace physiological arousal as the response elicited by the stimulus.

Sometimes called "exposure" training, this technique requires the phobic person to repeatedly approach close enough to the feared object or situation in order to expose himself or herself to the first feelings of increased anxiety, but not so close that he or she is overwhelmed by intense anxiety or panic. Gradually, the person will find himself or herself able to move closer to the feared object or into the feared situation. Eventually, the conditioned fear will disappear altogether.

Systematic desensitization training can be done in the imagination or in the real world. Often the former is preliminary to the latter form of training.

Systematic desensitization is highly effective when it is done carefully. It may be the only form of therapy required by an otherwise happy and healthy person with a single phobia. However, its greatest value in the more complex and pervasive problem of agoraphobia is that it can build self-esteem in a relatively short time and give people a sense of their own freedom as they start to expand their previously shrinking world.

Because it gives people the power to control their phobic reactions, systematic desensitization is one of the most valuable tools in the Self-Care Program.

Relaxation Training. Systematic relaxation training is often considered to be an integral part of assertiveness training and of systematic desensitization as well, although it is important for its own sake. Learning how to relax and "let go" of muscular tension—as well as of one's worries—is a vital part of recovery from any form of anxiety.

To help people learn how to relax, a variety of training techniques have been developed, including progressive muscular relaxation, guided visualization, and therapeutic meditation. All of these exercises follow a script, or set procedure, that may last 15 or 20 minutes, during which time the person sits or lies quietly. For this reason, cassette recordings are convenient—it is difficult to read a script and follow a relaxation procedure at the same time. In addition, listening to a soothing voice is in itself beneficial for the beginner.

We have included in the Self-Care Program sample scripts for three basic types of training, and we have listed a number of selected prerecorded tapes in the Suggested Cassette Tapes section. The goal of all of these techniques is the same: to help people learn how to achieve freely a state of relaxation and serenity.

When meditation is done for hygienic or therapeutic reasons (rather than as part of a religious or philosophical tradition), it is virtually indistinguishable from relaxation training. The simple breathing exercises in the Self-Care Program are similar to those used by beginners in meditative practices for the purpose of relaxation.

Scientific studies of practitioners of Zen and Transcendental Meditation have been conducted by, respectively, Dr. Tomio Hirai of the Tokyo University Hospital and by Dr. Herbert Benson of Harvard. These studies reveal a number of significant alterations in bodily conditions that accompany the profoundly relaxed or meditative state. These conditions include:

> Decreased sympathetic nervous system activity (lowered oxygen consumption, reduced respiration, and a decrease in the level of lactate in the blood).
>
> Increased alpha brainwaves, which are associated with the mental state of "letting go," "turning loose," or "floating."

Decreased bodily metabolism.

Decreased blood pressure (in people with high blood
    pressure).

In addition to the breathing exercises, we provide guidelines
in the program for those who wish to explore meditation
further.

There is a historical connection between relaxation therapy and drug therapy. Neuropharmacologist Vincenzo G.
Longo has noted that there is "a rather strict relationship"
between the muscle-relaxing properties of drugs and their
beneficial effect on anxiety. In recounting the rise of the
modern science of neuropharmacology in the 1950s and
1960s, Longo (who has played an active role in the field) described this rationale for the introduction of muscle-relaxing
drugs as tranquilizers: "A drug that diminishes muscular tension would presumably act through the same mechanism [as
Edmund Jacobson's progressive relaxation technique], with
the advantage that relaxation is obtained without the complex training connected with the progressive-relaxation
procedure."

Dr. Jacobson's pioneering technique, introduced in his
book *Progressive Relaxation* in 1929, showed that people
who suffer from high levels of anxiety can reduce their anxiety
by learning how to relax physically. True, it is a somewhat
time-consuming procedure. However, the important point is
that *it works*. Jacobson's pioneering work has led to the development of a number of simpler and less lengthy relaxation-
training techniques, among them the "quieting reflex" developed by Dr. Charles F. Stroebel, which is described in the
Self-Care Program.

Assertiveness Training.   Assertiveness training, or assertion training, directly addresses the issue of human freedom and thus can be extremely useful to the person who

seeks to recover from the limitations of self-defeating fears. For this reason we have incorporated some basic assertiveness exercises into our Self-Care Program.

Like systematic desensitization, assertiveness training has its roots in the principles of Pavlovian conditioning. It owes much to the work of Wolpe as well as psychologist Sherwin B. Cotler and others who have developed systematic assertiveness training procedures.

As explained by Cotler, assertiveness training has two distinct goals: anxiety reduction and social skill training. Cotler describes an assertive person as one "who can verbally and nonverbally express a wide range of both positive and negative feelings, emotions, and thoughts. . . . "

Cotler emphasizes the close connection between such free self-expression and the abilities to make decisions and free choices, comfortably establish close interpersonal relationships, and protect oneself from being "victimized" and taken advantage of.

As we pointed out in Chapter 4, true assertiveness is not accompanied by anxiety or guilt, because it avoids generating psychological stress in others through coercion, threats, or disrespect.

One fundamental assumption of assertiveness training (as stated by Cotler) is that each of us is "an important living being who is entitled to thoughts, emotions, and feelings which need not be sacrificed or negotiated away in a relationship with someone else (no matter whether the relationship is intimate or superficial)."

The goal of assertiveness training is (again in Cotler's words) to "learn to feel comfortable with yourself" and to recognize that "the most important thing in your life is *you*— only if you respect and take care of yourself will you be able to nourish others."

It is beyond the scope of the Self-Care Program to include material covering a whole course in assertiveness. The material we include is related to the most pressing issues that affect anxious people, particularly the expression of feelings long regarded as being "unsuitable" or "unacceptable." We urge readers to look upon the excellent books on assertiveness in the Suggested Readings section as a source for further training.

Flooding. Psychologist T. G. Stampfl, who developed implosive therapy, or flooding, believed that plunging into a feared situation in one's imagination would cause a phobic reaction to be extinguished. Stampfl did not mean just thinking about a feared situation; he meant subjecting oneself repeatedly to a prolonged story involving one's worst and most catastrophic fears.

In an experiment based on Stampfl's ideas, a group of female college students were selected who shared a common phobia, the fear of rats. The group was divided into two subgroups. The "experimental subjects" were induced to take part in a guided fantasy in which they visualized their worst fears come true. They vividly pictured rats attacking them, biting them, and so forth. The "control group" received no such training. The results of this experiment were remarkable: All of the women were subsequently asked to handle tame laboratory rats. Those who had received the training showed much less fear of rats than those who had not, as shown by their ability to touch the real animals.

No one has explained very well how or why such "implosive" or flooding training works, but some have suggested that the training is essentially cognitive and helps us to distinguish more sharply between fantasy and reality. When we engage in hypothetical what-if thinking, absolutist either-or thinking, or powerless have-to thinking, we are essentially living in the realm of fantasy. In flooding, we push our fantastic ideas to their logical limits and beyond, so that they no longer seem so relevant to the real world.

You can apply the same principle to dreaded experiences in your own life. Suppose you are invited to your cousin

Melanie's wedding and reception in two weeks. The prospect of the 80-mile round-trip drive, crowded church, noisy reception, relatives asking you personal questions—all fill you with dread. You suppose that you might have an anxiety attack on the freeway, in the church, at the reception, or possibly in all three places. Yet, you really like your cousin and don't want to disappoint her.

Flooding can help you turn this negative situation into a positive one—or at least into a neutral one.

You could construct a story incorporating all of the terrible things that could happen to you on the day of your cousin's wedding. For example:

> Your car could break down on the way to the church.
>
> You could arrive late and be seated in the last available seat—in the second pew, with 10 people on either side.
>
> You could start to hiccup loudly during the ceremony.
>
> You could burst into uncontrollable laughter when the person officiating asks if anyone present knows of any reason the wedding should not take place.
>
> You could drop three glasses of champagne at the reception.
>
> You could inadvertently knock the groom's mother into the swimming pool.
>
> Your Uncle Burt could say loudly, "Gee, these kids are making a lot more money than you are."

You can use your cassette recorder to record the story, or you can write down the key points. By playing the tape or reviewing your story once or twice a day for the two weeks before the wedding, you may completely transform the dreaded experience. At the wedding, you may come to see clearly how egocentric your anticipatory fears were. You may relax and notice many people who are overly concerned with how they look to others. You may smile when Uncle Burt asks you how much money you make, or when someone else drops a glass of champagne. And you may, just as your own private joke, go chat with the groom's mother at the edge of the pool. Overall, you may find that the reality of the day is far simpler to live through than your imagined fears.

It is important to keep in mind that flooding is a form of training that uses visualization to help you fully experience that which you fear and to thereby recognize the true nature of your fears. It is not a way of forcing yourself to do something unpleasant or something you don't want to do. For example, if you force yourself to go to your cousin's wedding, you are not training, you are simply trying—rightly or wrongly—to please your cousin or other family members. On the other hand, if you choose to use the wedding as an opportunity for training, then you are doing something for yourself.

Nutritional Therapy

In 1973, David Hawkins and Nobel Laureate Linus Pauling published *Orthomolecular Psychiatry*, a landmark book that described experimental methods of treating schizophrenia—a mental disease quite distinct from anxiety disorders—through optimum nutrition, especially the provision of "the optimum concentration of substances normally present in the human body."

Pauling has pointed out that "the proper functioning of the mind is known to require the presence in the brain of molecules of many different substances." For example, optimum mental functioning requires optimum concentrations in the brain of the following vitamins: thiamine (B-1), nicotinic acid or niacinamide (B-3), pyridoxine (B-6), cyanocobalamin (B-12), biotin (H), ascorbic acid (C), and folic acid. We have included nutrition in our Self-Care Program because we believe truly self-caring people would seek to ensure "an optimum concentration of substances" in their bodies to help them keep their physical and mental health at optimum levels.

Pauling places great importance on the biochemical individuality of human beings. He points out that different people need different amounts of vitamins and other essential foods to ensure the optimum functioning of their body's nat-ural protective mechanisms against illness. Since all forms of stress activate the body's defenses—and, as we know, psychological stress has been implicated in 50 to 80 percent of recorded illnesses—it makes sense that self-caring people would make certain that their diets include an adequate supply of the substances that help the body prevent and defend against illness.

In 1982, nutrition specialist Laraine C. Abbey reported, "The diets of agoraphobics are among the worst I've ever seen." Noting that most people with agoraphobia seemed to receive "three-quarters of their calories from processed foods—usually junk carbohydrates," she saw a common need for a "massive dietary overhaul." By contrast, our survey indicates that perhaps half of the people starting the Self-Care Program have already begun to reform their diets. In part this may reflect a general trend as Americans increasingly recognize the importance of nutrition. In any case, we have included in the program Pauling's recommendations regarding optimum amounts of vitamins and other essential foods as well as some other dietary guidelines that have a clear relationship to health and well-being.

Psychotherapy

Psychoanalysis.   Writer Janet Malcolm has described Sigmund Freud's theory of personal relations and the analytic therapy based on this theory in this way:

> According to the theory, we spend our lives playing out the same internal drama—that of our earliest parental and sibling relationships—indiscriminately casting the people we meet in the leading roles and doing our own rote performance of the part of the child, like an actor in a play with a very long run who years ago outgrew his part but whom nobody has thought to replace. Analysis proposes to show the patient (whose reason for seeking help is inevitably bound up with problems in his

personal relations) that he doesn't have to play this part any-more—that other parts are available to him now that he is an adult.

Freud recognized that anxiety attacks, self-defeating fears, obsessive worry, and other forms of severe anxiety are all related to *personal relations*—something that isn't always obvious to the acutely anxious person, who may think that the problem is a racing heart, a supermarket, or a high place.

Freud opened the door to the "unconscious mind" of his anxiety-ridden patients and began to explore the origin and development of phobias, self-defeating fears, and the other manifestations of severe anxiety. Judging from the limited evidence available, however, he and his followers have had little success in *treating* agoraphobia and similar problems, relying as they do mainly on a time-consuming abstract, in-tellectual analysis of their patients' verbal behavior and child-hood memories.

On the other hand, psychoanalysts like Karen ·Horney and Margaret Mahler, carrying forward the Freudian tradi-tion, have made valuable contributions in such areas as un-derstanding the nature of inner conflicts and the empirical investigation of early childhood development. The insights of Horney and Mahler have helped shape our understanding of agoraphobia and have thus influenced the Self-Care Program, although no explicitly psychoanalytic techniques are included.

Other Forms of Psychotherapy. In addition to the behavior-therapy techniques we have described, personal consultation with a clinical psychologist, psychiatrist, or psy-chiatric social worker is widely used in the treatment of ago-raphobia and other anxiety conditions.

As most of these professionally trained therapists will admit, psychotherapy is more an art than a science. The therapist's main function is to provide unconditional and un-critical acceptance of the client as a human being while serv-ing as an honest and informed sounding board for the client's thoughts, feelings, and problems. One of the shortest definitions of a good therapist we've ever heard is this: "simply and only an honest person." The main benefit of personal consultations with a good professional therapist is the clients' enhanced awareness as to how their own assumptions, beliefs, and habitual attitudes lead them into self-defeating behaviors.

When we consider that the most significant factor mitigating against psychological stress is friendship, we can see that the basically friendly and supportive stance of the therapist can be a very positive factor in the life of someone who is experiencing high levels of stress and needs someone to talk to.

Not everyone suffering from agoraphobia or other forms of anxiety requires the services of a professional therapist. However, everyone does need a support network of friendship, love, and moral support—and the presence of a professional therapist often can make the difference between an inadequate support network and one that is healthy and robust.

As we have explained, the Self-Care Program was originally developed out of necessity as a do-it-yourself approach to treatment for those who are unable to reach or be reached by treatment centers. For this reason, it includes several self-exploratory exercises that deal with thoughts, feelings, and problems—areas that are often the subject matter of personal consultations with therapists. It is desirable to have a strong support network in place and someone to talk to, possibly a therapist, while undertaking these explorations, since they are likely to create some transient anxiety.

Medical Care

Consultation with a Physician. Seeking medical assistance following an episode of sudden, unexplained physiological arousal (an "anxiety attack") is obviously a good idea. There are several medical conditions (such as hypoglycemia and inner-ear disfunction) that can create dizziness and other feelings to which sensitized phobic reactions can occur. In other words, such physical feelings can themselves serve as warning signals that trigger an emergency reaction. For example:

Disequilibrium   Dizzy   Startle reaction   Emergency
due to inner-ear ⟶ feeling   ⟶ and disruption ⟶ reaction
disfunction   of breathing   and panicky
                                             feelings

As a rule, no medical problem or illness can be found that would explain the patient's episodic physiological arousal. In such cases, the person may have such a low danger threshold that virtually any internal feeling can be perceived as threatening:

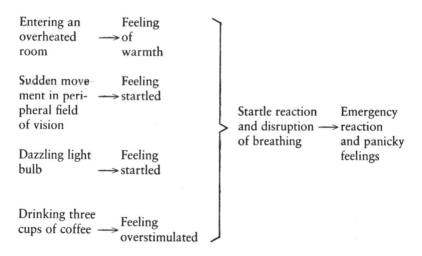

A low danger threshold is simply a way of looking at the world that is brought about by psychological stress and a philosophy of helplessness. In itself it is not a medical problem. It is basically a learned behavior and, as such, it is subject to voluntary modification. This is our assumption in the Self-Care Program.

Almost all of the people who have used the Self-Care Program had previously consulted one or more physicians concerning their panicky feelings. Half reported they received little or no help from such consultations. Although a few reported that physicians trivialized their problem and told them it was "all in their head," most were treated in a caring fashion. Some were disappointed with the verdict that there was "nothing wrong with them" from a medical standpoint. Because of their strong craving for certainty in an uncertain world, they felt disappointed not to have an illness that would explain their suffering. Instead of being grateful for a clean bill of health (as they realistically might have been), they felt that the physician had somehow let them down.

Drug Therapy.   Tranquilizers and other mild psychoactive drugs help many people through difficult episodes by enabling them to experience some degree of relaxation when they are acutely nervous.

For example, in 1980, medical researcher Dr. Charlotte Marker Zitrin and her associates, Dr. Donald F. Klein and Dr. Margaret G. Woerner, published a study of the use of the drug Imipramine (which inhibits the response of sympathetic nerve fibers to epinephrine) combined with systematic desensitization in the treatment of a group of 76 agoraphobic women. Moderate to marked improvement was observed in most of the subjects, who had suffered from agoraphobia for 8.6 years, on average. Certain benefits were reported for the use of the drug therapy in addition to behavioral therapy. The fact that significantly fewer subjects who received Imipramine dropped out of the study than did those who received a placebo was held to indicate that "Imipramine helps sicker patients to withstand the pressures of this therapy, thus enabling them to remain to the end."

Although drugs have been helpful in some circumstances, many medical specialists tend to overemphasize the role of biochemistry in the creation of panicky feelings. They tend to neglect the role optimum nutrition can play in maintaining an optimum internal environment and a subjective sense of well-being. They also avoid issues related to the subjective *meaning* of experiences—to psychological, philosophical, and spiritual distress—even though these issues are obviously relevant to the functioning of the whole human being.

From the various physiological changes we have discussed—a speeding heart rate, for example—it is clear that a chemical imbalance exists in the body of any person at the moment he or she is undergoing acute anxiety. A natural consequence of this is that some form of temporary chemical intervention, such as the traditional shot of brandy, may help by affecting the body's chemical balance and providing symptomatic relief. It is no less obvious that along with the chemical imbalance, a pervasive condition of psychological and philosophical imbalance coexists within the chronically fearful person. This condition, which contributes directly to extreme sensitivity to external events as well as to changes in bodily states, cannot be ignored by those who aim at full and complete recovery.

Recent evidence indicates that antianxiety drugs are helpful in the short term (for a few months, perhaps) in managing phobic symptoms but are not an effective long-term treatment. We believe that this is because they offer symptomatic relief at the physiological level but do not address the question of *why the acutely anxious person is feeling threatened.*

The point to bear in mind when you take a muscle-relaxing drug like Valium is that you can achieve the same results by learning to meditate or to perform a systematic relaxation exercise, like one of those included in the Self-Care Program. Of course, to do this, you must be willing to pause in the midst of your busy life and to devote some time to learning these self-care skills. We are not saying it is wrong to take medication in a crisis, but we are saying it is far better to learn to depend on yourself than to depend on a pill. Furthermore, the enormous amount of money spent on Valium in this country (in a recent year, Americans purchased 5

billion Valium and Librium pills) indicates that many people
don't realize that relaxation—like the other best things in
life—is free.

Buddhist Psychology

In October 1984, some 300 psychotherapists, experimental
psychologists, and other researchers gathered in Amherst,
Massachusetts, to hear the Dalai Lama discuss the Tibetan
view of the workings of the mind. It is no accident that
American psychology has begun to pay serious attention to
the Buddhist view of mental processes. Traditional meditative
practices achieve a degree of voluntary control of physiological processes that baffles and fascinates many American behaviorists. More importantly, Western understanding of
human freedom as a practical reality has been enriched by
the Buddhist teachings that are currently becoming easily
accessible in the West for the first time.

Broadly speaking, Buddhism is not a religion in the Western sense but a humanistic philosophy based on the rigorous
examination of the way thoughts and ideas arise in the mind.
It is an attempt to meet the harsh realities of life with all the
honesty and integrity that human beings can summon. In a
sense, it is an antidote to the philosophy of helplessness. In
the Buddhist view, a basic mistake people make is to wish
for reality to be different—because from this wish grows self-
deception. We pretend that reality is unreal and that our
illusions are real. For example, we try to make an "idealized
self" real and our true nature unreal. In psychoanalytic terms,
these illusions perhaps correspond roughly to neurotic defense mechanisms.

In the Buddhist view, human beings are actually strong
enough to face and accept reality without illusions. If we will
only abandon our illusions, we will discover that we have all
along possessed a mind that has no need of illusory defenses.
Again, in psychoanalytic terms, one might say that psychic
energy, tied up in unrealistic defense mechanisms, can be

liberated for more spontaneous and natural behavior if we can only find a way to discard the useless mechanisms.

Illusions are sustained by the fixed patterns of thoughts, the iron chain of associations that characterize ordinary consciousness. For example, chronically anxious people embrace the illusion that they can live in the future and thus ward off harm. They think the future is something that is about to happen to them, which they must struggle with and shape in advance. Meditative awareness was discovered by the Buddha ("the one who awakened") to be the means for breaking this chain of associations, for destroying illusions. The practice of Buddhist meditation takes various outer forms, but the state of awareness it nurtures is the essential characteristic that sets it off from other practices. Awareness requires constant discipline and sincere effort. Thus, when Buddhists speak of freedom and spontancity, thcy do not mean the self-conscious exhibitionism of cultists or faddists (for example, the excesses of "beatnik Zen") but rather the unselfconscious frccdom and spontaneity of the craftsman who knows his tools and materials so well that he is at one with them.

The task of the meditator is to expand meditative freedom from that brief moment into all of life, so that he or she becomes spontaneous, free, and open to the unfolding of life instead of being bound to preconceptions. For the anxious person, this means learning to live in the present rather than in the future.

The idea that we can bypass our conditioning and directly experience reality in this way strikes some people as antirational or antiintellectual because it challenges conventional ideas about the mind. It is neither, at least if one can judge by the unique personalities, spontaneous wit, and great perceptiveness of the Zen and Tibetan Buddhist teachers who have come to the United States in recent years. But it is a direct challenge to the prevalent Western belief that truth is solely the product of analysis (pulling apart ideas), synthesis (fitting together ideas), and disputation (arguing about ideas).

One does not have to follow the philosophy of Buddhism

or any other philosophy or religion to practice meditation, nor does meditation compromise any religious or philosophical beliefs. Zen Buddhist teacher Philip Kapleau describes *bompu,* or "ordinary" meditation, as "being free from any philosophic or religious content" and suitable for "anybody and everybody."

The Self-Care Program takes a number of ideas from Buddhist psychology, including these:

> We can gradually learn to regulate physiological processes that were long believed in the West to be machinelike, automatic, and beyond our control.
>
> Self-control and a state of well-being are natural consequences of mindful awareness. Calmly observing our thoughts permits us to break the chains of conditioning.
>
> Our inner freedom leads us naturally toward wisdom and compassion.

The program includes some instructions for beginning meditation exercises and some guidelines and suggested readings for those who wish to look more deeply into this subject.

THE GOALS OF RECOVERY

Recovery from agoraphobia or other anxiety conditions is not a one-dimensional event. It is a complex experience of a whole, multidimensional human being. It begins with basic physical self-care, including exercise and good nutrition, and has physical, behavioral, cognitive, and philosophical dimensions. Let us attempt to state the goals of the self-care program within each of these dimensions as concretely as we can. The goals have various interrelationships; in general, they are ranked within each category in order of how soon you can expect to reach them. (You will recognize a few of these goals that apply only if you suffer from anxiety attacks or agoraphobia.)

We have grouped the 24 goals of recovery into four categories labeled physical, behavioral, cognitive, and philosophical. In a sense, these categories represent a progression from short-term to long-term goals. This is not to say that you cannot find contentment within yourself, or enrich the quality of your life, or be genuinely compassionate until you have reached full recovery; however, these philosophical insights and attainments will be on a more solid basis after you have reached the physical, behavioral, and cognitive goals that precede them on the list.

Physical Goals

1. To increase your ability to relax physically (as you breathe naturally from your abdomen).
2. To increase your ability to substitute physical relaxation for physiological arousal.
3. To reduce the frequency and intensity of startle reactions.
4. To reduce the frequency and intensity of fight-or-flight reactions.
5. Overall, to increase the amount of time spent in a mentally alert, physically relaxed condition.

Behavioral Goals

1. To increase your ability to cope with startle or fight-or-flight reactions.
2. To increase your ability to go places and do things without experiencing such reactions.
3. To increase your ability to tell others what you do not need, want, or like.
4. To increase your ability to tell others what you do need, want, or like.
5. To decrease the amount of time you spend feeling guilty, ashamed, or embarrassed.
6. To decrease the amount of time you spend worrying.

Cognitive Goals

These goals have to do with gaining control through observation and awareness in the present moment. The act of calmly observing and understanding conditioned stimuli can eliminate their emotionally disruptive effects. (In other words, you can learn to be the "calm observer" rather than the "reactor" in these situations.)

1. To be able to relax and recognize the external stimuli that trigger startle reactions or fight-or-flight reactions.
2. To be able to relax and recognize the internal stimuli (thoughts and visceral feelings) that trigger these reactions, including self-diminishing and self-defeating assumptions, beliefs, and attitudes that "trap you in thought," such as:
    A. The idea that you are helpless and unfree.
    B. The idea that criticism or disagreement by others threatens your survival.
    C. The idea that something is fundamentally wrong with you.
    D. The idea that anxiety is a shameful secret.
    E. Either-or thinking.
    F. What-if thinking.
    G. Have-to thinking.
    H. If-only thinking.
3. To be able to relax and recognize thoughts and feelings that reflect an attempt to eliminate risk or uncertainty from life through avoidance, concealment, or deception.
4. To be able to relax and recognize thoughts and feelings that reflect an unrealistic craving for continuous expressions of love and admiration from others.
5. To be able to accept yourself and to care for yourself as you would for a beloved child or friend.

Philosophical Goals

If you replace the idea of your own helplessness with your actual freedom to accept reality honestly, these goals become attainable.

1. To accept yourself honestly, just as you are.
2. To accept responsibility for your own health and well-being—to be self-sufficient in this fundamental sense.
3. To find contentment within yourself.
4. To take the time to live fully and freely in the present moment—without missing the humor in the drama of life.
5. To use your freedom to enrich your life through friendship, unconditional love of others, and satisfying work.
6. To help others who suffer as you have suffered.

Drawing on the wisdom of the sciences and therapies we have mentioned, as well as on existential philosophy and Buddhist psychology, we have further identified seven skills that are essential in reaching the goals of recovery:

1. Voluntary physical relaxation, good posture, and natural breathing.
2. Coping with emotional distress.
3. Extinguishing learned reactions.
4. Achieving control through relaxed awareness and clear thinking.
5. Communicating assertively.
6. Cultivating inner freedom and discarding the idea of helplessness.
7. Maintaining a realistic and positive self-image.

The program itself consists of a collection of self-evaluation and self-training techniques and procedures that will help you develop these skills by directly experiencing them in practice.

Recovery Milestones

The goals we have listed are deliberately open-ended, because some people have further to travel than others to reach particular goals. This is why we use relative terms like "increasing abilities" and "reducing the frequency and intensity" of reactions. Naturally, you may wish to measure your progress against some more objective standard. For this purpose, we

will list some significant milestones on the road to recovery—
moments of clarity and recognition that are often experienced
by people as they outgrow anxiety attacks and agoraphobia.
Since everyone travels his or her own road to recovery, do
not expect to pass these milestones in exactly the sequence
in which they are listed. On the other hand, read this list
carefully, because you will indeed recognize many of these
milestones in coming weeks and months, and they will serve
to reward and encourage you:

> First success voluntarily reaching a state of noticeable physi-
> cal relaxation.
>
> First success voluntarily reaching a state of profound physi-
> cal relaxation.
>
> Recognition that you can reliably reach a state of profound
> physical relaxation.
>
> First successful use of desensitization training.
>
> First use of relaxed awareness to stop a fight-or-flight
> reaction.
>
> First satisfying assertive encounter with a stranger.
>
> First satisfying use of assertiveness to resolve a difficulty in a
> personal relationship.
>
> Those close to you notice that you "are different." (They
> don't necessarily like it—give them time to understand
> what you are doing.)
>
> First experience of easily sharing previously concealed feel-
> ings or experiences with a trusted friend or a therapist.
>
> Frequency of emotional distress reduced to once or twice a
> day.
>
> Frequency of emotional distress reduced to two or three
> times a week.
>
> First experience of rapidly regaining balance after an anxiety
> attack.
>
> First experience of responding to emotional distress by stay-
> ing in a situation, investigating and exploring it, and
> doing some on-the-spot desensitization training.

Calmly accepting the possibility of experiencing emotional distress and anxiety attacks occasionally in the future.

Reducing frequency of emotional distress to two or three times a month.

Spending an entire day or evening without thinking about anxiety attacks.

Reducing frequency of emotional distress to about once a month.

Spending an entire week without thinking about anxiety attacks.

Someone close to you remarks favorably on "how much you have changed."

Experiencing an anxiety attack and being more concerned with investigating the sources of psychological stress than with seeking external help. Remaining confident in your overall progress in spite of the attack.

Looking back at your progress over three months, six months, or a year, and noticing a great difference in the amount of freedom you experienced then and now.

6

Using the Self-Care Program

This program has been designed to be self-directed, self-paced, and open-ended. Many of the self-care skills and practices it describes are not meant for short-term use only but are intended to be incorporated eventually into your daily routine.

If you are confronted by recurrent anxiety, anxiety attacks, panic attacks, or agoraphobia, you are already taking care of yourself—somehow. By applying the principles in this program, you can improve the quality of your self-care and begin to reduce or eliminate the psychological stress that feeds your symptoms. The path of personal growth described here leads to a robust sense of personal autonomy, good mental health, and an enrichment of your compassion for yourself and for others.

This program works. Frankly, it works better than we realized it would when we first developed it for housebound sufferers from agoraphobia. To date, more than 300 people have used the program for at least a year. We have been delighted many times by phone calls and letters from people who wish to share the excitement and pleasure they feel as they pass through barriers that have limited their lives for months or years. Perhaps we should clarify the statement, "This program works." It works in the way a shovel works to dig a hole, a stove works to cook dinner, or a piano works to play music. There is no secret formula or magical cure contained within it that will change you. It simply comprises a set of tools (new assumptions, ideas, and skills) that you can learn to use.

The program works in the sense that it can help you use your freedom to activate your own innate self-healing processes. The more you practice with its tools, the better it will work for you.

If you find after trying them out that some of the tools are not particularly useful to you, don't use them. Deliberate redundancy has been built into this program because of our recognition that different tools work best for different people. It would be better for you to use 60 percent of the program wholeheartedly than 100 percent halfheartedly. There is no "busy work" in the program. Please don't fill out a log, an inventory, or any other form unless it seems important to you.

There is nothing in this program that can *make* you feel anxious. If you feel anxious, it is for one basic reason: you are drifting toward the idea of your own helplessness and away from your own freedom. If you feel anxious at any point, you need to pause and relax.

GETTING STARTED

Equipment and Supplies

You will need a notebook and supply of forms to write on. These forms can be prepared by making copies from the Blank Forms section at the end of this book. Suggested quantities of the forms to have on hand as you begin the program are given in the following checklist. The forms that are indicated by asterisks (*) are rather simple and could be easily copied by hand in your notebook to reduce the expense of copying.

It would be helpful to have a cassette tape recorder, a blank tape of 15 or 20 minutes' duration, and at least one relaxation tape for daily use as you begin the program.

A selection of relaxation tapes is listed in the Suggested Cassette Tapes section in the back of this book. If you already have a relaxation tape you like, use it. You may need to listen

to two or three tapes to find the type of relaxation procedure
that works best for you. (If you do not have a relaxation tape
or a cassette player, you can use the Quiet Sitting relaxation
exercise described in the Relaxation section.)

Equipment and Supplies Checklist
 Spiral-bound notebook, 8½ × 11 inches
 Folder for storing forms
 Calendar or datebook
 Small note pad or 3 × 5 cards
 Pocket alarm clock or watch (optional)
 Cassette tape recorder (optional)
 Tapes (optional):
  One blank tape
  One relaxation tape

Forms:
 Troubleshooting Checklist (1)
 Coping Checklist (1)
 Journal (5)
 Self-Evaluation (1)
 Nutrition and Medication Log (1)
 Inventory of Phobic Reactions* (1)
 Levels of Anxiety* (1)
 Situation Hierarchy* (3)
 Successive-Approximations Training* (3)
 Displeasure-Frustration Inventory* (5)
 Worry Inventory* (5)
 Guilt Inventory* (5)
 Assertiveness Log* (5)
 Negative Fantasies Inventory* (1)
 Negative Thoughts Inventory* (1)

Self-Evaluation Form

Before starting to use the program, you should fill out a Self-Evaluation form. Here is the way the form might be filled out by Tom K., a 29-year-old software development manager in Silicon Valley.

Self-Evaluation (of Tom K.)

	Date of Evaluation			
ITEM	Started reading this book (approx.):	Started using program:	Reached Level 3:	Reached Level 7:
	1 JAN.	*10 JAN.*		

PERFORMANCE
Use a number from 0 to 5 to rate your performance in each of the following areas.

0 = Completely unsatisfactory	3 = Mostly satisfactory
1 = Very unsatisfactory	4 = Very satisfactory
2 = Mostly unsatisfactory	5 = Completely satisfactory

ITEM				
Optimum vitamins and minerals in diet				
Fresh vegetables, whole grains, legumes, and fresh fruit in diet				
Minimum sugar and refined grain in diet				
Optimum amount of physical exercise	*5*	*5*		
Regular physical relaxation	*3*	*4*		
Mental alertness	*3*	*3*		

Self-Evaluation, (*continued*)

Ability to learn not to experience fear in specific places and situations	1	2	
Tolerance for bodily sensations	1	2	
Ability to remain relaxed when negative thoughts and feelings arise	1	2	
Ability to tell others about your strong feelings	1	1	
Ability to identify sources of psychological stress in your life	1	2	
Ability to maintain a realistic and positive self-image	1	2	

ASSUMPTIONS, BELIEFS, ATTITUDES, AND BEHAVIORS

Use a number from 0 to 3 to indicate how much you agree or disagree with each of these self-descriptive statements.

0 = Disagree	2 = Agree somewhat
1 = Disagree somewhat	3 = Agree

I hate to hurt the feelings of others so much that I neglect my own feelings	3	3	
I am unusually polite and considerate, even when I feel as though I am being dishonest	3	2	
Sometimes I am afraid to tell people how I feel	3	3	
I am a worrier	3	3	
I am too sensitive to criticism	3	3	
I usually know what to do in an emergency.	3	3	
Sometimes I am confused about my own feelings.	3	3	

Self-Evaluation, (*continued*)

Sometimes I ridicule myself	*3*	*3*		
I have a problem dealing with anger	*3*	*3*		
People often underestimate my abilities	*2*	*2*		
I have never felt entirely free from anxiety	*2*	*3*		
Sometimes I am full of self-contempt	*3*	*2*		

ROOTS

Which of these problems associated with persons close to you during your childhood (e.g., parents, siblings) do you believe contributed to your long-held assumptions, beliefs, and attitudes? (Check those that apply. Use a pen or pencil of a different color each time you review these items.)

	PERSON		
PROBLEM	*FATHER*	*MOTHER*	*BROTHER*
Argumentative	✔	✔	✔
Did not touch or hold you			
Indifferent			
Passive	✔		
Used ridicule	✔		✔
Nervous or anxious behavior		✔	
Overprotective			
Overly worried about your safety		✔	
Highly critical	✔		
Played favorites among family members	✔		
Worried about money a great deal	✔		

Tom has filled out the first two columns on the form at the same time. This helped him get a sense of the changes he has already made in the way he cares for himself and deals with psychological stress since he began reading this book. (He will fill out the two remaining columns when he has reached later stages in the program.)

He doesn't know a great deal about nutrition, and he hasn't yet read the Nutrition Guidelines section of this program, so he has entered a question mark following the first three items on the form. Tom has been a devoted swimmer for four years, so he has put a "5" (completely satisfactory) following the item regarding exercise.

Just reading this book has helped Tom relax a bit and develop some tolerance for physical sensations—even for the startle reaction he experiences when he perceives movement in his peripheral field of vision. Tom wears glasses, and when people lean over his shoulder to put something on his desk, it causes a "jump" in his peripheral field of vision as they pass the edge of the lens in his glasses. This still startles him, but he is less reactive to it.

In the remaining Performance items, Tom has noted some improvements in self-care and assertiveness.

In the next section, Tom notes that many of the self-descriptive statements listed there have applied to him in the past and still apply to him. He hesitates to admit it, but he recognizes that there are times he has feelings of contempt for himself.

In the last section of the evaluation, Tom has identified some of the childhood problems that caused him to develop a rather strict internal censor who stops him from sending out messages that might conceivably draw ridicule, disapproval, or criticism from others. Tom has had some awareness of this problem for a long time, but it is beginning to look to him more like something he can work with and change rather than something he cannot change.

The Journal

The Journal is the backbone of the Self-Care Program. It is a daily ongoing record of your self-training activities, important events in your life, and your progress toward recovery. Each Journal form can be used for a week and provides both structured checklists and open questions that will help you investigate the important issues in your life. Dated entries in your notebook can be used to supplement the Journal forms when you wish to write at length. The purpose of the Journal is to help you pause each day to reflect on the current conditions of your life as well as to monitor your progress and discover changes in your attitudes and behaviors.

Following we show the Journal form as it might be filled out by Jane B., a 30-year-old mother of two who has recently returned to school part-time. Jane is just beginning the program, so she is at Level 1 of the seven-stage program and has reached no program goals or milestones.

Journal (of Jane B.)

Date: _15 SEPTEMBER_

WEEKLY STATUS

Current level in seven-level plan (1–7): _1_

Number of program goals reached (1–24): _0_

Number of milestones reached (1–21): _0_

Current daily intake of vitamins and minerals:

Multivitamin tablet with minerals _✓_

Stress-B or Super-B tablet _✓_

A and D in multivitamin _10,000 /400 USP_

Amount of B vitamins in B tablet _B-1, B-2, B-6 50 MG_

Journal (*continued*)

Amount of extra C	_4G_
Amount of extra niacinamide/niacin	_200-300 MG_
Amount of extra E	_400 IU_
Amount of extra calcium and magnesium	_550/150 MG_
Amount of tryptophan	_0-500 MG_

Additional intake: IRON (FERROUS FUMARATE) 43 MG

DAILY PROGRESS

Self-Care Activity	S	M	T	W	T	F	S
Did you use the "to do" list (and calendar or datebook as needed)?	—	✓	✓	✓	✓	—	—
How many times did you practice relaxation or meditation?	—	1	1	2	3	—	—
How many times did you practice the Quieting Reflex or another coping technique?	—	3	3	3	3	—	—
How long did you exercise (in minutes)?	—	—	20	—	20	—	—
Did you take supplementary vitamins or minerals?	—	✓	✓	✓	✓	—	—
Did you refer to the carry-along checklists?	—	—	—	✓	✓	—	—

For the following items, enter a number from 0 to 5 to indicate the quality of your performance today.

1 = poor, 3 = good, 5 = excellent

	S	M	T	W	T	F	S
Nutrition	—	1	1	1	5	—	—
Coping with emotional distress	—	3	3	1	4	—	—

Journal (*continued*)

Desensitization training	—	—	—	—	—	—	—
Assertiveness training	—	—	—	—	—	—	—

Other training:

QUIET SITTING	—	3	3	3	5	—	—
Assertiveness in everyday life	—	2	3	1	3	—	—
Awareness of inner feelings	—	3	2	1	5	—	—
Maintenance of realistic and positive self-image	—	3	2	0	3	—	—
Enjoying the drama and humor of life	—	—	—	—	—	—	—
Overall self-care performance	—	—	—	—	—	—	—

For the following items, enter a number from 0 to 5 indicating the severity of problems experienced today.

0 = no problems, 3 = moderate problems, 5 = severe problems

Outdated assumptions, beliefs, and attitudes	—	3	3	5	2	—	—
The idea of helplessness or powerlessness	—	3	3	5	1	—	—
The idea that you are unworthy or flawed	—	3	3	5	0	—	—
The idea that everything must be perfect	—	2	2	5	1	—	—
The idea that security lies outside yourself	—	2	2	5	1	—	—
Negativity	—	2	2	4	2	—	—
Overreacting to or magnifying external events	—	2	2	5	1	—	—
Overreacting to bodily feelings	—	0	1	5	3	—	—
Passive or aggressive reactions	—	0	1	4	0	—	—
Nervousness or anxiety	—	0	2	5	1	—	—

Journal (*continued*)

Startle reaction	__	o	o	5	o	__	__
Fight-or-flight reaction	__	o	o	5	o	__	__
Anxiety attack	__	o	o	5	o	__	__
Other: _____	__	__	__	__	__	__	__

Use your notebook to discuss problems of moderate to severe intensity. What happened before the problem occurred? How were you feeling? Also use the notebook to discuss important events in your life and your honest feelings about them.

Jane has already begun to take vitamin and mineral supplements, so she has recorded the amounts in the weekly status section. Having glanced at the program's Nutrition Guidelines, she is considering increasing her intake of certain vitamins and minerals and may revise these entries on next week's Journal form.

It is now Thursday, and Jane has used a "to do" list every day since she started the program on Monday. Jane does not have a relaxation tape yet, but she has used the Quiet Sitting exercise in the morning and in the evening. Jane has started swimming regularly at school, but she has had a cold and thus is starting to gradually work back up to her selected length of time for swimming (20 minutes a day).

Yes, she has remembered to take her vitamins and minerals daily. She takes some with each meal, some between meals, and some at bedtime. She has also remembered to look at her carry-along checklists at stressful times each day (before she drives to and from school).

She thinks her nutrition is sometimes good but could be better, as indicated by her varying daily performance in this area. Wednesday was a rough day for Jane, as the "1" (for poor) indicates for that day for "Coping with emotional distress."

Jane has not yet started desensitization training or assertiveness training but she considers the Quiet Sitting to be training, so she keeps track of it in the "Other training" category. Jane was not very assertive on Wednesday, but on Thursday some of her inner feelings came into focus. Things looked black on Wednesday, as the low rating for "Maintenance of realistic and positive self-image" shows. Jane likes the idea of enjoying the unfolding drama of life—as well as its occasional comic relief—and she tries to remember this perspective.

Overall, she is not doing as well as she would like in taking care of her life, and this feeling is reflected in her entries following "Overall self-care performance."

Jane definitely found outdated attitudes getting in her way on Wednesday, and she identified a number of those old ideas and habits in the final 12 items on the Journal.

Wednesday night, she wrote down the difficult experiences of the day. When she woke up Thursday, she could see that what had happened on Wednesday occurred in part because she was trying to conceal a feeling of displeasure and resentment both from her husband and from herself. When she recognized the feeling, it seemed to be hardly worth the emotional disruption she had experienced. She spontaneously hugged her husband and told him, "You know, honey, I just realized why I got so upset yesterday. I was feeling bad because you had. . . . " Notice the "good" rating she has entered in the "Assertiveness in everyday life" for this simple, loving, and honest communication about her feelings. Jane also wrote about this incident in her notebook to remind herself that assertiveness is healthy. Later on, she can read this Journal form and her notebook to help her get a sense of the progress she is making toward recovery.

Setting Up a Recovery Network

The first task in the program is to ensure that moral support is available to you from people who understand your problem. We will ask you to examine your existing social support network of family and friends and to strengthen it as necessary to ensure that support and reassurance are always at most a phone call away. The purpose of the recovery network is simply to eliminate the worry that help will not be available when you need it.

Learning Essential Skills

The seven sections of the program correspond to the seven essential self-care skills listed at the end of Chapter 6.

The first section, Caring for Your Body, deals with relaxation, nutrition, and physical exercise. Nutrition and exercise are very important in their own right as hygienic factors in the life of any self-caring person. This section includes some simple relaxation and meditative exercises.

The second section, Coping with Emotional Distress, describes some immediate actions you can take when you feel subject to emotional distress. Most of these techniques offer short-term relief of your symptoms. Think of them as first aid.

The third section, Extinguishing Learned Reactions, explains what you need to know to eliminate phobic responses in specific places and situations.

The fourth section, Achieving Control Through Relaxed Awareness, makes use of your relaxation skill to explore honestly the self-diminishing behaviors, feelings, attitudes, beliefs, and assumptions that lead you into the trap of anxiety.

The activities in the fifth section, Communicating Assertively, involve relaxing and learning how to frame honest and assertive messages, rehearse them, then put them to use in overcoming communications problems.

The sixth section, Cultivating Inner Freedom, takes you further into the psychology and philosophy of meditation, a practice that has been followed by much of humankind for thousands of years. It invites you to rediscover the steady, alert, and wise observer of the here and now you really are. This observer is free from the conditioned desires and fears that control the idealized self that seeks to conceal helplessness behind exaggerated maturity and politeness.

The seventh section is called Maintaining a Realistic and Positive Self-Image. If you have lived for a long time with the either-or ideas of helplessness and exaggerated strength dominating your life, you may find yourself resisting the idea of a balanced middle way. If so, this section will help remind you that in the freedom that exists between the idea of helplessness and the idea of invincibility, you can always find your identity as a human being.

We will describe each of the seven sections in some detail to help you prepare to use the Self-Care Program, which contains the actual step-by-step instructions and procedures to follow as you practice essential recovery skills.

CARING FOR YOUR BODY

Relaxation

To overcome severe anxiety and phobic reactions, you need to learn what deep physical relaxation feels like. Relaxation can help you discover the secure core of identity that exists behind the various roles you play in your life.

Learning to relax is not the same as *trying* to relax. Often people report that they have been "working hard" at relaxing, but without success. Relaxation is what you experience when you stop working, stop trying, stop doing anything. It's letting go—not trying to make something happen.

Please remember this basic axiom: You can't be anxious and relaxed at the same time.

A common complaint among Christopher's clients is: "I didn't have the chance to practice relaxation this week." It may be hard to find 20 to 30 minutes in your day for relaxation training. To do so, you may have to say no to one or more persons who are used to your sacrificing your needs to them. This will mean confronting another important aspect of your problem—the fear of rejection and fear of criticism.

It's a good time for you to begin confronting these fears

and risk some criticism. If you mistreat yourself or allow others to mistreat you, you teach people that you don't care about yourself and that it is all right to make unlimited demands on you. If you say no to a friend who wants to come over and chat, because you want to do your relaxation exercises, you are being self-caring.

Occasionally, someone will experience anxiety during the relaxation training on the first try or two. This makes sense because, as we mentioned, one phobic characteristic is a fear of losing control. One of the truths this training will help you experience is this: Fighting your feelings and keeping yourself under tight control only perpetuates anxiety; a gradual "letting go" under your own control is safe, pleasant, and beneficial. It is safe to relax. Relaxation is not the same as losing control. It is simply refraining from active control for a while.

Should you experience some discomfort, stop the training; when you feel less anxious, try again, or try a different one of the suggested relaxation techniques.

The exercises should be practiced only in a quiet, restful place where you can give them your full attention. There is nothing intrinsically risky in simple relaxation exercises, yet it is possible to imagine a circumstance in which a very anxious person who is not fully familiar with the exercises could become distracted or confused by attempting to practice them while also attempting to drive a car or perform some other activity that requires mental alertness and concentration. For this reason we advise you not to practice these exercises in such situations. Once you understand the simpler techniques thoroughly, have complete confidence in your ability to remain mentally alert while using them to relax physically, and are comfortable taking full responsibility for their use, you may decide to use them any place you go.

Therapeutic Meditation

The Quiet Sitting exercise described in the program includes simple relaxation techniques commonly used by those who are beginning to practice Zen meditation. The advantage of this exercise is that it is easy to learn and does not require a cassette tape. Once learned, it can be done practically any place where you need to relax physically while maintaining mental alertness.

Nutrition

Nutrition is directly related to longevity and physical and mental well-being. The diseases and disabilities that arise from suboptimum nutrition produce physical stress on the body, which in turn can contribute to psychological distress and anxiety. Nutrition is thus of great importance to you both for the sake of your general health and in relation to any anxiety symptoms you may have.

One reason there is so much conflicting advice on the subject of nutrition is that, in a sense, there are *two* competing sciences of nutrition. One, represented by the United States Food and Nutrition Board and by the medical establishment in general, is based on the old idea that recommended daily allowances of vitamins should be the amounts that prevent vitamin deficiencies in most people. These recommended daily allowances (RDAs) are the ones listed on vitamin preparations manufactured in the United States. This approach to nutrition is analogous to the medical principle that the dose of medicine used should be the smallest amount that will cure the disease. This is obviously a wise approach in dealing with powerful drugs that are not normally present in the body and that produce serious side effects.

However, vitamins are not drugs. They are essential nutrient substances that are normally present in the body. The newer science of nutrition—which has been called "ortho-molecular medicine" by its preeminent spokesman, Linus Pauling—is based on the relatively new idea that the *optimum* intake of vitamins for human beings in general and for any person in particular may be much higher than the *minimum* amount that prevents a deficiency disease in most people.

Pauling, the recipient of two Nobel prizes (one in chemistry and one for contributions to world peace), coined the word "orthomolecular" to mean "the right molecules in the right amounts." He has defined orthomolecular medicine as "the prevention and treatment of disease and the preservation of good health by varying the concentration of these molecules in the human body." Pauling believes that optimum concentrations of nutrient substances like vitamins can strengthen the body's natural defense mechanisms against disease, can increase life expectancy by perhaps 20 years, and can similarly increase the period of health and well-being in most people's lives.

It is beyond the scope of this book to go deeply into the reasoning behind orthomolecular medicine, except to note the basic ideas on which the new science is built: (1) the modern human diet is not the one on which the human body is genetically adapted to thrive, (2) the biochemical individuality of human beings may mean that the optimum amount of certain nutrients varies by more than a factor of 20 from person to person, (3) resistance to disease can be significantly increased by increasing the intake of certain nutrients (especially ascorbic acid, or vitamin C) well above the RDA standards set by the Food and Nutrition Board.

At this point, no one really knows what the optimum intake of vitamins is, so the ultimate test is how we feel when we take different amounts of vitamins for a period of time. In the Self-Care Program we have listed the amounts Linus Pauling takes, as well as the ranges suggested by Richard A. Passwater in his book *Supernutrition.*

We also provide some basic dietary guidelines generally recommended by nutritionists and health-care specialists. We list substances that are suspected or known to contribute to the physical sensations commonly identified as anxiety symptoms, as well as natural substances that are held to have calming or tranquilizing effects. Finally, we recommend sources of information for those who wish to explore the subject of nutrition more thoroughly.

In regard to buying vitamin and mineral supplements, our advice is to look carefully for the best prices, since identical substances are sold at widely different per-unit prices.

We have also included a Nutrition and Medication Log (see the Blank Forms section at the end of this book) to help you become more aware of the effects of your nutritional habits, drugs, and other psychoactive substances (namely, alcohol and caffeine) on your day-to-day sense of well-being.

Physical Exercise

Regular exercise can contribute greatly to your overall sense of well-being and ability to relax. If you swim, jog, or engage in some other form of vigorous exercise regularly, you know what it feels like to exercise at the end of a long day of activity, when you feel mentally and physically exhausted. Out of a sense of duty, you may drag yourself to the swimming pool or reluctantly put on your running shoes. But after you have exercised, you feel invigorated. Even if your work involves real physical labor, exercise that stretches your body, especially swimming, can help take the kinks out. You feel far better than if you had simply collapsed in front of a TV or drank a beer or a martini in an effort to block your feelings.

If you do not exercise regularly, gradually adding exercise to your day-to-day routine would probably be a self-caring and beneficial action. However, you need to be mindful of several points:

1. No one should plunge into vigorous physical exercise suddenly. The "first snow" phenomenon is well known in the Northeast. Following the first snowfall, thousands of sedentary men labor mightily to shovel snow from driveways and walks. The result: significant increases in reported back injuries and heart attacks.

2. Overexertion and exhaustion can cause not only physical stress and injury but psychological stress and anxiety symptoms as well. For this reason, when you feel acutely anxious, you should probably avoid vigorous exercise, although gentle exercise, like stretching and walking, often seems to be helpful.

3. If you are under a physician's care, if you have physical or medical limitations, or if you have not exercised for a long time, you should obtain your physician's approval before you start a new exercise program.

4. If you have back problems or are physically disabled, a physician, physical therapist, or nurse practitioner may be able to suggest appropriate forms of exercise for you. Swimming or exercising in water is often recommended for those with back problems.

The Self-Care Program contains some suggestions and basic guidelines for those who are able to and wish to benefit from regular physical exercise. For more detailed information, we refer you to the Suggested Readings section.

COPING WITH EMOTIONAL DISTRESS

This second section of the program is intended to help you meet the sometimes pressing need for techniques and skills to call upon whenever the idea arises that you must seek help and you begin to experience acute anxiety.

Carry-Along Checklists

The Self-Care Program includes two checklists that can be copied and carried in your purse or wallet. The Troubleshooting Checklist helps you become aware of (and thus be in control of) the deeper feelings that have caused you to move toward the high end of the anxiety spectrum. The Coping Checklist summarizes the coping techniques and skills described in the Self-Care Program.

Coping Techniques

Coping techniques are ways of dealing with fearfulness and emotional distress at the time they are occurring. They are related to relaxation training, meditation, and desensitization training and have some features in common with each. The distinguishing characteristic of coping techniques is that they apply to the short-run situation. Relaxation training, meditation, and desensitization training are geared more to a longer-range approach to your problems, as is learning to be more aware of feelings and more assertive in communicating them.

Eventually, you will recognize that all of the various thoughts that trigger an emergency reaction are ultimately rooted in the idea of helplessness. You will learn to apply the antidote of your freedom whenever you recognize that sinking feeling that accompanies this idea. The techniques explained here are like first-aid measures that can be applied while you are still learning to go right to the heart of the matter.

Step-by-step instructions for several coping techniques are included in the Self-Care Program. In general, you can learn these techniques while you are relaxed in a quiet, comfortable location. You should rehearse them repeatedly in order for them to become fully effective in difficult situations. These coping techniques are learned behaviors that can be substituted for the fight-or-flight reaction fairly easily.

Meditating regularly has been compared to putting money in the bank—gradually developing the quiet awareness you will need to draw on in times of psychological stress. Of course, there are means of obtaining "instant credit" if you have little money in the bank. The coping techniques we present are such shortcuts to inner freedom. When you feel the signs of physiological arousal in the face of a threatening event or thought, you can use these techniques to substitute awareness and relaxation for agitation and alarm.

Simple Breathing Exercises. The point of practicing breathing exercises is not that you need to learn how to breathe properly and naturally, but rather that you may need to learn to refrain from allowing your natural rhythm of breathing to be disrupted when you are distressed or startled.

Anxious people tend to hold their breath or to over-breathe (hyperventilate) in such circumstances. Either behavior disturbs the vital levels of oxygen and carbon dioxide in the body and can lead to the physical sensations associated with anxiety. For example, overbreathing drives carbon dioxide out of the lungs too rapidly, causing an abnormal decrease in the level of carbon dioxide in the blood. As reported in the *Harvard Medical School Health Letter* (January 1985), a group of British researchers holds that this sets off "a series of chemical changes in the body" that cause the typical symptoms of an agoraphobic episode: "light-headedness, nausea, chest pain, palpitations, a smothering feeling, and all too frequently an overwhelming sense of impending death."

To test their idea, the researchers trained a small group of agoraphobic patients "to breathe with their diaphragms, keeping their chest walls as immobile as possible." (When you breathe with your diaphragm, your abdomen will protrude slightly as you inhale and your chest walls and shoulders will remain at rest.) When this group was reexposed to frightening situations, they had far fewer panic attacks than before.

The British researchers concentrated their attention on overbreathing. By contrast, Dr. Charles F. Stroebel, professor of psychiatry at the University of Connecticut Medical School, found that most people tend to hold their breath during an emergency reaction. Like overbreathing, holding one's breath obviously triggers a series of significant chemical changes in the body that could lead to heightened physiological distress.

Thus a basic technique for coping with any form of emotional distress is breathing naturally from the abdomen (which means "with the diaphragm") and thus avoiding either form of disrupted breathing.

The Quieting Reflex. The quieting reflex was developed by Dr. Stroebel. The result of careful scientific research, it is resonant both with the principles of conditioned learning and medical stress psychology. It is more than a coping technique, since it actually teaches you, over a period of weeks and months, to respond more appropriately to events in your environment.

Stroebel explained to writer Barbara Lang Stern that he and his associates carefully analyzed the behavioral components of the emergency startle (fight-or-flight) reaction. They found five definite stages of arousal occurring within a 6- to 10-second period:

First, the activity of the sympathetic nervous system increases. (For example, the pupils of the eyes dilate, "trying to collect more information on what there is to be afraid about.") Second, muscle tension increases, "initially in the face around the eyes, and mouth, and then extending gradually over the entire body." Third, typically, most people hold their breath, although a few begin to breathe too rapidly (hyperventilate). Fourth, cold hands or feet indicate that "the body is redirecting the blood to the deep muscles that would be used for running or fighting." Fifth, the jaw is clenched. "It's equivalent to the dog's baring his fangs going into battle, although more subtle."

Stroebel's idea is that you can learn to modify your behavior by substituting a set of incompatible behaviors for those we have just described. The new behaviors are contained in a six-second exercise, called the quieting reflex, that you perform consciously whenever you observe the startle reaction arising. According to Stroebel, these new behaviors can eventually become an automatic reflex for most people if used regularly for four to six months.

The quieting reflex is an excellent technique for coping with the symptoms of psychological stress. In addition, it helps you become aware of the types of stimuli you perceive to be threatening. You can gain much self-knowledge and self-understanding by examining these stimuli closely. For example, how often are you reacting to what-if thoughts? How often do comparisons of yourself to other people trigger your alarm? How often do you begin to be afraid when you feel insulted or treated with disrespect? How often are you reacting to a perceived threat to your freedom? As you gradually become aware of such patterns, they lose their power to throw you off-balance.

One woman in her 70s liked the quieting reflex the first time she tried it on a shopping trip. "I've always felt anxious while I'm driving," she said, "and I've always told myself,

'Be alert, be alert.' Now, when I say, 'Mind alert, body calm,' I can feel my shoulders settle down, and I relax."

Answering Your Inner Child.   In the process of accepting our freedom and outgrowing chronic anxiety, it is sometimes important to remember the child we once were. We now understand that to love a child means to facilitate—and not interfere with—its growth toward freedom and independence. This applies to the small child we remember ourselves to be. To love ourselves, as a truly self-caring person would, means to give ourselves—and the child within—the freedom to outgrow self-diminishing assumptions, beliefs, attitudes, and behaviors.

Emotional reactions of regret, sorrow, and shame directed toward the child we once were stem from the idea that in the earliest stages of our life, we should have been stronger, more courageous, wiser, and more articulate than we were.

This is neither realistic nor fair. At the time the infant we once were began to adopt the counterphobic ("coverup") strategies of concealment, distrust, and avoidance, it lacked the experience that would have given it wisdom, and it lacked the language that would have made it articulate. As for strength and courage, that infant put every ounce of its strength and courage into what it saw as a life-and-death struggle. It made terrible sacrifices, but it fought to survive. If we want to be realistic and fair, we need to recognize that the infant we once were did the very best it could in dealing with what it perceived to be a life-threatening situation.

Ten, twenty, thirty, forty or more years later, when we look back at that psychologically incomplete being, do we say, "Thank you. Thank you for fighting for my survival. Thank you for putting every ounce of your strength and courage into the struggle to survive! You did the best you could. I accept you as part of me."

Or do we say, "You miserable little brat, you should have been stronger, tougher, wiser, more articulate, more bold, and more courageous. I am ashamed of you. You are not part of me—I reject you!"

As we enter into the process of honest introspection, it is easy to become impatient with ourselves and with the child we once were. We need to see clearly how rejecting that child keeps us off-balance and at war with ourselves. We need to learn to pause and embrace that child within when feelings of insecurity arise. We need to treasure it, soothe it, and respond to it when it feels unloved, isolated, and alone. We need to tell that child that it can relax and sleep peacefully in the warmth and love of our heart.

The suffering caused by chronic anxiety can be seen as the belated "growing pains" of someone who, at any age, is struggling to become a more balanced, independent person.

Once anxious people are able to accept responsibility for themselves and for their problem, they find they have taken control over their own lives. They now have the power to change their beliefs and actions and the power to redefine themselves in significant ways. They do not necessarily feel "above it all." Instead, they feel authentic, balanced, flexible—and more confident than they have ever felt before.

If they can embrace the child within and give it the continuous and unconditional love it craves, they are on the road to freeing themselves from self-sabotaging fear and anxiety.

The coping techniques in the Self-Care Program include simple breathing exercises, Stroebel's quieting reflex, Weekes's "four concepts," answering your inner child, stretching and movement, self-affirmation, visualization, focusing, talking, humor, and acceptance and compassion.

EXTINGUISHING LEARNED REACTIONS

Desensitization is the process by which you systematically reeducate your nervous system so that it will not automatically respond with anxiety to a specific object or place.

Desensitization employs the principles of conditioned learning to extinguish the connection between a conditioned response (salivation, anxiety, etc.) and a conditioned stimulus (a tone, department store, freeway, elevator, etc.).

In the desensitization process itself, you are not directly concerned with *why* you had an anxiety attack; you are concerned only with disconnecting an unproductive anxiety response from an inappropriate stimulus. Your goal is to reduce and eventually eliminate an anxiety response that is restricting your freedom in some way. Your method of disconnecting the response from the stimulus will not be as painful or traumatic as making the connection was. Desensitization can be done with very little anxiety, at your own pace, and under your own control.

Successive Approximations

In systematic desensitization, a nonfunctional behavior is gradually modified and converted into a desired behavior through a series of successive approximations. This approach uses successive approximations of a desired behavior to gradually shape that behavior. If your goal, for example, is to be able to climb a ladder to put up the storm windows, but you get very nervous on the ladder, you would break your eventual goal into a series of subgoals. The first rung of the ladder would be your first subgoal, the second rung would be your second subgoal, and so on. By the time you reach the fourth or fifth rung of the ladder, after many training trials spaced out over a few days, you might have a setback and be unable to go higher than the third rung. This is a normal part of training. If it happens, just continue training at the third-rung level until you are comfortable trying the fourth once again. It is not uncommon to make rapid progress for a while after you have successfully coped with a setback.

One man, who liked to go running on an ocean beach every day, found that he suddenly had a phobic reaction when he walked onto a fishing pier that extended some distance from the beach. He felt dizzy and weak as soon as he was over the surf breaking on the beach below the pier.

He set as his goal being able to walk all the way to the end of the pier without experiencing dizziness and anxiety.

Analyzing his experience, he decided he was sensitive to at least four aspects of the total situation: (1) distance from the shore, (2) being over water, (3) the other people on the pier, and (4) the panoramic scene.

The basic problem, he felt sure, was distance from the shore. Noticing that there was a series of 14 or 16 lampposts on the pier, he decided to use the lampposts as markers and to see whether he could gradually extend the distance he could walk without feeling uncomfortable.

He knew that for him, cold feet, a feeling of warmth, and sweaty palms indicated mild anxiety; a sick feeling in the pit of his stomach and cold hands indicated moderate anxiety; and chills indicated a high level of anxiety.

Following the first rule of successive approximation, he knew that *he should try not to exceed a mild level of anxiety* at any point in his training. (Accidentally exceeding mild anxiety does not necessarily cause training to fail, but it does not help, nor does it feel good!)

The first step would be to find a starting place for his training. This he did the next time he went running on the beach. Walking slowly out onto the concrete pier, he observed no symptoms at all as he passed the first two "easy" lampposts. Just beyond the third lamppost, he began to experience mild anxiety. He had found his starting place.

He stood by the third lamppost and carefully observed the scene. For a few moments, he watched the beach beneath him, where occasional waves washed over the sand. He watched the swirling patterns on the surface of the water. He shrugged his shoulders and then allowed his back and neck muscles to relax. When other people walked by, he looked at their faces and briefly met their eyes. For a while he focused on distant objects, trying to pick out familiar buildings in nearby towns on the coast.

Feeling no anxiety symptoms at all, he decided to approach the fourth lamppost. Striding confidently along, he began to experience mild anxiety symptoms halfway to his goal. Following the second rule of successive approximation—*to withdraw immediately from a situation when you experience mild anxiety*—he turned around and walked back to the third lamppost, whistling nonchalantly.

After a few deep breaths, some muscular tensing and relaxing, and a few moments spent observing the scene, he began to walk, a bit more cautiously this time, toward the fourth lamppost. He made it this time and spent a few moments relaxing there and congratulating himself on a job well done.

He decided that on every following day he would add at least one more lamppost to his "safe territory" on the pier. He began to do so, and the following days were much the same, except that he now had to get used to being over deep water.

Stormy winter weather complicated the situation and slowed his progress, but he decided to treat the wind and big waves simply as one more element to get used to.

By the time he finished his training—and had overcome his phobic reaction—he liked to walk out on the pier toward sundown, enjoy the view and ask the fishermen how they were doing. Even in stormy weather he enjoyed walking all the way to the end of the pier. He felt like a Viking, watching the ocean waves and feeling the rain and sea spray in his face. Anyone who saw him out there all alone on a stormy day may have thought he was crazy, but he didn't care.

Step-by-step instructions for this systematic desensitization training will be given in the Self-Care Program.

Flooding

As we explained earlier, flooding involves deliberately evoking a phobic reaction in your imagination and allowing it, in a sense, to wear itself out, so that eventually you no longer experience it in the presence of the feared object or situation. Many people like to use flooding in combination with field work using the successive-approximations approach.

ACHIEVING CONTROL THROUGH RELAXED AWARENESS

As you begin to feel more physically relaxed and mentally alert and to gain some degree of control over phobic reactions and acute anxiety, you will naturally want to look more deeply at the habitual behaviors, feelings, attitudes, beliefs, and assumptions that have moved you toward the high end of the anxiety spectrum in the past.

This investigation can in itself create some psychological stress because it requires you to confront the idea of helplessness as well as the idealized self-image you may have developed to defend against that idea.

We have already described the role of a good therapist in helping people overcome their ignorance of the sources of their suffering. Whether or not you should include a professional therapist in your recovery network is your decision. The point is not that you have to report your feelings to someone, simply that it is important to have someone to talk to—to have a mature, supportive person to act as a sounding board. It is often difficult for family members to be objective and nonjudgmental enough to play this role well, and children should not be burdened with it. A valued and trusted friend may be of help if he or she understands that what you need is not answers and judgments but simply support in honest self-exploration.

One thing family members and friends can provide is friendship and love that will help you through feelings of sadness and loss that may arise as you work to free yourself from the trap of anxiety.

The rewards of enlarging your awareness in this way are great. Moments of clarity and insight, when you understand and transcend the neediness of the infantile self, lift great burdens from your shoulders. You become able to recognize old self-diminishing ideas without being moved by them. At such times you may find yourself seeing the world with new eyes, enjoying its beauty, and feeling a common bond with others—perhaps understanding human suffering in a more realistic way.

The Self-Care Program includes five inventory forms on which you can objectively list the following information:

> The places and situations in which you have experienced phobic reactions.
>
> Current sources of frustration and displeasure in your life.
>
> The things you worry about.
>
> The things you feel guilty about.
>
> Ways in which you diminish or defeat yourself while talking to others. (The Assertiveness Log will help you identify these.)

The benefits of making such inventories include:

> Becoming aware of the scope and limits of your problems; seeing them in perspective.
>
> Distinguishing between realistic and unrealistic concerns, so that you can set better priorities.
>
> Getting ideas for dealing with your problems.
>
> Accepting and confronting your problems instead of avoiding them; in a sense, earning the right to set them aside for a time, to relax, and to live in the present moment.

COMMUNICATING ASSERTIVELY

Assertiveness

To assert your honest feelings is to own yourself. To own yourself is an antidote to anxiety and the basis of real security and freedom. As we have explained, a comprehensive discussion of assertive communication is beyond the scope of the Self-Care Program. We highly recommend the books by

Pamela E. Butler and Thomas Gordon in the Suggested Readings section if you wish to look more closely at this important self-care skill. (Also, at some time, you might wish to review the section Assertiveness Training in Chapter 5.) In a way, Gordon's book, *Parent Effectiveness Training,* is especially appropriate, since the task of anxious and phobic people is first of all to become good and caring parents to themselves and secondly to allow the compassion of this inner good parent to radiate outward toward others. Butler's book, *Self-Assertiveness for Women,* deals with feminist issues that arise from the way contemporary society is organized, but men will find much in her book that applies to them.

Anger

Anger is one of the most valuable guides you will meet on the road to recovery. Recognizing hidden anger can reduce anxiety. Expressing anger appropriately can be a powerful affirmation of the self. Although it may be a "no" to another person's request or demand, it is a "yes" to the self.

Suppose that you recognize—or at least concede the possibility—that your problem with anxiety is related to the suppression of feelings of frustration, displeasure, or anger. What should you do about it? Throw a temper tantrum? Yell at people when they displease you? Become an angry, unpleasant, selfish person?

We are emphatically *not* advising you to create psychological stress for other people by acting in an aggressive or threatening manner. What we are telling you is that very few people who recover from anxiety conditions do so without accepting, understanding, and learning to express their negative feelings. Unfortunately, many people, largely through a lack of experience with assertiveness, tend to express their displeasure aggressively (threateningly), which more often than not provokes defensive responses and results in their own subsequent feelings of guilt. Such guilty feelings appear to confirm the idea that expressing anger does not work; so they go back to being passive and holding on to their anger. This is why assertiveness (which permits the nonthreatening expression of displeasure) is so vital to recovery. You need to learn how to express negative feelings occasionally without feeling guilty afterward.

We discussed the value of assertiveness in overcoming anxiety in Chapter 4, Self-Expression: Telling the World Who You Are. The Self-Care Program includes a log form on which to monitor the assertiveness, aggressiveness, and passivity in your communications with others and the consequences of these three stances.

The Self-Care Program also provides guidelines for framing assertive messages, rehearsing what you want and need to communicate, and analyzing and solving communications problems.

CULTIVATING INNER FREEDOM

Where Is Your Mind?

In *The Three Pillars of Zen*, Philip Kapleau writes, "Ask the ordinary Japanese where his mind is and the chances are he will point to his heart or his chest."

In Japan, the expression "to act from the *hara*" suggests wholehearted action; literally, action that comes from the gut. Kapleau clarifies this concept: "*Hara* literally denotes the stomach and abdomen and the functions of digestion, absorption, and elimination connected with them. But it has parallel psychic and spiritual significance. . . . *Hara* [is considered to be] a wellspring of vital psychic energies."

The student of Zen Buddhist meditation "is instructed to focus his mind constantly at the bottom of his hara (specifically, between the navel and the pelvis) and to radiate all mental and bodily activities from that region."

Most of us Westerners (including Americans of Japanese heritage) would probably tend to locate our minds someplace behind our eyes and between our ears. We tend to equate our mind with the visual images we perceive, except when we close our eyes and listen to music, in which case our mind seems to move over closer to our ears than to our eyes.

We cannot help suspecting that this somewhat top-heavy Western tendency is related to the fallacious division of mind and body that has distorted Western thought for centuries. The ancient Greeks understood the unity of "a sound mind in a sound body," but modern people tend to emphasize one at the expense of the other and to regard the body as a machine and the mind as somehow external to the body. Indeed, as children many of us fantasized a little person up in our head, looking out through our eyes and controlling the body's actions.

Centering oneself in the *hara* is a way of eliminating this kind of internal division and alienation and experiencing the essential unity of body, breath, and mind and the sense of freedom that comes with this experience.

Choosing Versus Falling into Traps

In a way, thoughts are like baited fishhooks. When a thought arises, we can blindly "take the bait" or choose not to. Consider these thoughts, for example:

> "Here comes that overpass on the freeway where I felt pan-
>   icky last August."
> "I can't remember the last three blocks I just walked past!"
> "The new department head doesn't seem to understand the
>   problems any better than the last one did."
> "I've wasted a lot of years with the problem of anxiety."

If we believe we are helpless and unfree beings—and are in this sense alienated from ourselves—then we must habit-ually fall into the traps of thought created by our unrealistic assumptions about ourselves and our world:

The thought "*Either* I feel perfectly relaxed while I drive on this overpass *or* I will feel anxious for the rest of the trip" may lead us to start feeling anxious.

The thought "*What if* there's something seriously wrong with me?" may lead us to worry for days about having a fatal illness.

The thought "But I *have to* work for him!" may lead us into an imaginary argument with our new supervisor.

The thought "*If only* I had started this when I was younger" may lead us to have feelings of self-contempt.

Eastern and Western thinking complement each other in many helpful ways that few people have had the opportunity to appreciate. We believe that the meditative tradition and the human psychology associated with it can greatly enrich Western psychology—which in some ways has reached an impasse—and can help all of us learn to live more from the inside out and less from the outside in.

In this section of the Self-Care Program, we emphasize the value of meditation as a means of cultivating inner freedom and eliminating the idea of helplessness as the driving force of our behavior. We offer some guidelines for those who wish to receive practical training in meditation and also refer you to some excellent books on the subject.

MAINTAINING A REALISTIC AND POSITIVE SELF-CONCEPT

Some people believe that when you experience psychological pain or suffering, it is your own fault for not thinking positively. Others believe that suffering is entirely the result of external conditions and what others do to you.

It is easy to fluctuate between these two points of view while you are recovering from an anxiety condition. As long as a particular approach is working, you may feel optimistic—indeed, at times, euphoric. This joy is well earned; however, any setbacks, obstacles, or difficulties—any discontinuities in the smooth course of progress—may tempt you to throw up your hands in despair and decide that the particular approach cannot work for you after all.

Realistically, you need to recognize that there are bound to be setbacks and negative experiences in the recovery process, as in any human endeavor. You also need to recognize the necessity and value of these experiences. Recovery, like any process of self-regulation, occurs through alternating cycles of self-observation and self-adjustment. This feedback process cannot take place in the absence of detectable "errors"—deviations from ideal conditions. This means it is essential to have some errors to observe. Naturally, as your awareness and ability to observe gradually improve, you will be able to detect deviations from ideal conditions sooner, while they are small, and thus smooth out the course of recovery.

In sum, it is better to seek to be a good observer of yourself than to seek to make no mistakes. A realistic and positive self-concept allows room for mistakes.

Most of us are living out the self-image we acquired as children. We say "most of us," because it is possible for us to change our self-concept and even to replace a negative self-concept with a positive sense of self. In fact, this is an important part of outgrowing anxiety conditions.

It is not always obvious that we are living out a self-image acquired so many years ago. Yet, subconsciously, we see the world according to an assumption we have made about who we are. This assumption, unless challenged later in life, stems from our very earliest experiences of ourselves as separate and distinct individuals.

If you learned a negative self-image of yourself in childhood, then your personality—your expectations and reactions—reflect that negative attitude. Indeed, other people in your life may to some extent come to share your belief in your negative image.

Some psychotherapists like to compare recurrent thoughts and attitudes to tape recordings. Why play the old, negative tape, they ask, when you can replace it with a new, positive one?

Self-affirmation is a way of making new tape recordings for yourself—of developing new thoughts, attitudes, and a positive self-image. Instead of playing the old, self-defeating tape, you can choose to play a self-affirming one.

Your old tape might be telling you things like: "You are weak and fearful." "You can't take care of yourself." "You need someone to rescue you." "You can't learn to do things properly." Listen to the things overly protective, domineering, or anxious family members sometimes say to children. A negative self-image is constructed of such messages.

Your new tape can say things like, "You are an affectionate and caring person." "You deserve care and affection." "You are OK." "You are strong and resourceful." "You are intelligent." "You can learn to do things properly." "You are free to make choices." "You can take care of yourself."

There is no EJECT or ERASE button for changing tapes on your internal tape recorder. But you can patiently and deliberately repeat the positive thoughts you choose for yourself over and over for a period of days and weeks—until one day the new messages have replaced the old ones. It took time for you to learn the negative self-image recorded on your old tape. It will also take time for you to learn the new message.

It's not necessary to worry too much about writing a new tape. Loving yourself is not something you have to work at. It is the natural consequence of letting go of negative thoughts. If you allow your more complete, positive, caring self to emerge, you will feel more secure, and a sense of well-being will follow.

In the Self-Care Program, we will provide some guidelines for transforming a negative internal tape into a positive one. We will ask you to actually record your new tape (if you have a cassette recorder) and to play it along with other calming, comforting, and self-affirming tape recordings listed in the Suggested Cassette Tapes section.

Part 2

Your Self-Care Program

*"Habit is habit, and not to be flung out of the
window by any man, but coaxed downstairs a
step at a time."*

—Mark Twain, *Pudd'nhead Wilson*

Whenever you work on the program, it would be a good idea
to sit in a balanced posture and to begin by taking two or
three complete breaths from your abdomen. (If you're not
sure what this means, just yawn.) Now, let's get started.

THE SEVEN-LEVEL PLAN

Since the program is self-paced, it would not make sense for
us to give you an arbitrary schedule. On the other hand, it
would not make sense to hand you a set of tools without any
instructions about how to go about using them. For this
reason, we have prepared the Seven-Level Plan. It tells you
how to get started and gradually introduces all of the self-
care skills and techniques in the program.

All of the forms mentioned in the Seven-Level Plan can
be found in the Blank Forms section at the end of this book.

Those whose problems are moderate may be able to reach
Level 7 within seven to nine weeks. Those with severe and
pervasive problems may take quite a bit longer. In the case
of agoraphobia, recovery generally takes place over a period

of months, not weeks, and full recovery may take a couple of years. Our operational definition of full recovery from agoraphobia is this: you have recovered when (1) you no longer worry about having an anxiety attack, and (2) if you do have an anxiety attack on a rare occasion, you take it not as a life-or-death threat but as an invitation to reflect on the current psychological stress in your life and on your self-care practices.

Read through the entire Seven-Level Plan to get an idea of the program's scope and of the way the pieces fit together. Then start working through the plan, item by item, at your own pace.

THE SEVEN-LEVEL PLAN (CHECKLIST)

Level 1

General

___ Obtain the equipment and supplies listed on the Equipment and Supplies Checklist in Chapter 6.

___ Make copies of the forms listed on the checklist.

___ Set aside a special place for your self-care materials near a desk or table where you can work on them in private.

___ Begin using the small note pad or a 3 × 5 card each evening to make a "to do" list of self-care activities for the following day. Check your calendar or datebook for activities that should go on the list. If appropriate, transfer unfinished items from one day's list to the next before discarding the old list. Items should be short imperative sentences that precisely specify the task you wish to do—they should not be single words or phrases.

___ Begin using your notebook to record insights, ideas, significant experiences, books to read, and so forth—anything related to coping with distress or reducing stress.

___ Begin using your calendar or datebook to schedule self-care activities that you plan more than one day in advance.

— Use a pocket alarm clock or watch to remind you of scheduled activities if you wish.

— Set up your recovery network, putting all pertinent information (names, telephone numbers, comments, and so forth) in your notebook.

— Begin using the seven-day Journal form every day. There is room for brief notes on this form; longer notes can go into your notebook. Save all completed forms in the front of your folder of forms for future reference.

— Fill out a Self-Evaluation form and save it in the front of your folder.

Caring for Your Body

— Before you begin relaxation training or meditation, start a program of physical exercise, or increase your intake of vitamins and minerals, you may need to consult a physician. (See the section on Setting Up a Recovery Network.)

— As soon as you obtain a relaxation tape, begin using it twice a day.

— If you do not have a relaxation tape, use the Quiet Sitting exercise for a few minutes twice a day.

— Begin keeping a one-week Nutrition and Medication Log.

— Review the discussion of physical exercise in the program and consider whether you wish to begin an exercise program.

Coping with Emotional Distress

— Put a copy of the carry-along checklists in your purse or wallet.

— Select a simple breathing exercise and begin practicing it four to eight times a day. Do it following use of the relaxation tape or the Quiet Sitting exercise.

Extinguishing Learned Reactions

— Use the Inventory of Phobic Reactions to pinpoint the situations and locations to which you have become sensitized.

Control Through Awareness

__ Use the Displeasure/Frustration Inventory to help pinpoint sources of psychological stress in your life. Do this after reviewing Chapter 4 (see next item).

Communicating Assertively

__ Review Chapter 4, Self-Expression: Telling the World Who You Are. Use your notebook to make notes concerning how this chapter applies to you.
__ Start using the Assertiveness Log to help you pinpoint possible communications problems.
__ Review the section on Telling Your Spouse or Companion About the Self-Care Program.

Level 2

General

__ Continue using daily "to do" lists.

Caring for Your Body

__ Continue regular daily relaxation exercises.
__ Check your posture whenever you do a breathing exercise— are you habitually putting undue stress on any portion of your spine or neck?
__ Review your completed Nutrition and Medication Log in light of the nutritional guidelines in the Self-Care Program.
__ Decide on some positive changes in nutrition. For example, do you want (1) to reduce your intake of caffeine or sugar? (2) to increase your intake of fresh vegetables? (3) to begin starting each day with a hearty and nutritious breakfast? Record your decisions as positive goals in your notebook. Put reminders in your calendar or datebook.
__ Consider increasing your intake of vitamins and minerals to orthomolecular levels. Record your decision in your notebook

and use your calendar or datebook to remind you to obtain necessary vitamin and mineral preparations.

Coping with Emotional Distress

— Review the sections describing the various techniques for coping with emotional distress.

— Begin practicing the quieting reflex. Rehearse the entire procedure at least twice a day over a period of days, until you begin to use it automatically whenever you are startled or distressed or observe a troublesome thought. If you wish, use tally marks on your "to do" lists to keep track of the rehearsals.

Extinguishing Learned Reactions

— Review the sections in chapters 5 and 6 on desensitization and successive-approximations training.

— Use the Levels of Anxiety form to identify your symptoms at different levels of anxiety. Cultivate the habit of identifying your current level of anxiety by number.

— Select one or two of the "easiest" (most accessible) places or situations on your Inventory of Phobic Reactions, and prepare Situation Hierarchy forms for them.

— While you are relaxed, begin rehearsing in your imagination a visit to one of the places or situations for which you have prepared Situation Hierarchies. To start with, focus on the easiest goals on the hierarchy. Rehearse at least 21 times over a period of days—until you feel thoroughly relaxed while visualizing the entire series of goals. Use the simple breathing exercise or the quieting reflex to help you remain calm and relaxed during these rehearsals.

Control Through Awareness

— Use the Worry Inventory to help pinpoint sources of psychological stress in your life.

— Use the Guilt Inventory to help you pinpoint sources of psychological stress in your life.

Maintaining a Realistic and Positive Self-Image

___ Use the Negative Thoughts form to identify ideas that contribute to feelings of helplessness, inadequacy, and insecurity. Also use it to describe self-diminishing ways in which you tend to see yourself and portray yourself to others.

___ Use your notebook to begin to describe your ideal (not idealized) self—the person you really wish to be.

Level 3

General

___ Continue using daily "to do" lists.

___ Use your calendar or notebook to schedule additional uses of the Assertiveness Log, the Displeasure/Frustration Inventory, the Guilt Inventory, and the Worry Inventory forms.

___ To gain more time for self-care activities, review your television viewing habits. Schedule your favorite programs and other special programs you wish to see in your calendar or datebook and daily "to do" lists. Turn on your television set at scheduled times, relax, and enjoy these programs wholeheartedly—as though you are giving yourself a treat. Keep the set off at other times.

___ Review your Self-Evaluation form and enter current answers.

Caring for Your Body

___ Continue daily relaxation exercises.

___ At this point, you may wish to try out a different relaxation tape. (See the Suggested Cassette Tapes section.)

___ Check the Suggested Cassette Tapes section for other useful tapes.

___ If you have a physician's approval to begin an exercise program, use your calendar or datebook to schedule short periods of exercise every other day for the next two weeks.

___ If you are beginning to exercise, avoid overexertion and exhaustion.

— If you wake up with aches and pains, it could be because of your sleeping positions. Consider obtaining an orthopedic pillow that will support the natural curve of your neck while you sleep.

— Also, consider changing your sleeping positions. Try sleeping on your back with a pillow under your knees, and on your side with a pillow between your knees. For most people these positions avoid stress on the lower back. If you have back or other health problems, you should consult your physical therapist or nurse practitioner before making changes. No single measure is right for everyone.

Coping with Emotional Distress

— Continue practicing the quieting reflex at least once or twice a day.

— Start using the quieting reflex to cope with startling events and unpleasant events and thoughts.

Extinguishing Learned Reactions

— Once you are relaxed while visualizing the goals on your first Situation Hierarchy, use your calendar or datebook to schedule a series of 15 visits to the place you have selected to do the training. Space the visits out over a period of a week or two.

Control Through Awareness

— Set aside an hour when you are relaxed, and list in your notebook all of the internal and external sources of psychological stress in your life. Write them down in any order, just as they come to mind. Use the completed forms and any other notes you may have made.

— Set aside another hour to work in your notebook. Identify seven or eight of the greatest sources of psychological stress on your list. Use the notebook to make notes concerning how you might reduce or eliminate stress from any of these sources. Identify specific self-care skills that can help.

Cultivating Inner Freedom

___ Review Chapter 3, The Key Issues: Freedom and Responsibility. Use your notebook to make notes concerning how this chapter applies to you.

Maintaining a Realistic and Positive Self-Image

___ Review the section in Chapter 6 on recording a new "tape." Use your notebook to write a series of realistic and positive self-affirmations for use on a self-affirmation tape.

Level 4

General

___ Continue using daily "to do" lists.

Caring for Your Body

___ Continue regular daily relaxation exercises.
___ Review your progress toward the nutritional goals you noted in your notebook. Try to pinpoint any factors that may be interfering with reaching these goals.

Coping with Emotional Distress

___ Review Chapter 2, Growing Up Anxious. Use your notebook to make notes concerning how this chapter applies to you. What applies and what does not? How are your early experiences related to your emotional reactions?
___ Review the sections describing the various coping techniques. Continue practicing the quieting reflex and/or select another coping technique to practice regularly.

Extinguishing Learned Reactions

—— Begin desensitization field training at the "easiest " (most accessible) location selected for initial training.
—— Once you have started field training, try to do it at least every other day if possible, until you have trained at all of the places listed on your Inventory of Phobic Reactions.

Control Through Awareness

—— Use your notebook to review your list of psychological stressors. How much stress is produced by your own tendencies to be overreactive and to anticipate future harm?

Communicating Assertively

—— Review your Assertiveness Log and select one or two situations in your life in which you have difficulty communicating (for example, ordering in a restaurant, talking to an answering machine). When you are feeling relaxed, use your notebook to record the things you usually say in these situations. Now frame simple assertive messages you can begin to use instead.
—— Schedule several 15- to 20-minute rehearsals over the next week or two, and use your blank cassette tape to practice saying the assertive messages you have framed. Say them as though you really mean them. If you become nervous, stop and use a simple breathing exercise or the quieting reflex. Resume practice when you feel relaxed.

Maintaining a Realistic and Positive Self-Image

—— Use the blank cassette tape to make your own self-affirmation tape. Record the program goals as well as the self-affirmation statements from your Journal. Express yourself in a warm, wholehearted way, as though speaking to a beloved child or a cherished friend. Before recording, make the affirmative sound

"umm-hmmm" several times to help you locate your natural voice. Revise your tape until you are satisfied with it.
— Use your calendar or datebook to schedule times to listen to your self-affirmation tape. Listen to it several times over the next two weeks.

Level 5

General

— Continue using daily "to do" lists.
— Use your calendar or datebook to schedule monthly review and planning sessions. Allow an hour for each session. Begin the sessions by bringing the list of stressors in your life up-to-date.
— Make sure you have a recovery partner to give you moral support during field training. You may want the person to accompany you at first, or you may just want the partner to be available by telephone.

Caring for Your Body

— Continue regular daily relaxation exercises.
— Continue regular physical exercise. If you stop exercising for a while, gradually work back up to the level at which you stopped; do not attempt to resume exercising at the same level.

Coping with Emotional Distress

— Continue practicing a coping technique daily.

Extinguishing Learned Reactions

— Prepare one or two more Situation Hierarchy forms and schedule desensitization training at a second location.
— Set aside half an hour to rewrite your list of psychological stressors. Are there any new sources of stress in your life? Have you been successful in reducing or eliminating any of the old ones?

Communicating Assertively

— Continue framing and rehearsing assertive messages three or four times a week.

Cultivating Inner Freedom

— Review the sections on meditation.
— If you wish, try substituting meditation for your morning relaxation tape.

Level 6

General

— Continue using daily "to do" lists.
— Continue regular daily relaxation exercises (or meditation).
— Again, you may wish to try a new relaxation tape.

Coping with Emotional Distress

— Continue practicing a coping technique daily.

Extinguishing Learned Reactions

— Continue regular desensitization training.
— Review the section on Flooding in the Self-Care Program. If you want to try the flooding technique, use your calendar or datebook to schedule a training session.

Communicating Assertively

— Continue framing and rehearsing assertive messages three or four times a week.

Cultivating Inner Freedom

__ Use your calendar or datebook to schedule reading books (and listening to tapes) that will help you improve your self-care skills. Use the lists of Suggested Readings and Suggested Cassette Tapes. Some libraries and treatment centers have these or similar tapes available on loan.

Level 7

General

__ Continue using daily "to do" lists.
__ Review your Self-Evaluation form and enter current answers.

Caring for Your Body

__ Continue regular relaxation exercises (or meditation).

Coping with Emotional Distress

__ Continue practicing a coping technique daily as long as you wish. When you discontinue daily training, schedule refresher training every week or every other week.

Communicating Assertively

__ Continue framing and rehearsing assertive messages three or four times a week for as long as they are helpful to you.
__ Review section on Improving Communications with Your Spouse or Companion.

Maintaining a Realistic and Positive Self-Image

__ Listen to your self-affirmation tape. Make notes to see whether you can improve it and make it say what you want to say more simply and more clearly. Schedule another review of the tape in two or three weeks' time.

The skills and habits acquired in this Seven-Level Plan can pay off in positive gains over the coming weeks and months. They are meant to be used for a lifetime. Naturally, you can return to this plan whenever you feel the need for a "refresher course."

FINDING A RECOVERY PARTNER AND SETTING UP A RECOVERY NETWORK

When you are ready to begin desensitization-training field work at the places where you have experienced phobic reactions in the past, you may need your recovery partner to accompany you. Or it may be sufficient for this person to be available by telephone while you are doing the training.

The role of a recovery partner is to help you train (and perhaps make suggestions to help you plan your training)—not to take charge of the training. Recovery Partners must not be overprotective or impatient, and they must understand the nature of desensitization; they should be aware that progress in training is often very slow and gradual at first and that setbacks are common and to be expected. By giving you encouragement and moral support—but not sympathy—they can help you stick to the training during the most difficult early stages.

Here is a checklist for selecting a recovery partner. Make sure it is someone:

You can trust and feel comfortable with, who will quietly support your efforts without attempting to direct them.

Who is genuinely interested in helping you.

Who understands or is willing and able to learn about desensitization training.

Who is available to help at least once or twice a week.

Guidelines for a Recovery Partner to Follow are included in the subsequent section, Extinguishing Learned Reactions. Ask your partner to read these guidelines.

A recovery partner can be a family member (if he or she is not overprotective or impatient, as family members sometimes are); a friend or acquaintance (ditto); a volunteer worker; a graduate student in social science, nursing, or psychology; or someone who has fully recovered from phobic reactions through desensitization training. Naturally, we are not ruling out help from a professional behavioral therapist or one of his or her interns, if it is available in your area.

Family

People with agoraphobia or similar problems often have grown into an unbalanced relationship with a spouse, companion, or parent. The other side of the coin, of course, is that spouses, companions, and parents also grow into the same relationships, even at a cost to their own freedom.

If you are engaged in such a relationship, your decision to move away from the idea of helplessness and toward freedom may appear to the other person like a decision to move *away from him or her.* This is not necessarily true at all. People who are free can actually be closer to others than can those who are preoccupied by the problems of being dependent.

In the section Communicating Assertively, we offer you some help in the important task of explaining your self-care activities to your spouse, companion, or parent. This person is part of your recovery network. His or her wholehearted support can be a great help. At the very least, these people close to you need to understand that what you are doing is for the sake of your own happiness and is not directed against anyone else.

A spouse, companion, or parent is not always an ideal recovery partner, because he or she may be overly protective and overreact to your anxiety symptoms during training, and because you may feel self-conscious about training in this person's presence.

Do you have family members living nearby? Perhaps one of them could be your recovery partner, or could at least provide understanding, support, and encouragement if you explained your situation. Also, your relatives might be able to help you find a recovery partner. Whether or not you find a recovery partner among members of your family, we hope very much that you find loving acceptance and support. It can be a big help.

As we mentioned before, you should not rely on children for emotional support. To do so would interfere with their own growth toward freedom and autonomy. Helping your child toward independence and freedom is the right way to help yourself toward the same goals. Bear in mind that freedom does not separate people, it brings them closer together by eliminating obstacles to communication and understanding.

Friends and Acquaintances

Can you think of someone you know who might be a good recovery partner? If so, give him or her a call. Are you drifting away from any friends because of your anxiety or phobic reactions? If so, consider explaining your situation to them; they may have thought you were being unfriendly when you avoided going places with them. Friendship and love are two of the best antidotes to psychological stress. We all need friends.

Of course, friendship is a matter of giving as well as of receiving. If you live in any major American city, you have probably encountered some of the homeless and miserable people who live in the streets. Perhaps feeling unable to help them, you have ignored them. If, instead, you do what you can to help them in some small way, it will leave you with a warm feeling. It will be a small demonstration of the freedom you possess to overcome suffering.

Caring for others and being helpful to them—through some form of volunteer work, for example—is a good way to make a friendly connection with other people, as long as it is done for the satisfaction of doing it, and not out of some idea of self-sacrifice or self-punishment.

Professional Helpers

There are at least four good reasons why someone seeking to recover from agoraphobia, anxiety attacks, or related problems should have a personal physician as part of his or her recovery network.

First, a physical examination may pinpoint medical conditions as causes of dizziness and other physical sensations or may eliminate them. In the former case, medical treatment of some kind may be called for. In the latter case, you can set aside worries about your physical health and focus your attention on the causes of psychological stress in your life.

Second, a physician can advise you about an appropriate exercise program. If you have not been exercising regularly—especially if you are over 40—you should consult a physician concerning the kind and amount of exercise that is appropriate for you.

Third, if you wish to increase your intake of supplementary vitamins and minerals to ensure that you are receiving an optimum amount, your physician can explain any possible interactions between vitamins and medications you may be taking, and can also tell you whether it is advisable for you to avoid certain forms of specific vitamins.

Fourth, the reduction of physiological stress achieved by changes in patterns of relaxation and exercise may significantly affect your need for prescribed medications. This is especially important if you take insulin for diabetes or medication for high blood pressure, epilepsy, or a thyroid condition. (Dr. Stroebel cautions those with these conditions to consult their physician before beginning to use the quieting reflex.) For example, according to Barbara B. Brown in *Stress and the Art of Biofeedback,* biofeedback relaxation procedures in several cases have "apparently caused physiological changes that rendered insulin dosage excessive, causing undesirable effects of insulin overdosage." If you have any of these conditions or receive regular medication for any reason, you need to consult your physician about possible physiological changes produced by changes in your self-care practices, so that your dosage can be adjusted accordingly.

Just as you would seek advice from a specialist for various medical questions, it is wise to seek nutritional counseling from a registered dietician or from a medical doctor with special training in nutrition. In the following Organizations and Services section, we explain how you might locate such a counselor.

Even though you may not require the services of a professional psychotherapist, you should at least locate professional therapists in your vicinity who specialize in anxiety attacks, phobias, or agoraphobia and keep their names and addresses in your notebook in case you decide to seek professional help at some point. The Organizations and Services section will help you locate the nearest therapists who specialize in treating these problems. Sometimes, counseling by telephone is available to housebound agoraphobic people. Also, there are a few residential treatment programs that temporarily transplant a housebound agoraphobic person into a new environment in which he or she receives intensive training and therapy.

If you are an agoraphobic mother who keeps your children home from school as companions, you need to get the children back into school on a regular basis. You are inadvertently teaching them to be anxious and fearful by keeping them at home. A professional therapist or social worker can help you take this important step.

Organizations and Services

Various organizations and services can help you locate (1) medical doctors who take an orthomolecular or holistic approach to nutrition, (2) therapists who specialize in the treatment of anxiety attacks and phobias, (3) recovery partners, and (4) support groups.

1. Finding a physician who practices orthomolecular medicine or who specializes in nutrition. Key terms to look for are "orthomolecular medicine," "megavitamin therapy,"

"preventive medicine," and "holistic medicine." If you already have a physician, ask him or her for a referral to such a specialist. Or look in the yellow pages of your phone directory. Following the "Physicians" section, you may find a section labeled "Guide to Physicians and Surgeons, M.D." Within this section there may be a subsection labeled "Nutrition," listing nutrition specialists.

The following organization may be able to help you locate a medical doctor who specializes in nutrition or who practices orthomolecular medicine in your area:

> The Society for Orthomolecular Medicine, c/o American
> Academy of Medical Preventics, 6151 W. Century Blvd.,
> Suite 1114, Los Angeles, CA 90045

2. Finding a therapist. Ask your physician for a referral, or write to the Phobia Society of America and order a copy of their treatment directory. As of this writing, the directory costs $2.50. Make checks payable to the Phobia Society of America. Address: PSA Publications Department, 5820 Hubbard Drive, Rockville, Maryland 20852.

You might also try looking in the "Mental Health Services" section of the yellow pages of your telephone directory for specialists in phobias, agoraphobia, or anxiety disorders. Or you might look in the white pages of your telephone directory for a "Mental Health Information and Referral" listing. Legitimate therapists have advanced training at accredited academic institutions and have served an internship or have had equivalent training. They will be able to provide you with the names of other health-care professionals as references. Be cautious—many states do not have strict licensing requirements for psychotherapists.

Many physicians and therapists have a sliding scale of payments to permit unemployed people and those with fixed or limited incomes to have access to treatment. (If you ask about this, please be direct and assertive, not apologetic.)

3. Finding a recovery partner. If you cannot locate a recovery partner among your family or friends, find out if there is a volunteer group at a local hospital that could help you locate a partner. Or call the social work, nursing, or psychology department at a nearby college or university and see if they can help locate a student who could help you—perhaps for pay.

A therapist who specializes in phobia treatment may be able to help you locate volunteer or paid help. Requesting such help from a therapist would be a good way to get a "feeling" for him or her should the need arise for personal counseling at some point.

You might also try placing an advertisement in the classified section of your newspaper:

> Volunteer needed to be my "support person" while I do phobic desensitization training. References needed.

If you find someone through an advertisement, be sure to talk to two or three personal references on the telephone. You want a recovery partner who is trustworthy and mature.

4. Support groups. Support groups are helpful for those who are doing field training to overcome phobic reactions. It has been noted that those who suffer from agoraphobia are unusually supportive of other people with the same problem. For example, the study we cited by Dr. Zitrin and her colleagues found that

> . . . unlike many other patients, agoraphobics immediately coalesce into a group. At the first session [of group therapy], they discover that they are kindred spirits; they are excited and relieved to find that there are others so like themselves and that they are not unique and not crazy; they share symptoms and experiences in common; they offer each other pointers and helpful hints to deal with difficult situations; they commiserate with one another and are extremely supportive.

There is definitely a role for the mutual caring and encouragement provided by support groups in the process of recovering from anxiety attacks and agoraphobia. For help in locating such a group in your area, contact the nearest treatment center listed in the Phobia Society treatment directory.

Some agoraphobic people have successfully started their own groups with a newspaper advertisement. It would be wise—we think essential—to have a health-care professional as an adviser or sponsor of such a group.

Here are some suggestions for getting the most out of a support group:

1. Maintain a positive spirit.
2. Avoid overloading the group with discussion of other kinds of personal problems. Concentrate on behavioral problems, such as, "I am having trouble shopping in stores." A support group is not a therapy or encounter group.
3. Avoid dwelling on physical symptoms. Many people with agoraphobia are sensitive to hearing about them.
4. You might want to publish a telephone directory for group members. Calls among group members should be to share successes and offer encouragement—not to substitute for therapy.
5. The group should be action-oriented and goal-oriented. Talking is valuable, but just sitting and talking can become avoidance. At the end of each meeting, plan the next session. Sometimes it's feasible for the entire group to go on a field trip together. If there is time, it is a good idea to share experiences after the field trip.
6. It works well to rotate leadership among the members. This prevents the group from becoming aimless, as well as being good experience in assertiveness for the leader.
7. Often, fear and anxiety can be diminished by factual information. People who have phobias related to driving on freeways, for example, will often say, "I don't know what I would do if I had car trouble while driving alone," or, "What if I made the wrong turn?" Knowing what one would actually do

can take the mysterious "what if" out of the situation. One of Christopher's groups invited experts to their meetings, including an elevator company representative to explain safety features and advise what to do in emergency situations, and a mechanic to explain and demonstrate how to change a tire.

8. Have a professional counselor or therapist instruct your support group in assertiveness training.

The Benefits of Pets

As Alan Beck and Aaron Katcher have reported in *Between Pets and People: The Importance of Animal Companionship,* carefully planned programs introducing pets into nursing homes and prisons have produced beneficial results. The reason seems obvious. With a pet bird, fish, or other animal comes love. An animal will unconditionally accept you as you are and will expect to be accepted unconditionally, just as it is. Cats, dogs, and birds show their affection for those who care for them; there are even owners of tropical fish who are sure that their baby tetras regard them fondly at feeding time. It is a rare person who can resist loving pets in return. Selecting an appropriate pet for your circumstances, caring for it, and loving it can create a circle of love and acceptance in your life. Pets are terrific antistressors.

CARING FOR YOUR BODY

Relaxation

The skill of voluntary physical relaxation is related to almost every one of the 24 goals of the self-care program. Here are a few guidelines that may be of help:

> Pick a quiet, restful place to listen to your relaxation tape, to practice Quiet Sitting or meditation, or to rehearse the

exercises listed in the Coping with Emotional Distress section.

Many people find that the early morning and the evening are the best times to practice relaxation or meditation.

If you live in a noisy environment, try using earphones to listen to your tape. Also, simple wax earplugs (available at most pharmacies) will reduce the noise level while you are doing other relaxation activities.

Wear loose clothing.

If you lie down to listen to a relaxation tape, lie on your back, with pillows supporting the curve of your neck and your knees.

If you are sitting, be aware of your spine in a natural curve—with your buttocks sticking out just a bit. Point the top of your head straight up, so that your chin is lowered slightly. It may be helpful to gently tense and relax your shoulders two or three times before you begin. Also, if you sway your body gently from side to side and then from front to back when you sit down, this may help you find the most balanced position.

Except when you are asked to close your eyes during visualization exercises, keep your eyes open and let your gaze rest comfortably on the wall or ceiling you are facing. If you wear glasses, leave them on. Don't force yourself to stare at one spot for very long periods—this will tire your eyes.

Remember to consult a physician concerning the possible effects of relaxation or meditation on the required amounts of prescribed medications.

Increasing Awareness of Muscular Tension and Muscular Relaxation. This technique teaches you to be more aware of how each muscle group feels when it is tense and when it is relaxed. To give you an idea of what it is like, see the script at the back of the book that we used for the training tape we produced. (It is best to use a tape recording or to have someone read to you rather then to try to read and relax at the same time.)

Autogenic Training. This technique uses simple phrases and visualization with the eyes closed to help you gain voluntary control of processes underlying physiological arousal. We adapted our script from one developed by Elmer E. Green, Alyce M. Green, and E. Dale Walters of the Research Department of the Menninger Foundation. See our script at the back of the book to give you an idea of what this technique is like.

Visualization. This technique uses features of muscular relaxation and autogenic training and adds guided fantasy that calls on all of your senses as you visualize a series of peaceful scenes and situations. (See back of book.)

Quiet Sitting. If you do not have a cassette player or a relaxation tape, you can still perform this simple meditation technique (which predates cassette players and tape recordings by at least 2,500 years). (See back of book.)

Nutrition Guidelines

We cannot give you detailed advice about your diet, especially if you have allergies or are taking medications. Our focus here is simply on identifying some basic nutritional issues as well as some common nutrition-related problems. We do invite you, as a self-caring person, to consider these fundamental questions: (1) Does your diet offer you optimum protection against physical stress, psychological stress, and disease? (2) Does it in any way contribute to actual or potential health problems, especially problems related to psychological stress?

Because certain vitamins and minerals can interact with certain medications, you should consult your physician before increasing your intake of vitamins and minerals while you are taking a prescribed medication. (This can probably be done by a phone call to your doctor.) For the same reason, when your doctor prescribes a medicine, you should tell him or her what supplemental vitamins and minerals you are taking.

If you have problems related to nutrition, we suggest you consult a medical doctor who practices orthomolecular or preventive medicine for advice in developing a personal nutrition plan.

Don't try out vitamins at random to see what they can do for you. Even normally harmless substances can be harmful in large enough amounts. Some vitamins or minerals taken alone in large amounts can deplete other vitamins or minerals and create undesirable side effects. Although most vitamins—except A and D—are not known to be toxic even in large amounts, some, like niacin, can have unpleasant side effects. With other vitamins, C and E, for example, your intake should be reduced gradually rather than suddenly if you decide to cut down from large doses. Still other vitamins and minerals—like the B-complex vitamins; calcium and magnesium; calcium and phosphorus; potassium and sodium; and many other combinations—work synergistically in your body and should be balanced in your supplements. This is why the same ratio of certain B vitamins is used in various vitamin preparations.

What's Wrong with the Normal American Diet?   One of the foundations of the concept of orthomolecular medicine is the idea that the modern human diet is significantly different from the one to which our bodies are physiologically adapted. It is fairly certain that our earliest forebears ate large quantities of plant food as well as some meat and fish. From the plant food, they obtained on average—as Linus Pauling has calculated—at least 2,300 milligrams (mg.) of ascorbic acid (vitamin C) daily, in contrast to the 5 to 15 mg. a day which will prevent death from vitamin C deficiency, or scurvy. (Modern-day gorillas, who, like human beings—and unlike most other animals—do not possess the ability to manufacture vitamin C in their bodies, obtain *several grams* of vitamin C daily from their basically vegetarian diet.) This is quite significant in view of the role this vitamin plays in many of the body's natural defense and healing mechanisms. Burn patients are frequently given several grams of ascorbic acid intravenously each day to promote healing of damaged tissues.

These facts not only lead us to consider supplementing our diet with extra ascorbic acid but also raise the question of whether we should seek to emulate the diet of our forebears in other ways as well. Physician Dean Ornish has developed a diet somewhat along these lines—although it does not include vitamin or mineral supplements—with the objective of reducing the risk of coronary heart disease. It is generally agreed that coronary heart disease is connected to nutrition in some way. Noting that "most people throughout the world have eaten primarily vegetarian foods until recently," Ornish designates certain complex carbohydrates that human beings have been eating for thousands of years as the "most nourishing" foods. These are listed in Table 1. Most nutritional experts—even those who disagree with Ornish's belief that the consumption of animal fat and cholesterol is a leading factor in coronary heart disease—would probably agree that these foods are underrated in our diets today.

Table 1
The Complex Carbohydrates—Underrated Foods

WHOLE GRAINS	Including barley, corn, oats, unrefined rice, and unrefined wheat products.
LEGUMES	Including soybeans, black-eyed peas, chick-peas (garbanzos), kidney beans, lima beans, navy beans, and pinto beans.
FRESH VEGETABLES	Including "starchy" ones like potatoes.
FRESH FRUIT	All varieties. (Ornish plays down the fatty ones—avocados and olives.)

Source: Adapted from Dean Ornish, *Stress, Diet and Your Heart*, New York: Holt, Rinehart, and Winston, 1982.

As Ornish points out, it is a modern myth that we must eat meat to obtain essential amino acids—the building blocks of protein. We can obtain the essential amino acids by eating a wide variety of *combinations* of vegetable foods (eaten together or at least eaten on the same day). These include not only the often-cited example of rice and beans but also a dozen other combinations, including rice and wheat; wheat with rice and soybeans; and legumes with corn, rice, wheat, sesame seeds, barley, or oats.

Another modern myth, according to Ornish, is the idea that complex-carbohydrate foods like potatoes, rice, and beans are especially fattening. These foods contain exactly the same number of calories per gram as protein: 4. Fats and oils store 9 calories per gram, and thus are considerably more fattening per unit of weight. The bad reputation of complex carbohydrates seems to be a case of guilt by association. The *simple* carbohydrates—refined sugar and flour—are extremely recent additions to the human diet that contribute "empty calories" (calories but no nutrition). These substances displace nourishing foods in our diets, and their metabolism depletes the body's supply of vitamins and minerals. The metabolism of sugar, for example, depletes the body's supply of niacin.

Sugar constitutes 15 to 20 percent of the daily caloric intake of the average American, who eats a third of a pound of refined sugar (pure sucrose) every day. According to Linus Pauling, the average American of 150 years ago ate only two pounds of sucrose (mostly from honey and other natural sources) *each year.*

This leads us to the current debate between those who believe sugar is more to blame for the prevalence of heart disease in 20th century America and those who blame the animal fats and cholesterol in our diets.

Compare the statistics concerning sugar with this statement by Ornish in his book *Stress, Diet, and Your Heart*: "The rise of coronary heart disease in the United States paralleled the changes in U. S. dietary habits. As the consumption of animal fat and cholesterol began to rise during this century, so did the incidence of coronary heart disease." In other words, the consumption of both sugar and cholesterol-bearing animal fat apparently rose at the same time heart disease was becoming the most prevalent crippling and killing disease in the United States.

Pauling and nutritionist Richard A. Passwater take the position that it is the refined sugar in our diets, not the animal fat or cholesterol, that is most clearly linked to heart disease. On one point, however, Passwater and Ornish agree: people on high-fat diets who are subject to *emotional* (psychological) *stress* are more at risk for heart disease than those who are not.

Our own feeling is that the available evidence indicates that a stringent low-fat, low-cholesterol diet is not as valuable an idea as is a diet that emphasizes optimum amounts of vitamins and minerals and therefore tends to leave out "empty" foods like refined sugar and refined flour. On the other hand, there is no denying that fat is fattening, especially for people who are not physically active. In any case, we include books representing both points of view (low-fat and low-sugar) and leave the final decision on this subject where it must rest—in your hands.

Suboptimum Amounts of Vitamins and Minerals.

In Table 2, we list substances that are known to be linked to vitamin and mineral deficiencies. In compiling this table, we relied on Passwater's book and on *Earl Mindell's Vitamin Bible,* both of which are included in the list of Suggested Readings.

In Table 3, we list some bodily sensations that have been linked to vitamin and mineral deficiencies. This will be of special interest to those who are sensitized to some degree to their own bodily sensations.

In Table 4, we provide a list of substances considered to be "natural tranquilizers." Pharmacist Earl Mindell recommends an open-face turkey sandwich and a glass of milk as a bedtime snack that includes the "natural tranquilizers" tryptophan, calcium, and magnesium.

Table 2
Substances Linked to Vitamin and Mineral Deficiencies

Substance	Effects
ALCOHOL	Can lead to a decrease in blood-sugar (glucose) level, causing feelings of fatigue, irritability, anxiety, shakiness, or faintness.
	Can deplete the body of vitamins B-1, B-2, B-6, and B-12, folic acid, vitamin C, vitamin K, zinc, magnesium, and potassium. Linked to personality disorders in large amounts.
REFINED SUGAR	See the first comment above, in the "Effects" column.
	Displaces foods that contain vitamins, minerals, amino acids, and fatty acids. Depletes body of vitamins and minerals, including niacin.
REFINED GRAINS	Lack most B vitamins found in natural grains. Displace whole grains that contain full range of B-complex vitamins.
CAFFEINE	See the first comment above, in the "Effects" column.
	Can inhibit iron absorption and deplete body of vitamin B-1, potassium, and inositol. Linked to personality disorders in large amounts. Linked to nervousness (particularly in social settings), in smaller amounts.
NICOTINE	See the first comment above, in the "Effects" column.
	Introduces oxidants (toxins) into the body. Depletes body's supply of vitamin C.

Source: Adapted from *Earl Mindell's Vitamin Bible.*

Table 3
Bodily Sensations That May Be Associated with Vitamin and Mineral Deficiencies

As Earl Mindell notes, "The supplements recommended are not intended as medical advice, only as a guide in working with your doctor."

Possible Deficiency	Earl Mindell's Recommended Daily Supplements
DIZZINESS	
Manganese (found in nuts, green leafy vegetables, peas, beets, egg yolks).	Niacin, 50–100 mg., 3 times a day. Vitamin E, 400 IU.
EAR NOISES	
Manganese (see above). Potassium (found in bananas, watercress, green leafy vegetables, citrus fruits, sunflower seeds).	Same as for dizziness.
HEART PALPITATION	
Vitamin B-12 (found in liver, beef, pork, organ meats, eggs, milk and milk products).	A high-potency multiple vitamin with chelated minerals, preferably time-release. Vitamin C, 1,000 mg., with bioflavanoids, rutin, hesperidin, rose hips; time-release. One of each to be taken with breakfast or dinner. Vitamin B complex, 100 mg., time-release, morning and evening. Niacin, 100 mg., 1–3 times a day. Lecithin, 3 capsules 3 times a day.

Table 3, (*continued*)

Possible Deficiency	Earl Mindell's Recommended Daily Supplements

INSOMNIA

Potassium (see discussion of potassium above).	Tryptophan, 3 tablets half an hour before bedtime.
Vitamin B complex (found in yeast, brewer's yeast, dried lima beans, raisins, cantaloupe).	Chelated calcium and magnesium, one tablet 3 times a day, plus 3 tablets half an hour before bedtime.
Biotin (found in brewer's yeast, nuts, beef liver, kidney, unpolished rice).	Vitamin B-6, 50 mg., half an hour before bedtime.
Calcium (found in milk and milk products, meat, fish, eggs, whole-grain cereals, beans, fruit, vegetables).	Also see the first item listed above in this column for Heart Palpitation.

NERVOUSNESS

Vitamin B-6 (in dried nutritional yeast, liver, organ meats, legumes, whole-grain cereals, fish).	Stress B with C, 50 mg. of all B vitamins, 3 times a day.
Vitamin B-12 (see discussion of vitamin B-12 above).	Tryptophan, 3 times a day, and 3 tablets at bedtime.
Niacin (in liver, lean meat, brewer's yeast, wheat germ, peanuts, dried nutritional yeast, white meat of poultry, avocado, fish, legumes, whole grain).	Chelated calcium and magnesium tablets, 3 times a day. Also see first item listed above in this column for Heart Palpitation.
PABA (same as vitamin B complex, see above).	
Magnesium (found in green leafy vegetables, nuts, cereals, grains, seafoods).	

Table 3, (*continued*)

TREMORS	
Magnesium (see discussion of magnesium above).	B complex and Vitamin B-6, 50 mg. 3 times a day.
	Calcium, 1,000 mg., and magnesium, 500 mg., divided among 3 meals.

Source: *Earl Mindell's Vitamin Bible* (1979).

Note: Earl Mindell cautions that you should not "double dose"—that is, duplicate a supplement if you have more than one symptom for which the same supplement is recommended. One supplement is enough.

Table 4
Nature's Tranquilizers

Small supplemental amounts of these substances, which are normally present in the human body and the human diet, are often reported to promote a feeling of well-being, to help people feel calm, and to promote sleep. These substances are all available in tablets. The *Nutrition Almanac* and *Understanding Vitamins and Minerals* (see the Suggested Readings section) can be used to determine which foods contain them.

Substance	*Comments*
Dolomite or chelated calcium and magnesium in 2:1 ratio.	Avoid excessive daily intake (more than 2,000 mg.) of calcium.
	Reduces muscle fatigue.
Niacinimide	An important B vitamin.
Choline	Another important member of the B-complex family. Found with inositol in lecithin. Lecithin should be taken in balance with calcium.

Table 4, (*continued*)

Substance	Comments
Tryptophan	An essential amino acid. Can be used by the body to manufacture niacin. Tablets should not be taken in milk or with other protein; should be taken in water or juice.

Source: Compiled from *Earl Mindell's Vitamin Bible.*

The evidence for the effectiveness of these substances as tranquilizers is largely anecdotal. Many of Christopher's clients have tried tryptophan, one of the essential amino acids, on their own initiative and say it is helpful. Mindell mentions one scientific study at the Maryland Psychiatric Research Center that found tryptophan to be helpful for insomnia. Incidentally, Mindell mentions that the body can manufacture niacin from tryptophan, which may be the basis of its tranquilizing effect.

Optimum Amounts of Vitamins and Minerals.   All of us are in the same perplexing situation in regard to determining the optimum amounts of vitamins and minerals to include in our diets. No one knows for certain what they are, although the minimum amounts needed to avoid deficiency diseases are fairly well established, as are toxically high levels of certain vitamins (A and D, fat-soluble vitamins that tend to remain in our bodies).

Those who follow the old science of nutrition are of no help because they scoff at the idea of optimum nutrition for optimum health. They say things like, "You'll get all the vitamins you need if you eat a normal, well-balanced American diet," and, "Those water-soluble vitamins pass right through you, you know."

On the other hand, the new science of orthomolecular or preventive nutrition does not have all the answers, either, because it is still in the process of inventing itself. Unfortunately, as Linus Pauling points out, very little research has been aimed at answering the question of optimum amounts of vitamins. Most research is aimed at fighting diseases, not at promoting good health.

Table 5 shows the best guidelines we can find on the subject of vitamins. In the first column are listed the vitamins that are most commonly taken in supplements. The second column shows current RDA amounts. The third column shows the "supernutrition (orthomolecular) range" cited in Passwater's book *Supernutrition*. (Incidentally, Passwater's book provides a systematic approach to finding your optimal level of intake for each vitamin.) The fourth column shows Linus Pauling's daily intake of vitamins (as of 1985), which reflects his thinking about optimum amounts. Finally, the last column shows the adult toxic level for vitamins.

This is how Pauling takes his vitamins:

Two super-B tablets, each with 50 mg. of B-1 (thiamine); 50 mg. of B-2 (riboflavin); 50 mg. of B-6 (pyrodoxine); and 100 mg. of niacinamide.

Usually an additional 300 to 400 mg. of nicotinic acid in separate tablets. (Niacinamide and nicotinic acid are forms of the same vitamin.)

A super multivitamin tablet with traces of minerals that includes 10,000 international units (IU) of vitamin A.

A relatively large amount (12 grams) of vitamin C in the form of fine crystals of ascorbic acid dissolved in water or fruit juice. This is consumed throughout the day.

A relatively large amount (800 IU) of vitamin E.

In 1980, Pauling gave a talk in which he explained his reason for taking relatively large amounts of vitamins. A reprint of this talk is included in literature available from Bronsons Pharmaceuticals (4526 Rinetti Lane, La Cañada, California 91011-0628). We do not endorse or recommend

Table 5
General Guidelines for Daily Adult Vitamin Intake

Vitamin	RDA	Supernutrition Range	Linus Pauling's Intake	Adult Toxic Level
A	5,000 IU	10,000–35,000 IU	40,000 IU	75,000 IU
D	400 IU	400–1,000 IU	[1]	40,000 [2] [3]
C (Ascorbic acid)	60 mg.	500–4,000 mg. (4 g.)	12 g.[8]	[3]
B-1 (thiamine)	1.5 mg.	10–100 mg.	100 mg.	[3]
B-2 (riboflavin)	1.7 mg.	10–100 mg.	100 mg.	[3]
B-6	2.0 mg.	10–100 mg.	100 mg.	[3,4]
B-12	6 mcg.	5–100 mcg.	[1]	[3]
Folic acid	0.4 mg.[5]	[0.1–2.0 mg.]	[1]	[3]
Biotin	0.3 mg.	[6]	[1]	[3]
Niacin (or niacinamide)	20 mg.	50–300 mg.[7]	200–500 mg.	[3]
Pantothenic acid		10–100 mg.	[1]	[3]
E	30 IU	200–800 IU	800 IU	[3]

Sources: RDA figures are from *Earl Mindell's Vitamin Bible* (1979); Supernutrition Range and toxicity figures are from Richard A. Passwater, *Supernutrition* (1976); Linus Pauling's intake figures are from a lecture he gave at San Francisco State University on February 14, 1985.

1. Pauling does not specify an amount for this vitamin; however, it is found in the super multivitamin tablets and super-B tablets he takes.

2. The toxic level for children is 2,000 IU.

3. No toxic level has been found; however, this does not indicate that it is necessarily reasonable or safe to consume unlimited quantities of this vitamin.

4. One recent report indicated that very large amounts of Vitamin B-6 (in the 2000–4000 mg. range) taken over a period of months or years can cause a loss of feeling in the toes, which appears to be reversible when the dosage is reversed.

5. The RDA is set at this level, according to Passwater, because larger amounts make it difficult to diagnose pernicious anemia. The figures in the second column show Passwater's estimate of daily human requirement.

6. Passwater points out that very large amounts of biotin (150–300 g.) are normally ingested in food and manufactured by intestinal bacteria.

7. When niacin, or nicotinic acid, is suddenly taken in a large amount, it can cause flushing of the skin and itching. For this reason, an alternate form of the vitamin, called niacinimide or nicotinamide, is often substituted.

8. Pauling points out that an adult male goat with a body weight of 80 kg. manufactures 13 g. of vitamin C each day in its body. He believes that intake of vitamin C is beneficial up to that point that a laxative effect is observed.

Bronson products or believe them to be superior to the products of other pharmaceutical companies. We mention them because of the Pauling article and because they sell crystalline ascorbic acid and other vitamins by mail, which may be of special interest to housebound readers.

Medication and Drugs. Medications (tranquilizers, antidepressants, sleeping pills, etc.) are clearly useful and justifiable in at least two circumstances:

> A crisis, in which immediate relief is necessary. (For example, when someone is overwhelmed by such stressful events as a death in the family.)
>
> Life situations that call for practical medical help—for instance, if you may lose your job as a result of anxiety attacks or missed work.

Just what medication, if any, is appropriate for you must be determined by you and your physician. You should participate in the prescribing of drugs. Do not passively accept your doctor's decisions without knowing:

1. How does this drug act?
2. What can I expect to feel?
3. What are the possible side effects?
4. Are there possible interactions with other medications or with vitamins and minerals?
5. How long do the effects last?
6. How long does it take the drug to produce an effect?

Drugs can become a crutch and mask feelings that you need to deal with. A rule to remember is: *Never substitute medication or drugs for self-caring or psychotherapy.* Confronting a problem is ultimately far easier and more productive than avoiding it through the use of drugs or alcohol.

Alcohol sometimes becomes a complication for phobic and anxiety-ridden people. They may initially use alcohol to relax in order to function out in the world. The drinking, however, may itself become a problem along the way. If drinking has become a problem, you need to deal with that as your first priority before you can deal with phobic reactions effectively.

Nutrition and Medication Log. Remember to use the Nutrition and Medication Log to monitor your intake of various substances at the beginning of the program. You can use the log again later on for the sake of comparison.

Physical Exercise Guidelines

Here are some basic guidelines in regard to physical exercise:

If you have not been exercising regularly or if you have a medical condition, review the precautions discussed in Chapter 6 before starting to exercise. *The New Aerobics* by Dr. Kenneth H. Cooper provides a thorough and careful approach to starting a physical fitness program that is particularly helpful for those over 30.

Approach exercise in a gradual, self-caring manner. Do not force yourself to do too much too fast. Avoid overexertion and undue physical stress. If you are starting to jog, alternate jogging and walking. If you are starting to swim, alternate easier strokes with the crawl.

An excellent morning stretching exercise for the spine is simply to stand up straight, with your arms and feet apart, and (1) inhale as you rotate your upper body 90 degrees to your left, then exhale as you return to the original position, then (2) do the same thing rotating to the right. As you turn to the left, allow the heel of your right foot to lift up, and vice versa. Most people will find 30 repetitions to be satisfactory. (Rev. Ekai Koremotsu of San Francisco teaches this exercise to his Zen meditation students.)

Precede jogging and similar exercise with a few minutes of warm-up stretches. When you stretch, do not bounce or jerk.

If you are capable of vigorous exercise, gradually work up to
at least 12 to 15 minutes of vigorous activity every day
or every other day for the sake of a good cardiovascular
workout. As an alternative, consider walking for 30 or
45 minutes.

COPING WITH EMOTIONAL DISTRESS

Carry-Along Checklists

These checklists have been designed to be copied and carried
along with you in your purse or wallet. The Coping Checklist
reminds you of techniques for coping with fearfulness and
emotional distress while they are occurring. The Troubleshooting Checklist helps you pinpoint the origins of the psychological stress that has built up into an episode of emotional
distress. (See the back of the book.)

Simple Breathing Exercises

Some people overbreathe, or hyperventilate, when they are
distressed or startled. If you have ever done this, you've probably already been given the most sophisticated medical advice
available: breathe slowly into your cupped hands or into a
paper bag for a moment to reduce your intake of oxygen
temporarily. The suggested remedy for mild hyperventilation
is simply to breathe through your nose rather than through
your mouth. Recently, as we mentioned in Chapter 6, a group
of British doctors trained agoraphobic patients to breathe
with their diaphragms to avoid the effects of hyperventilation.
   (If you have become sensitized to the act of concentrating
on your own breathing, you may find the following simple
breathing exercises to be somewhat troublesome and need
some help from a therapist in working on them. Biofeedback
therapy, which allows you to closely monitor your physiological processes, might be helpful.)

The following exercises can help you relax physically whenever you feel distressed and whenever the idea of helplessness or inadequacy arises. It is best to select one exercise at a time and to rehearse it six or eight times a day for a few days. Rehearse in a quiet, restful place. Wear clothing that does not constrict your body. It is best to breathe through your nose if possible, with your tongue relaxed and touching the roof of your mouth, just behind your teeth. Your teeth should not be clenched together. You can lie down on your back or sit. Review the guidelines for relaxation techniques listed under the Relaxation section.

Slow, Complete Breathing. Take a few complete breaths. Breathe in gently and deeply, so deeply that you can feel your abdomen protruding slightly as you inhale. Allow your chest walls and shoulders to remain at rest. As you breathe out, focus your attention on your exhalation, prolonging it until your lungs are almost empty. Do not force or strain your breathing. If you make a mistake, you will find that your breathing will naturally correct itself. Just concentrate on the prolonged, smooth, slow exhalations as you breathe gently and deeply a few times.

Slow, Deep Breathing with Shoulder Relaxation. This is the same as the first exercise, except that each time you exhale, focus on slowly relaxing your shoulder muscles. Try to relax them more and more each time you exhale. Learn to let your shoulders and chest walls rest as your abdomen moves gently in and out. (It may help to begin this exercise by raising your shoulders up to your ears for a moment and then relaxing them slowly.)

Counting Breaths. This is the same as the first exercise, except that you don't need to deliberately prolong your exhalations. Just follow them attentively and count them slowly from one to ten as they occur: "Onnne. Twooo. Threee. Fooour. . . . " Let your inhalations take care of themselves.

Keep your sense of humor handy as you attempt to follow the next instruction: Try to count 10 exhalations without being interrupted by arising thoughts. If a thought arises, you can either continue counting or start over. Go ahead and try it. . . . If you made it all the way to 10 without a thought arising, you had beginner's luck. Thoughts are like bubbles that are always arising, and that is something this exercise helps us to accept. Its object is not to eliminate disturbing thoughts but, in a sense, to help us become desensitized to them. This is a basic exercise often used in meditation training.

Following Your Breathing.   This is the same as counting breaths except that instead of counting exhalations, you slowly repeat a word like "relax," "calm," or "one" each time you exhale to help keep your attention on your breathing. When you focus on your breathing in this way, you will find that it often becomes somewhat slower and deeper by itself. This can be very restful for a moment or two.

Circling Your Breaths.   This exercise is done seated. It is like slow, complete breathing except that you are moving the focus of attention in a circle that runs around your body. As you start to inhale, you slowly bring your attention up the ventral centerline of your body from the groin to the navel, chest, throat, and face, until you reach the crown of your head. As you exhale, slowly move your attention down the back of the head, down the neck, and all the way down the spine. This exercise could be done two or three times before doing one of the other breathing exercises.

Focusing on the Hara.   This exercise is also like slow, complete breathing, except that the focus of your attention during both inhalation and exhalation is on the *hara,* which is located in the abdomen, somewhat behind and below the navel.

All of these exercises are excellent coping techniques in themselves and are also good preparation for learning how to be habitually physically relaxed while remaining mentally alert.

Stroebel's Quieting Reflex

There are four steps to the quieting reflex developed by Dr. Stroebel:

1. Become aware of the stimulus you are responding to as clearly as you can. (Is it a bright light, a loud sound, or just the jumble and confusion of a crowded place? Is it a "what if" thought or something someone said?)

2. Give yourself the suggestion, *"Alert mind, calm body."* (The idea is to pause and use your inner freedom. If you don't really need to fight or run, then you don't need to tense up your muscles.)

3. Smile inwardly with your eyes and mouth to reverse their tendency to go into a grim set.

4. Inhale slowly and easily to a count of two, three, or four, imagining your breath coming in through the pores in the bottom of your feet. A feeling of "flowing warmth and flowing heaviness coming up through the middle of your legs" may accompany this mental image. "As you exhale, let your jaw, tongue, and shoulders go limp, feeling that wave of heaviness and warmth flowing to the toes. And then resume normal activity."

Weekes's Four Concepts

In Chapter 5, we described the four concepts at the heart of the coping technique developed by Dr. Claire Weekes. For a more detailed look at Dr. Weekes's approach, refer to the materials listed in the Suggested Readings and Suggested Cassette Tapes sections.

Answering Your Inner Child

Instead of fighting against the childish idea that you are help-less and powerless, you can try embracing the child within—the child you once were who lives on both in the positive aspects of your personality and in old, self-diminishing as-sumptions, attitudes, and habitual behaviors. This child is the part of you that thinks in catastrophic terms. It sees every loss, separation, or criticism as a potential threat to its very existence.

Queenelle Minet, a San Francisco–based therapist, de-veloped this technique for use by her phobic clients:

> Picture yourself as you were when you were three or five. Then imagine that this child lives within you. It does. We all have a part of us which has never completely matured. Your child, like any real child, feels small and helpless. Like any real child, your child often engages in irrational thinking. And, like any real child, your child gets scared when there is no adult around to take care of it. When you get overwhelmed with phobic anxiety, the basic problem is that your inner child has completely taken over your personality. The adult in you is nowhere in sight.
>
> Get in touch with the adult part of you, and make a com-mitment to take care of your child. Make a commitment to be there for your child 24 hours a day. No leaving it with baby-sitters. That won't work. Pay attention to your insides, and whenever you feel yourself becoming tense and anxious, listen to what your child is saying. Probably it's scared about some-thing. Now assume the position of a loving and strong, trust-worthy parent and answer your child. Be sure to correct your child's irrational thinking.
>
> For example, a woman who had an elevator phobia had the following conversation with her child:
>
> *Child:* I don't want to get on. The elevator might get stuck and I'll suffocate to death.
>
> *Adult:* No. Look up there. The elevator has an air vent. They don't make elevators airtight. It probably won't get stuck, but even if it did, you wouldn't suffocate.

A man who felt afraid to drive into any unfamiliar part of the city had this conversation with his child:

Child: I don't want to go. I'm afraid I'll get lost and never find my way home again.

Adult: No you won't. You're forgetting about the map. Even if you can't remember how you came, you can use the map to find your way back.

Child: But what if I have a panic attack? If I get really scared, I won't even be able to read the map.

Adult: I don't think you need to worry about that. You've already learned plenty of good techniques to prevent your anxiety from spiraling out of control. You can relax your body and keep breathing deep down into your abdomen. You can keep your mind focused on things that are happening in the here and now—the scenery, the people on the street—or on pleasant memories, or on everyday affairs like what you're going to have for dinner. And if you do get scared, I'm here to reassure and calm you.

Child: But, what if I *do* have a panic attack?!

Adult: That's an old fear. Remember to use these tools and you won't, but even if you did, a panic attack is not the end of the world. Sure, they feel awful. But they don't go on forever, and you're not going to die or go crazy. If worst comes to worst, you can pull over, let the anxiety run its course, and then use the map to get yourself home. And remember, kid, I'm always here. I'll never leave you.

Always talk to your child in a calm, loving, supportive way. Never criticize your child or demand that he or she shape up and stop having these troublesome fears. Be patient. Your child's fears are deeply ingrained. You may have to have the same conversation with your child hundreds of times before she or he finally learns that there is nothing to fear. Be alert. You're probably not used to listening for your child's small voice. Don't let his or her fears build up before you, as adult, step in and take charge of the situation.

Stretching and Movement

As we know, physiological arousal is your body's way of telling you that it wants to do something physical—run, jump, yell, scream, or throw something, for example. Does that mean you should engage in some vigorous exercise when you are feeling fearful and emotionally distressed? It doesn't seem like a good idea in view of what is known about the physiology of anxiety.

To some extent, vigorous activity might actually cause the body to sustain a high level of arousal (until fatigue sets in). We know that when people are anxious, they tend to have a relatively high amount of lactate in their blood. This blood lactate is known to play a role in causing the nervous system to be overactive, probably by depleting the amount of calcium available to nerve cells. Heavy muscular activity would produce more lactate and thus would seem to be ill-advised for someone who is acutely anxious.

On the other hand, it's hard to sit still or lie down while you are feeling nervous or "twitchy." Also, some movement might help use up the oversupply of epinephrine produced by the fight-or-flight reaction.

Therefore, it seems best to choose a middle course between vigorous exercise and inactivity. Gentle stretching and yoga-type exercises, combined with deep breathing, might help, as might walking. If you must walk indoors, you could walk very slowly and deliberately around a room while using one of the simple breathing exercises—this is similar to a form of meditation often used in Buddhist monasteries. If you must remain seated, see the guidelines in the following section for ways to stretch while seated.

Exercises for Relaxed Travel

These guidelines appeared in *American Way,* the in-flight magazine provided to passengers by American Airlines:

> Some simple exercises, all done with your seat back upright and seat belt fastened, can make a long airline flight more

comfortable by stimulating circulation and relaxing muscles.

The exercises can be done so discreetly that your fellow passengers may not realize what you are doing. But if the kids are along, have them follow the leader or do as "Simon says."

1. Lean head forward as far as possible. Feel a stretch down the back of your neck. Lean head to the side (keep face front) and feel the stretch down the side of the neck. Lean head to other side.

2. Let head drop back (jaw relaxed), and look up at the overhead compartment of the row behind yours. Arch upper back as you look up. Feel stretch under your chin.

3. Hug yourself (right hand on left shoulder, left hand on right shoulder). Lean head forward, cave in upper chest, and pull your shoulders forward. Feel stretch down the back of the neck and between your shoulder blades.

4. Push shoulders forward and cave in upper chest and stomach. Push shoulders back and arch lower back. Keep head straight. This exercise moves the rib cage to front and loosens muscles in the center back.

5. Relax your shoulders and arms and make a circle with one shoulder at a time by moving it forward, raising it up, pushing it back, and down. Then move it back first, reversing the exercise.

6. Press elbows down onto armrests and press shoulders down as hard as you can. Feel stretch across top of shoulders.

7. Grasp the right armrest with your left hand and turn your upper body around to the right to look behind you. Turn to the left grasping the left armrest with your right hand. Feel stretch down each side of your back.

8. Reach up toward light or air vent without rising from your seat. Breathe in as you reach up and exhale as you lower your arm. Stretch as you reach, using one hand and then the other.

9. Loosen seat belt slightly, and lean over to the floor as if to pick up something you've dropped or to adjust packages

under the seat in front of you. Reach down as far as possible, and then sit up slowly. This stretches lower back and back of thighs.

10. Sit up straight and pick one foot up off the floor by raising your whole leg about an inch off the seat. While maintaining this position, make circles in the air with the raised foot by rotating your ankle. Circle your foot to the right eight times and to the left eight times. Place the foot back on the floor and repeat with other foot. This one exercise stretches not only the ankle but all sides of the lower leg as well. (An added benefit is that while you are holding your leg up, you are pulling in and tightening the stomach muscles.)

In doing all exercises, move the part of your body as instructed as far as possible to feel the greatest stretch. Push your head forward as far as it will go, raise your shoulders or push them back as far as they will go, etc. Even circle your foot as far as it will circle to stretch your toes and arches. Repeat all exercises, right and left, as many times as you need to really feel them working.

Self-Affirmation

At moments of emotional distress, the small, ego-centered self feels like it is shrinking to the point of disappearing. The purpose of the self-affirmation technique is simply to remind yourself of who you really are through the use of positive and realistic self-affirming statements. Such statements may come up as you work in your notebook or in the Maintaining a Positive and Realistic Self-Image section, in which you are invited to record a set of such statements on a cassette tape. The statements can also be reduced to a few key words and used with the Following Your Breathing technique in the Coping with Emotional Distress section of the program.

Here are some examples of self-affirming statements and key words that can be used with the breathing exercise:

Statement	Key Words
Pure gold need not fear the furnace.	(Pure gold.)
You are a perfect human being.	(You are perfect.)
You value wisdom and compassion.	(Wisdom and compassion.)
You enjoy the adventure of life.	(Enjoy the adventure.)
You are worthy of love and respect.	(You are worthy.)

Statements you compose yourself or borrow from your favorite songs, poems, books, or prayers will be most meaningful to you. Remember to concentrate on their *meaning* when you repeat them. They are not "busy work."

Visualization

We include a visualization exercise in the Relaxation section. You can use visualization as a coping technique quite effectively by vividly calling to mind a pleasant scene, the face of a kindly and wise teacher or relative, a friendly animal, or any image that carries associated meanings of serenity, peacefulness, and happiness: a warm, sandy beach. A cozy cottage in the country. A comfortable apartment in the city. Your grandmother baking a cake. Whatever says "relax" to you.

In your imagination, try to add as many sensory details as you can: The sound of the surf. The smell of a wood fire and the warmth of the fireplace when you hold your hands up to it. The clink of crystal glasses. The taste of the cake batter as you lick the spoon.

Focusing

Some public speakers stand before groups of hundreds of people and deliver their speeches to two or three friendly faces in the crowd. This is an example of focusing your attention on something or someone specific outside yourself.

On a crowded street, you can focus your attention on the buildings you are walking past if the movement in the street begins to seem overwhelming. On a bus or airplane, you can focus your attention on an interesting book or magazine article—or on the in-flight movie if you are flying.

The act of focusing your attention on something or someone in your environment and being an active observer can help you remember who you are so you will not feel as though you are losing yourself.

Anything that involves simple, repetitive actions—such as knitting, crocheting, or braiding—can absorb your attention in situations in which you must spend some time waiting.

Talking

A department manager for a company was unexpectedly called upon to speak before a group of 20 or 30 of the company's most important distributors and clients. He could feel the anxiety mounting within him as he approached the podium, which had been placed at least 15 feet from the nearest person in his audience. By the time he reached the podium, his knees were shaking. What could he do? What should he say?

He smiled at a couple of the friendly faces in the audience and said, "You know, I get really nervous sometimes when I have to speak to a group like this, and I'm feeling nervous right now. I'm afraid I may not do too well if I just stand up here and talk. So if it's all right with you, I'd like for you to ask me questions about your concerns, and this can be more of a conversation than a speech. Does anyone have any questions?" Two or three hands went up. Leaving the podium, the speaker moved to a chair much closer to his audience, sat down, and began to answer their questions. The discussion went on for 15 or 20 minutes, and a number of valuable ideas emerged.

It's not always necessary or appropriate to tell people that you are feeling nervous—but it's always a choice that you have. Sometimes it is relaxing simply to ask people about something they are interested in and to focus on what they have to say. People often like to share their knowledge and interests. Casual conversations about a sports team, local history, or what-have-you are simple and human ways of sharing a few moments of sociable relaxation and can help you overcome a feeling of isolation and aloneness.

Humor

The good feeling of laughter goes right down to your bio-chemistry. *Anatomy of an Illness as Perceived by the Patient* is Norman Cousins's account of his holistic, self-caring approach to a crippling disease that doctors believed was irreversible. Cousins conquered the disease in part by watching his favorite slapstick comedies on a screen set up in his hospital room—and later in a hotel room into which he moved. Using the comedies to replace a pain-killing drug, he found that "ten minutes of genuine belly laughter had an anesthetic effect and would give me at least two hours of pain free sleep." Cousins writes:

> How scientific was it to believe that laughter—as well as the positive emotions in general —was affecting my body chemistry for the better? If laughter did in fact have a salutary effect on the body's chemistry, it seemed at least theoretically likely that it would enhance the system's ability to fight the inflammation. So we took sedimentation rate readings just before as well as several hours after the laughter episodes. Each time, there was a drop of at least five points. The drop by itself was not substantial, but it held and was cumulative. I was greatly elated by the discovery that there is a physiological basis for the ancient theory that laughter is a good medicine.

There are many ways to use gentle, ironic humor as a coping technique at times of fearfulness and emotional distress. Humor helps you to see things in perspective and to keep a sense of proportion.

If you can pause and accept the humorous aspect of certain habitual thoughts and thought patterns, you can take away their power to move you. One man recognized that every day, on the way to his highly stressful workplace, he would get into an imaginary argument with someone about something. Often, the argument would be with a supervisor or a co-worker. "Wait a minute," he would tell himself, "this is an *imaginary* argument." A moment later, he would be back at it again, in the same imaginary dispute or in another one. Finally, he started counting them: "Ah. This is imaginary argument number one for today." "This is number two," and so on. The very act of counting in this way diminished his tendency to engage in such thinking. The same principle can be applied to what-if thoughts, either-or thoughts, and other kinds of habitual thoughts that pull us away from the here and now.

Here are a few other principles you can play with:

Magnification. "This the world's highest elevator!" (Of an elevator in a three-story building.)

Miniaturization. "This is actually a *tiny* little bridge across a mud puddle." (Of a two-mile-long bridge.)

Mock egocentricity. "This bridge was actually built for *my personal convenience,* so that *I* could get from back there to over there."

Mock anger. "I am *furious* with whoever designed this elevator (building, bridge, etc.)."

Mock suspicion. "*Somebody* planned this. It can't be happening to me by accident."

Mock philosophical observations. "Well, it could be much worse—but I can't think how."

Reverse intention. Have you ever stopped a child's hiccups by requesting "the world's greatest hiccup"? You could fantasize that you really *like* having startle reactions—for example, "That was a really good one."

This all may sound silly, but it is a painless way to help yourself become more aware of the illogical and inconsistent aspects of phobic reactions.

Acceptance and Compassion

In the long run, acceptance of your feelings of distress and compassion for yourself and for others are the simplest ways to cope. Such simplicity and directness come with the patient cultivation of one's inner freedom and self-honesty.

EXTINGUISHING LEARNED RESPONSES

Successive-Approximations Training

The successive-approximations method is somewhat like gaining immunity to a disease through a series of vaccinations. The term "successive approximations" refers to the fact that this kind of desensitization training incorporates many small steps that bring you closer and closer to the eventual goal of being entirely free from a particular phobic reaction. With each successive step, your behavior more closely approximates what you want it to be.

Step 1. Inventory of Phobic Reactions. The first step in training is to use the Inventory of Phobic Reactions form to list the places and situations in your life that are associated with anxiety. Making this inventory will give you a clearer understanding of the boundary line between the "safe" part of your world and the seemingly "unsafe" part.

Rank the anxiety-linked places and situations by accessibility—i.e., from the one that is easiest to approach and withdraw from, to the one that seems to be most difficult in this respect. Then select the easiest one to work on first: someplace like a fishing pier or a supermarket or a situation like driving, where you can come and go relatively easily. Places where you are not so free to come and go are more difficult to work on and should be left until later when you have acquired some skill and confidence. You will know when you have enough confidence to board an airplane, a train, or a boat for a short trip.

Step 2. Levels of Anxiety Form. The experience of anxiety is hardly ever the same for two different people. Before you can start successive-approximations training, you must have a clear, precise understanding of the way you physically experience anxiety. Use the Levels of Anxiety form to define five levels of anxiety in terms of your own anxiety symptoms:

5   Panic (Maximum Anxiety)
4   High Anxiety
3   Moderate Anxiety
2   Mild Anxiety
1   Minimum Anxiety
0   Total Calm

We see below how Elsie S., a woman who has experienced anxiety while shopping in her supermarket, might fill out the Levels of Anxiety form.

Levels of Anxiety (Elsie S.)

Date: _____

Use this form to identify how you experience (physically feel) anxiety. The five levels you define here will be used in desensitization training. Common anxiety responses include sweaty palms, cold hands or feet, warmth over face or neck, rapid heartbeat, weak feeling in legs, tightness in throat, dizziness, dryness in mouth, diarrhea.

Levels of Anxiety	Your Symptoms
5 Maximum Anxiety (Panic)	*Hyperventilation -- hard to catch my breath. agitation.*
4 High Anxiety	*Dizziness. "Jelly" legs.*
3 Moderate Anxiety	*Heart beats faster.*
2 Mild Anxiety	*Sweaty palms.*
1 Minimum Anxiety	*Tingling skin. Feelings of warmth.*

Step 3. Situation Hierarchy Form. Use the Situation Hierarchy form to analyze the reactions you experience in the place or situation you have selected. In other words, break down the total experience into manageable pieces or smaller situations.

We will provide two sample Situation Hierarchy forms. The first will show the way Elsie S. might fill one out for training in her local supermarket. The second will show the way a young baseball player, Bart T., might fill out the form for training in restaurants, where he has experienced anxiety attacks.

Here's the way Elsie's form looked after she had first selected the least anxiety-provoking part of the total situation and the most anxiety-provoking part.

Situation Hierarchy (Elsie S.)

Date: _____

Use this form to break down an anxiety-arousing place or situation into
manageable pieces or smaller situations. Start with the least anxiety-
arousing aspect (1) and the most anxiety-arousing aspect (9). Fill
in intermediate situations (2–8). These will be successive goals in
successive-approximations training.

Describe Location or Situation

9 *Waiting in a long line at a checkout stand.*

8 _____

7 _____

6 _____

5 _____

4 _____

3 _____

2 _____

1 *Standing just outside the door.*

Elsie decided that approaching the front door of the supermarket would be fairly easy, and standing in a long line with
a lot of groceries would be the hardest thing to do.

Having identified the bottom and the top of a nine-step
Situation Hierarchy, Elsie then filled in the intermediate steps.

She decided to work in pencil and to write the steps on separate 3 × 5 cards first so that she could easily revise the sequence until she was satisfied. When she had the sequence worked out, her form looked like this:

Situation Hierarchy (Elsie S.)

Date: _____

Use this form to break down an anxiety-arousing place or situation into manageable pieces or smaller situations. Start with the least anxiety-arousing aspect (1) and the most anxiety-arousing aspect (9). Fill in intermediate situations (2–8). These will be successive goals in successive-approximations training.

Describe Location or Situation

9 Waiting in a long line at a checkout stand.

8 Purchasing a number of items without waiting very long.

7 Purchasing one item without waiting.

6 Walking around several aisles in the back of the store.

5 Walking all the way down one aisle and back out.

4 Walking into the shopping area and right out again, as though looking for someone.

3 Walking across the front of the store to the opposite side doors.

2 Standing just inside the door.

1 Standing just outside the door.

Bart used two copies of the form, doing his rough work and revisions on one and making a clean copy on the other when he had finished. His completed form looked like this:

Situation Hierarchy (Bart T.)

Date: _____

Use this form to break down an anxiety-arousing place or situation into manageable pieces or smaller situations. Start with the least anxiety-arousing aspect (1) and the most anxiety-arousing aspect (9). Fill in intermediate situations (2–8). These will be successive goals in successive-approximations training.

Describe Location or Situation

9 Ordering a full dinner with some people I don't know.

8 Ordering dinner with friends at a table some distance from the exit.

7 Ordering food and sitting some distance from exit.

6 Ordering a drink and sitting some distance from exit.

5 Ordering food and sitting near exit.

4 Ordering a drink and sitting near exit.

3 Ordering food to go and sitting at a table while waiting for it — near exit.

2 Ordering a drink to go and sitting at a table while waiting for it — near exit.

1 Ordering a drink to go at a counter.

Step 4. Successive-Approximations Training Chart.
The next step is to transfer the nine subgoals (in abbreviated
form) to a training chart. Here's the way Elsie's looked:

Successive-Approximations Training (Elsie S.)

Date: _____

You can keep a record of your progress in successive-approximations training on this chart.

Trial

GOAL	1	2	3	4	5	6	7	8	9	10	11	12	13	14	15	16	17	18	19	20	21
1 Outside door.																					
2 Just inside.																					
3 Across front.																					
4 In and out.																					
5 One aisle.																					
6 Several aisles.																					
7 No wait.																					
8 Short wait.																					
9 Long line.																					

Step 5. Training. Now you are ready to begin training.

Without training, people tend to deal with their phobic anxiety in one of two ways. Either they stay away from the object or place as much as possible (this is why they become such great excuse-makers), or they try to endure the anxiety-provoking situation for somebody else's sake, no matter how miserable they feel. This is an either-or approach.

By contrast, successive approximation requires a gradual approach-withdrawal-approach method:

1. *Advance toward* the first goal in the Situation Hierarchy.
2. When you experience Level 2 symptoms, *withdraw* from the situation.
3. Allow yourself to *relax.*
4. Then *advance toward* the same situation again.
5. Repeat this a number of times as you visit the place that is the goal of your training.

It is the *repetition* of exposures to a situation that builds your confidence and reduces the anxious anticipation associated with that particular situation. The purpose of withdrawing is to achieve relaxation; it is preparation for reexposure. Withdrawing is not defeat or failure. All good coaches know when the team should take a time-out to regroup before resuming play. This is an important point to understand before this technique can succeed.

Do not let the worry over what others might think keep you from working properly on this problem. The graduated steps in the situational hierarchy are designed to help you build up your confidence and to help you experience the feeling of not being trapped—of being free.

Suppose you are training in a coffee shop. The easiest goals in the situational hierarchy for restaurants allow you to feel free to leave by ordering food or drink to go. It is important to realize in this situation that feeling trapped is a result of your own thinking or perception. If you say to yourself, "Oh, once I sit down here and order a meal, I'm stuck, and if I have an anxiety attack I couldn't leave," you have trapped yourself. Therefore, in desensitization training, you are confronted by one of the phobic personality characteristics that you must address—namely, an oversensitivity to what others think.

You may actually need to leave the restaurant briefly in order to experience directly that it is all right to do so. If you are working with a recovery partner, it is easy to practive going out, relaxing, and coming back to the table. If you choose to leave when you begin to experience Level 2 anxiety, you will have the important experience of choosing to leave and choosing to return. If, instead, you wait until you are feeling panicky (Level 4 or Level 5), then you may feel that you "had to" leave and that you were not in control, and you will not want to come back. So, when you catch yourself saying, "I can't get out of here—what will people think?" simply tell yourself, "I can always leave and come back. People don't really care what I'm doing. They won't think anything of it."

Naturally, you may be concerned about making sure that you can pay for your order without having to wait. When you sit down, you might say simply that you may have to leave in a hurry and ask for the check in advance. Also, you can carry the right denominations of money so that you can pay in a hurry.

It is very important to have the right attitude in applying this procedure. Do not complicate things by allowing yourself to be upset because you "had to" leave; you did not "have to" leave—*you chose to leave and return because you are a self-caring person who is working on a problem.* If you were diabetic and left a situation in order to give yourself an insulin injection, you would feel justified; it is the same with the problem of phobic reactions.

Take One Thing at a Time. We advise that you begin with only one phobic situation at a time. It's easier to master the training technique if you do not try to use it in too many different situations. Start with a simple problem and then go to the next one, which may be somewhat more difficult. In addition, it can tire you out if you try to work on department stores in the morning, freeways in the afternoon, and restaurants and movies at night.

Be Prepared to Make a Few Mistakes.   The president of a large corporation once remarked that he had always hoped to be right in his decisions "at least 51 percent of the time." His point (and our point) is that any great enterprise (and surely the quest for health and equanimity *is* a great enterprise) requires that we be prepared to make a few mistakes. Mistakes can be seen as opportunities for discovery, increased understanding, and personal growth.

At any step in preparation for desensitization and at any point in your training, you may not get things exactly right. This is perfectly all right and is to be expected, given the nature of the problem you are dealing with.

Now you're ready to start training by approaching Goal 1 on your situation hierarchy, following the four rules listed above.

You or your recovery partner should keep a record of each trial (each time you enter the situation) on the training chart. Here is Elsie's completed training chart for the supermarket:

Successive-Approximations Training (Elsie S.)

Date: _____

You can keep a record of your progress in successive-approximations training on this chart.

GOAL	Trial																				
	1	2	3	4	5	6	7	8	9	10	11	12	13	14	15	16	17	18	19	20	21
1 Outside door.			x	x	x	x	x	x	x	x											
2 Just inside.		x	x	x	x		x	x	x	x											
3 Across front.				x			x	x	x	x											
4 In and out.						x	x	x	x												
5 One aisle.							x	x													

(continued)

Successive-Approximations Training (Elsie S.) *(continued)*

GOAL	Trial																				
	1	2	3	4	5	6	7	8	9	10	11	12	13	14	15	16	17	18	19	20	21
6 Several aisles.																					
7 No wait.																					
8 Short wait.																					
9 Long line.																					

Flooding

Review the information about flooding in Chapters 5 and 6. Here are a few guidelines to help you use the flooding technique:

> Flooding is done in the imagination. Usually it is done at home or in a therapist's office.
>
> Try to vividly picture—in color if possible—all of the worst things you fear in a situation. Use your notebook to list them.
>
> Put all of these fears into a story. Again, use your notebook. You can actually record the story on a cassette tape if you wish.
>
> Visualize the story (or play the tape) several times over a period of days before you confront (visit) the actual situation.
>
> When you visit the actual situation, compare your fantasy with the real experience.

If you wish, you can combine flooding and successive-approximations training by using the visualization technique to rehearse the goals on your Situation Hierarchy form and to identify all of the things you fear in connection with each goal.

Guidelines for a Recovery Partner

> Use this book to become familiar with successive-approximations training and flooding training.
>
> Your job is basically to be a warm, friendly, and relaxed human being. Sounds easy so far, doesn't it?
>
> The hard part is that you must be very patient and uncritical and must refrain from trying to direct the training or to tell the person doing the training what to do.
>
> When the person doing the training becomes anxious, ask if he or she wants to pause for a moment and use a breathing exercise or other coping technique. The idea

of "the pause" is important. Even during flooding, it is all right to withdraw to a more comfortable location and to use a coping technique for a while.

When the person doing the training wants to end a training session, don't argue. It's important for her or him to have the experience of being in control. However, it's all right to ask, "How about pausing and using your coping technique for a while, and then making up your mind whether to end the session for today or to do one or two more trials?"

Accentuate the positive. Even mistakes in training can be instructive and useful.

Discourage any sense of urgency in the training. Human beings are complex and take time to learn things. You are not trying to set a record on an assembly line.

Observe the training process closely. It's fascinating. Enjoy yourself, and encourage the person doing the training to feel a sense of accomplishment after each session.

It's all right to offer suggestions, but remember to leave the responsibility for decisions—and for the success of training—in the hands of the person you are helping.

There are tremendous rewards in being a recovery partner, as you watch the person you are helping rediscover a sense of personal freedom. To help someone get in touch with freedom is one of the finest things you can do for another human being.

ACHIEVING CONTROL THROUGH RELAXED AWARENESS

These three inventories can be helpful in monitoring negative feelings:

The Displeasure-Frustration Inventory
The Worry Inventory
The Guilt Inventory

The Displeasure-Frustration Inventory

We often hide displeasure and frustration from ourselves. Healing occurs when we take note of them and bring them out into the sunlight.

The Worry Inventory

Worrying is an inefficient way to deal with the world. When we write our worries down, we are able to sort out the fantasy in them from the reality, and to stop worrying and start solving problems.

The Guilt Inventory

Guilt takes you away from the here and now toward the past. Guilt can be an honest feeling or it can be a way of avoiding the present. As you trust yourself more and are able to be more relaxed in the present, you will find that you spend less time living in the past.

COMMUNICATING ASSERTIVELY

Framing Assertive Messages

Here are some general guidelines for making statements that are direct and assertive and that avoid the pitfalls of passivity and aggressiveness. We will deal here mostly with negative feelings, since they are the ones with which you probably have the most trouble.

Clarify Communications.   You are not trying to win anything or to gain anything. You are simply trying to be understood by another person and to understand him or her.

Describe How You Feel.   Describe the things that belong to you: your feelings, thoughts, and behaviors. For example, if you are disturbed or even outraged because someone is late in arriving someplace, you could say, "I am disturbed because you are late," or, "I am outraged because you are late."

Avoid Labeling Someone Else's Behavior, Feelings, or Thoughts. What the other person has done or said does not belong to you. There is no point in describing these actions. Don't bother to say, "By your inconsiderate behavior," or, "By your totally selfish and insensitive behavior. . . . " Similarly, the other person's thoughts and feelings don't belong to you. It is pointless to say, "No, that's not what you were thinking. You were thinking. . . . "

Be Responsible Only for What Belongs to You. Don't give away your ownership of your own feelings by saying, "You make me feel . . . " or, "I feel this way because you. . . . " Instead, you could say, "I feel this way *when* you do such and such."

Don't accept responsibility for the other person's feelings or actions. If someone says to you, "Now look what you've done to me, I'm all upset," gently hand the responsibility back. You could say, "What are you feeling right now?" or, "Can you tell me more about how you are feeling?"

Avoid Self-Canceling Messages. Don't invalidate something you have just said by adding, "It's not really important" or "I don't really care that much about it" if it really is important or if you really do care about it.

Also, if you wish to reassure a person, be careful not to cancel out a reassuring statement by contradicting it through the use of a word like "but" or "however" (for example, "You know I really like you, but. . . . ").

Pause, Then Respond. The eventual goal of assertiveness is to be spontaneous and natural. While you are still learning to be assertive, it is often helpful to pause, take a deep breath, and reflect a moment before sending a message.

Passive or aggressive reactions tend to be blurted out mindlessly. As you know, they can lead to anger, worry, and depression. By contrast, assertive responses are made after a free choice, they express true feelings, and they lead to a feeling of satisfaction.

Here is a simple checklist that may help you remember the preverbal pause:

Preverbal Phase (Pausing and Reflecting)

__ Take a deep breath.

__ "How do I honestly feel right now?"

__ "How do I want to communicate that feeling?"

Verbal Phase (Speaking)

__ Let the other person know you have heard what he or she has said, if appropriate.

__ Tell the other person how you feel.

__ Invite the other person to help resolve the issue, if appropriate.

Don't Work Too Hard. People who are learning to be more assertive sometimes express a sense of failure when they react passively or aggressively and do not perform "correctly." One said, "It's so hard to be assertive, I have to think so much—maybe it's just too difficult to do it *all* the time." Another told Christopher, "Well, I'd have to be assertive all the time from what you say. That could be too much work!" The mistake these people have made is to work too hard at designing a "proper" or "correct" sentence instead of simply reflecting on how they feel. Assertiveness is the easiest and most natural way to communicate. It just takes some getting used to.

Telling Your Spouse or Companion About the Self-Care Program

Here are some points to bear in mind when you tell your spouse or companion about the Self-Care Program:

> Be as clear as possible about what agoraphobia is and how it is treated.
>
> Your phobia does not cancel out the positive aspects of your personality or your achievements, although it may have limited your activities in many ways.
>
> Ask your spouse or companion to take your problem seriously and to understand your suffering.
>
> Explain that you need to be more open in sharing your feelings and that you need to be able to tell him or her when you feel frustrated, misunderstood, or sad.
>
> Show him or her relevant sections of this book or other books or articles on the subject.
>
> If you are consulting a therapist, it would be useful for the therapist to talk to your spouse or companion, to help increase understanding of the problem and to help your partner learn how to support your progress.

The Assertiveness Log

Use the Assertiveness Log to monitor your interactions with others to help you see more clearly the consequences of assertiveness, passivity, and aggression.

Here are some guidelines for handling displeasure or anger more effectively:

> Cultivate awareness of negative feelings by using the Displeasure-Frustration Inventory and by writing down angry feelings in your Journal. Remember, control comes through awareness. Sometimes, it may take you several hours or even a day to recognize a feeling of frustration or resentment that you experienced as anxiety.

Look for the roots of feelings of resentment and frustration. Many negative feelings originate in the philosophy of helplessness and in the natural consequences of that philosophy. The frustration of not being in control is combined with resistance to expressing one's displeasure. The result is what has been aptly called "the fury of impotence." It has its roots in:

Perceived dependence on others.

Passivity.

Avoidance of confrontations.

People-pleasing behavior.

Hypersensitivity to what others think.

Unexpressed feelings.

It is not necessary to raise your voice or to shout to express anger. You can simply say, "I am angry." (Some people are surprised and pleased to discover this simple truth.)

Be assertive at the time negative feelings are occurring if possible. This will help bring them to completion.

If it is not possible or appropriate to express the feelings when they occur, try to express them as soon as you can, while they are still fresh in your mind.

If it is not possible or appropriate to express the feelings at all to the other person, it is helpful to find another way to express them and to bring them to completion. For example, if you are angry at an elderly person who should not be disturbed because of fragile health, you could put all of your feelings into a letter and then burn the letter in the fireplace or destroy it in some other manner in your own personal ceremony. You might choose to tear it up and bury it—the way native Americans buried the hatchet. This could help you recognize and acknowledge the reality of the feelings, then relinquish them.

The physical expressions of old anger and resentments can sometimes be helpful if they are used constructively. Punching a pillow or beating a rug, for example, might help. One man bought a punching bag but reported that it gave him little release from his anger because "the darn thing just kept coming back at me." He chose instead to tear up his concrete patio with a sledgehammer—a project he had been wanting to do for a long time anyway. He needed a feeling that his anger had some result.

It is important that you, perhaps with a friend's or therapist's help, learn to accept negative feelings and to bring them to a satisfactory conclusion by expressing them assertively if possible or at least by dealing with them constructively and not struggling to ignore them.

Sometimes, people will say, "I couldn't be assertive, I was too angry." It is an error to consider assertiveness as simply being tactful or "saying something in a nice way." Assertiveness is not limited by these requirements. It is not reserved for just some feelings and not others.

Once you are able to deal effectively with negative feelings like anger, they will lose the exaggerated importance they may now have in your life.

"Win-Win" Negotiations

An emotional trap for the agoraphobic personality is the tendency to take an either-or view of personal interactions. Others are often seen as being either *good* or *bad*, *right* or *wrong*. To be able to appreciate that differences can exist between people without destructive conflicts is to utilize a powerful healing process. The simple fact that you feel one way and I feel another way is not, in itself, a conflict. It becomes a conflict if one of us insists that one position must be right and the other wrong.

One way to get away from either-or thinking is to make use of the "no-lose" technique for resolving differences that is recommended by Thomas Gordon (author of *Parent Effectiveness Training,* 1970, and *Leader Effectiveness Training,* 1977).

According to the either-or approach to conflict, *either* I win and you lose *or* you win and I lose. Many people view even the most trivial differences of opinion as contests to see who will win and who will lose. Figure 7–1 is a diagram that shows this black-and-white view of something as simple as a disagreement about whether two people should go to a movie or to a concert.

Gordon asks the intelligent and very human question: Why do we need to waste time fighting for victories and suffering defeats in our everyday lives? Figure 7–2 shows Gordon's more businesslike approach to resolving differences.

In a nutshell, Gordon's approach is for each person to behave in a way that keeps problems out of the other's "problem zone," and for both persons to look for ways to do things that avoid both their "problem zones."

My Way	We go to a movie. (My Choice)	I Win
Your Way	We go to a concert. (Your Choice)	You Win

Figure 7–1. Either-Or Approach to Conflict.

Either-or thinking makes life look like a series of win-lose contests. (A) I win if I get my way. (B) You win if you get your way.

Dealing with Criticism

We can always learn something useful from criticism—sometimes about ourselves and sometimes about the way the person doing the criticizing sees things and feels about them. Even an angry, finger-pointing attack can be an opportunity to clarify communications between two people. Here are some guidelines to apply when you are the recipient of criticism.

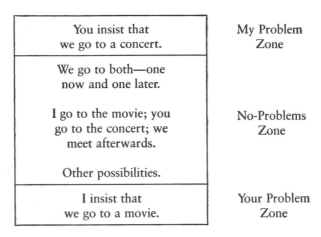

You insist that we go to a concert.	My Problem Zone
We go to both—one now and one later.	
I go to the movie; you go to the concert; we meet afterwards.	No-Problems Zone
Other possibilities.	
I insist that we go to a movie.	Your Problem Zone

Figure 7–2. Gordon's "No-Lose" Technique.

As you pause and take a complete breath before you respond to the other person, consider whether any of these points apply:

Set Limits.   Is the criticism cruel, punitive, or abusive? If so, you may need to clarify your limits. For example, "I do not like it when you talk to me in that way. If you want me to respond to you, let's both try to be polite."

Accept Valid Criticism.   If you agree with something, accept it. For example, "I accept that. It's true I've been late getting here the last three mornings."

Buy Time.   If you need time to think about the criticism, say so. For example, "I need some time to think about this. Could we discuss this in the afternoon?"

Repeat Valid Points.   Don't be afraid of sounding a bit like a broken record, if the other person ignores a point you are making that you feel is important and valid. Invite him to acknowledge your point. For example, "It really was my understanding that that job was no longer my responsibility. Do you see why I thought that?" This is an important point.

If You Are Not Sure. If you are not sure whether a criticism is valid or if you do not feel strongly about it, say so. For example, "Sometimes I may be too excitable."

Rehearsal

You need to find a way to practice talking in an assertive manner if you are not used to doing so. Your cassette recorder can be useful for this purpose.

First, use your notebook or some 3 × 5 cards to assemble a set of seven or eight challenging statements or situations. These should be arranged from least challenging to most challenging. They will vary from person to person, but here are some examples:

"You put too much salt in this soup!"

"You are too excitable."

"You are lazy."

You want to take a nap. Your daughter says: "You don't want to take a nap now. Come on, we're going shopping."

Your husband or wife says: "Come on, honey, don't be a party-pooper. We're all going to ride up the outside elevator."

Two policemen come up to you in a restaurant: "Are you the person who's been causing all the trouble?"

Next, record the set of statements on a cassette tape. Read them with feeling. Space them out, leaving 15–20 seconds between each item. Repeat the entire series six or seven times.

Now, lie down or sit quietly, listen to the tape, and *talk back to it*! Note whether your responses are assertive, aggressive, or passive. Stop the tape for a moment if you need time to decide. Refer to the Framing Assertive Messages section if need be. Carry on this process with the objective of gradually shaping your responses so that they are consistently assertive.

This rehearsal technique can be used in conjunction with flooding training. For example, you could rehearse several situations that you expect to occur at your cousin's wedding, such as Uncle Burt asking you how much money you make or Cousin Ruth asking you whether you've gained any weight since she's seen you last.

Improving Parent-Child Communications

We highly recommend Gordon's book *Parent Effectiveness Training* to all parents who feel the need to improve communications with their children. Gordon's message is that attempting to coerce children into acceptable behaviors simply doesn't work—and consumes too much of the parent's energy. Ignoring children is obviously not the answer, either.

The approach Gordon recommends is to use clear and simple communications about those aspects of the child's behavior that are truly important to you, to refrain from labeling or criticizing the child's behaviors or feelings, and to use the "no-lose" negotiations technique to help resolve problems.

A basic consideration is to make the limits of your "problem zone" as clear as possible. For example, "I don't care when you put the dishes away, as long as you get it done before your bedtime. I hate to walk in the kitchen in the morning and find the dishes on the counter." Or, "I really want you to put the dishes away right now. I really like for us to keep the kitchen in good order."

Remember, what your children learn now will help shape the way they will live in the future. If you want your children to be independent and healthy adults, allow them to own their own feelings and encourage them to investigate the world around them. In this way, you will show them that you love them just as they are, with no strings attached.

CULTIVATING INNER FREEDOM

Centering

While you are doing a breathing exercise or the Quiet Sitting exercise, you may wish to quietly and calmly shift your attention down to the pit of your belly.

Take a few slow, deep breaths. Feel the exhalations all the way down in the pit of your belly. You may notice some interesting things happening in your body. What happened to your shoulders? To your throat and neck? To your jaw? To the muscles of your face? It is likely that this simple shifting of attention to your center of gravity caused the upper part of your body to relax considerably. Furthermore, you gained some distance on whoever was chattering away in your head— the measurements and judgments probably continued, but you were watching or listening to them from a distance, with some degree of objectivity. You were, in effect, digesting, absorbing, and eliminating the thoughts and feelings that happened to arise.

Guidelines for Meditation Training

We have gone as deeply as we can in this program into beginning meditative techniques. Many people need personal instruction and guidance to help them get the most out of meditation. Our advice in seeking personal instruction can be summed up in these guidelines:

> Do not pay for meditation training. Good training is given freely. An exception to this would be small fees charged for organized classes.
> Avoid any practice or group that does not respect your freedom and dignity. Coercion and meditation are mutually exclusive.

Meditation is not an escape from life, it is a way of living. You can be meditative and alert even in the hustle and bustle of a busy downtown street.

You don't have to change the way you dress or wear your hair if you meditate—although loose clothing helps.

If you are exposed to the outer forms of Japanese, Tibetan, or Indian culture, enjoy them. But remember, there is room for meditation in the context of American and European culture as well. You don't need to give up being who you are.

We have listed several excellent books about meditation and meditative psychology in the Suggested Readings section. One you may wish to start with if the subject is new to you is *Freedom in Meditation* by Patricia Carrington, an American clinical psychologist who has produced an authoritative guide to meditation from a Western perspective. Carrington discusses the benefits of meditation and also the problem of overdependence and misuse of meditation. As in everything else we have discussed, our recommendation is to take into consideration your own unique situation and then to take a gradual, common-sense approach to finding the path that is right for you.

MAINTAINING A REALISTIC AND POSITIVE SELF-CONCEPT

Negative Fantasies Inventory

It is interesting and useful to monitor your negative fantasies for a time. It is not necessary to make a record of every one— you may be too busy to do this. Just write down those you remember. See if you can classify them.

Are there many fantasized arguments? Are they with people you know or with strangers? Do they involve life-or-death issues?

Do you ever enjoy negative fantasies in the sense that they have some entertainment value for you?

When did you first experience such fantasies? Can you trace any of them back to the circumstances of your childhood?

When you started having such fantasies, were you bored? Worried? Lonely?

There is no need to do anything in particular about fantasies other than to be aware of them, digest them, and let them pass on. However, there are interesting ways to work with them.

You can in a sense take charge of negative fantasies by writing new endings for them, in which you bring the fantasy to a conclusion by being relaxed, mentally alert, and assertive with others. Think through your new ending and experience it in the same way you experienced the original fantasy.

Negative Thoughts Inventory

You can approach negative thoughts in the same way. Just as you can write new endings for your fantasies, you can prepare positive and realistic thoughts to substitute for negative ones, so that when a habitual negative thought arises, you can respond by saying to yourself, "Yes, I recognize this negative thought, but I prefer this more realistic and positive one:. . . . "

Self-Affirmation Tape

When you reach Level 3 of the Seven-Level Plan, use your cassette recorder to make a tape of the self-affirmations you have written in your Journal. Express yourself in a warm, wholehearted way.

Revise the tape, over a period of days if necessary, until you are satisfied with it.

Whenever you find yourself beginning to frantically climb up the tree of anxiety, pause and remember the power of relaxed, quiet sitting and natural, complete breathing—as well as the importance of optimum nutrition. They help you locate your psychological center of balance within your own freedom. Remember also that the fear and hostility that drove you up the tree arose from illusions produced by the past conditions of your life. As you cut through these illusions with the sharp blade of objectivity and honesty, you will be able to find your way back to the here and now. Once your feet are planted on the earth, you will see that self-respect and self-care are indivisible from respect and care for other people—and, indeed are inseparable from respect and compassion for all living beings. This is a wonderful realization. You may even be grateful for the anxiety that came like a bolt from the blue.

Checklists

Troubleshooting Checklist

This set of questions can help you pinpoint the external and internal factors contributing to psychological stress. Investigate your yes answers with an open, accepting attitude, as though you were helping a cherished friend or child.

	Yes/No
Have you been holding your breath or hyperventilating?	____
Have you been ignoring your need to relax physically regularly?	____
Have you ignored what you know about good nutrition?	____
Have you neglected your body's need for physical exercise or activity?	____
Are you trying to ignore any of these feelings: dissatisfaction? frustration? displeasure? anger? fear of losing friendship? (love? your job?)	____
Have you allowed yourself to feel "trapped in thought" by: Hypothetical what-if thinking? Absolutist either-or thinking? Powerless have-to thinking? Worrying about something that is beyond your control? Worrying instead of acting or planning?	____
Have you been "nice" lately at the expense of being honest?	____
Have you been acting on the assumption that you are helpless and powerless—that you cannot do anything to improve or enrich your own life or to give emotional support to others or to help them?	____

From *Managing Your Anxiety* by Christopher J. McCullough and Robert Woods Mann. Published by Jeremy P. Tarcher, Inc. Copyright © 1985 by Christopher J. McCullough and Robert Woods Mann.

Coping Checklist

These coping techniques can be helpful when you are feeling emotionally distressed. Use the ones that work best for you.

Take a few slow, abdominal breaths through your nose. Breathe out slowly.

Use Dr. Stroebel's quieting reflex ("Alert mind, calm body").

Think of yourself as a cherished friend or child.

If you feel like a helpless child, imagine yourself putting your hand into the hand of a kindly, all-wise, all-compassionate parent.

Focus on something in your environment, such as a picture, a building, or an object you can handle. Allow yourself to become interested in it.

Remember a peaceful scene in which you felt very calm. Can you remember what you saw, heard, felt, and smelled?

Accept and observe thoughts and feelings without fighting them. Ask yourself: Who is it that reacts to these thoughts and feelings? Who is it that observes these thoughts and feelings? Is it necessary for me to react to them?

If you continue to be disturbed by an unrealistic thought, take a deep breath, focus on your solar plexus, and very simply and firmly order the thought to "get out" as you exhale.

Move around a bit or do some gentle stretching. If you are on a bus or plane, gently contract and relax the muscles of your arms, legs, buttocks, abdomen, shoulders, neck, and face.

Talk to a relaxed person.

Take small amounts of calcium and magnesium, tryptophan, and niacinamide. Or eat a snack containing these substances (such as a turkey sandwich and a glass of milk).

Blank Forms

Journal

Date: _____

WEEKLY STATUS

Current level in seven-stage plan (1–7):   _____

Number of program goals reached (1–24):   _____

Number of milestones reached (1–21):   _____

Current daily intake of vitamins and minerals:

    Multivitamin tablet with minerals   _____

    Stress-B or Super-B tablet   _____

    A and D in multivitamin   _____

    Amount of B vitamins in B tablot   _____

    Amount of extra C   _____

    Amount of extra niacinamide/niacin   _____

    Amount of extra E   _____

    Amount of extra calcium and magnesium   _____

    Amount of tryptophan   _____

    Additional intake:

From *Managing Your Anxiety* by Christopher J. McCullough and Robert Woods Mann. Published by Jeremy P. Tarcher, Inc. Copyright © 1985 by Christopher J. McCullough and Robert Woods Mann.

Daily Progress

Self-Care Activity	\tDays of the Week						
	S	M	T	W	T	F	S
Did you use the "to do" list (and calendar or datebook as needed)?	—	—	—	—	—	—	—
How many times did you practice relaxation or meditation?	—	—	—	—	—	—	—
How many times did you practice the quieting reflex or another coping technique?	—	—	—	—	—	—	—
How long did you exercise (in minutes)?	—	—	—	—	—	—	—
Did you take supplementary vitamins or minerals?	—	—	—	—	—	—	—
Did you refer to the carry-along checklists?	—	—	—	—	—	—	—

For the following items, enter a number from 0 to 5 to indicate the quality of your performance today.

1 = poor, 3 = good, 5 = excellent

Nutrition	—	—	—	—	—	—	—
Coping with emotional distress	—	—	—	—	—	—	—
Desensitization training	—	—	—	—	—	—	—

Checklists

Daily Progress, (*continued*)

Assertiveness training   — — — — — — —

Other training:

_____ — — — — — — —

Assertiveness in everyday life   — — — — — — —

Awareness of inner feelings   — — — — — — —

Maintenance of realistic and
    positive self-image   — — — — — — —

Enjoying the drama and humor
    of life   — — — — — — —

Overall self-care performance   — — — — — — —

For the following items, enter a number from 0 to 5 indicating the severity of problems experienced today.

0 = no problems, 3 = moderate problems, 5 = severe problems

Outdated assumptions, beliefs
and attitudes   — — — — — — —

The idea of helplessness or
powerlessness   — — — — — — —

The idea that you are unworthy
or flawed   — — — — — — —

The idea that everything must
be perfect   — — — — — — —

The idea that security lies
outside yourself   — — — — — — —

Negativity   — — — — — — —

From *Managing Your Anxiety* by Christopher J. McCullough and Robert Woods Mann. Published by Jeremy P. Tarcher, Inc. Copyright © 1985 by Christopher J. McCullough and Robert Woods Mann.

Daily Progress, (*continued*)

Overreacting to or magnifying external events	—	—	—	—	—	—	—
Overreacting to bodily feelings	—	—	—	—	—	—	—
Passive or aggressive reactions	—	—	—	—	—	—	—
Nervousness or anxiety	—	—	—	—	—	—	—
Startle reaction	—	—	—	—	—	—	—
Fight-or-flight reaction	—	—	—	—	—	—	—
Anxiety attack	—	—	—	—	—	—	—
Other: _____	—	—	—	—	—	—	—

Use your notebook to discuss problems of moderate to severe intensity. What happened before the problem occurred? How were you feeling? Also use the notebook to discuss important events in your life and your honest feelings about them.

Self-Evaluation

Date of Evaluation

ITEM	Started reading this book (approx.):	Started using program:	Reached Level 3:	Reached Level 7:

PERFORMANCE

Use a number from 0 to 5 to rate your performance in each of the following areas.

0 = Completely unsatisfactory   3 = Mostly satisfactory
1 = Very unsatisfactory   4 = Very satisfactory
2 = Mostly unsatisfactory   5 = Completely satisfactory

Optimum vitamins and minerals in diet				
Fresh vegetables, whole grains, legumes, and fresh fruit in diet				
Minimum sugar and refined grain in diet				
Optimum amount of physical exercise				
Regular physical relaxation				
Mental alertness				
Ability to learn not to experience fear in specific places and situations				
Tolerance for bodily sensations				
Ability to remain relaxed when negative thoughts and feelings arise				

From *Managing Your Anxiety* by Christopher J. McCullough and Robert Woods Mann. Published by Jeremy P. Tarcher, Inc. Copyright © 1985 by Christopher J. McCullough and Robert Woods Mann.

Self-Evaluation, (*continued*)

Ability to tell others about
your strong feelings

Ability to identify sources of
psychological stress in
your life

Ability to maintain a realistic
and positive self-image

ASSUMPTIONS, BELIEFS, ATTITUDES, AND BEHAVIORS

Use a number from 0 to 3 to indicate how much you agree or disagree
with each of these self-descriptive statements.

0 = Disagree	2 = Agree somewhat	
1 = Disagree somewhat	3 = Agree	

I hate to hurt the feelings of
others so much that I
neglect my own feelings.

I am unusually polite and
considerate, even when I
feel as though I am being
dishonest.

Sometimes I am afraid to tell
people how I feel.

I am a worrier.

I am too sensitive to criticism.

I usually know what to do in
an emergency.

Sometimes I am confused
about my own feelings.

Sometimes I ridicule myself.

I have a problem dealing with
anger.

Self-Evaluation, (*continued*)

People often underestimate
my abilities.   _____ _____ _____ _____

I have never felt entirely free
from anxiety.   _____ _____ _____ _____

Sometimes I am full of self-
contempt.   _____ _____ _____ _____

ROOTS

Which of these problems associated with persons close to you during your childhood (e.g., parents, siblings) do you believe contributed to your long-held assumptions, beliefs, and attitudes? (Check those that apply. Use a pen or pencil of a different color each time you review these items.)

PROBLEM	PERSON		
Argumentative	_____	_____	_____
Did not touch or hold you	_____	_____	_____
Indifferent	_____	_____	_____
Passive	_____	_____	_____
Used ridicule	_____	_____	_____
Nervous or anxious behavior	_____	_____	_____
Overprotective	_____	_____	_____
Overly worried about your safety	_____	_____	_____
Highly critical	_____	_____	_____
Played favorites among family members	_____	_____	_____
Worried about money a great deal	_____	_____	_____

Nutrition and Medication Log

Use this form for one week to monitor your daily intake of listed substances. When the form is complete, put it alongside your Journal form for the same week and see if you find any connections between your diet and your feelings. Use your datebook or calendar to schedule another use of this form in six or eight weeks.

Substance	Days of the Week						
	S	M	T	W	T	F	S

PRESCRIBED MEDICATIONS (Use check marks. Your physician can advise you concerning possible interactions between medications and other substances.)

Enter
Amount

Valium	_____	—	—	—	—	—	—	—
Xanax	_____	—	—	—	—	—	—	—
Other _____	_____	—	—	—	—	—	—	—
_____	_____	—	—	—	—	—	—	—
_____	_____	—	—	—	—	—	—	—

VITAMIN AND MINERAL SUPPLEMENTS (Use check marks.)

Enter
B Vitamins   Amount   — — — — — — —

Vitamin B_1	_____ mg.	—	—	—	—	—	—	—
Vitamin B_2	_____ mg.	—	—	—	—	—	—	—
Vitamin B_6	_____ mg.	—	—	—	—	—	—	—
Vitamin B_{12}	_____ mg.	—	—	—	—	—	—	—

Nutrition and Medication Log, (*continued*)

Niacinamide/ niacin	_____ mg.	— — — — — — —
Extra niacin- amide/niacin	_____ mg.	— — — — — — —
Vitamin C		
Ascorbic acid	_____ mg.	— — — — — — —
Sodium ascorbate	_____ mg.	— — — — — — —
Calcium ascorbate	_____ mg.	— — — — — — —
Vitamin E	_____ mg.	— — — — — — —
Calcium and magnesium (2:1)		— — — — — — —
Calcium	_____ mg.	— — — — — — —
Magnesium	_____ mg.	— — — — — — —
Tryptophan	_____ mg.	— — — — — — —
Vitamin A	_____ mg.	— — — — — — —
Vitamin D	_____ mg.	— — — — — — —
Multivitamin and mineral tablet		— — — — — — —
_____	_____	— — — — — — —
_____	_____	— — — — — — —
_____	_____	— — — — — — —

UNDERRATED FOODS

Green, leafy vegetables   — — — — — — — —

Other fresh vegetables   — — — — — — — —

Nutrition and Medication Log, (*continued*)

Whole grains of all kinds   — — — — — — —

Legumes (peas and beans)   — — — — — — —

Fresh fruit   — — — — — — —

SUBSTANCES ASSOCIATED WITH VITAMIN AND
MINERAL DEFICIENCIES

(Use numbers to indicate how many individual servings, cups, glasses,
cigarettes, you had.)

Alcohol   — — — — — — —

  Beer   — — — — — — —

  Wine   — — — — — — —

  Hard liquor   — — — — — — —

Refined sugar

  Canned foods   — — — — — — —

  Jam, jelly, sugar   — — — — — — —

  Chocolate   — — — — — — —

  Other candy   — — — — — — —

  Cake, pie, pastries, doughnuts   — — — — — — —

  Ice cream   — — — — — — —

  Other desserts   — — — — — — —

Refined and "enriched" grains

  White bread   — — — — — — —

  Polished rice   — — — — — — —

From *Managing Your Anxiety* by Christopher J. McCullough and Robert Woods
Mann. Published by Jeremy P. Tarcher, Inc. Copyright © 1985 by Christopher J.
McCullough and Robert Woods Mann.

Nutrition and Medication Log, (*continued*)

Caffeine

   Cola drinks — — — — — — —

   Coffee — — — — — — —

   Certain teas — — — — — — —

   Cocoa — — — — — — —

   Chocolate — — — — — — —

Nicotine

   Cigarettes — — — — — — —

   Other tobacco products — — — — — — —

Aspirin
(indicate amounts per day) — — — — — — —

Aspirin substitutes
(indicate amounts per day) — — — — — — —

Antacids
(Indicate amounts per day) — — — — — — —

Proscribed psychoactive
substances
(indicate amounts per day) — — — — — — —

   Marijuana — — — — — — —

   Cocaine — — — — — — —

   Other — — — — — — —

Inventory of Phobic Reactions

Date: _____

List specific places and types of situations where you have
experienced phobic reactions. Rank them from the "most difficult"
to the "least difficult" from the standpoint of physical access (that is,
how easy is it to get there and back? to get in and get out?). Use
additional copies of this form if necessary.

Rank (1 = Most Difficult)	Situation or Place
_____	_____
_____	_____
_____	_____
_____	_____
_____	_____
_____	_____
_____	_____
_____	_____
_____	_____
_____	_____
_____	_____
_____	_____
_____	_____

Levels of Anxiety

Date: _____

Use this form to identify how you experience (physically feel) anxiety. The five levels you define here will be used in desensitization training. Common anxiety responses include sweaty palms, cold hands or feet, warmth over face or neck, rapid heartbeat, weak feeling in legs, tightness in throat, dizziness, dryness in mouth, diarrhea.

Levels of Anxiety	Your Symptoms
5 Maximum Anxiety (Panic)	
4 High Anxiety	
3 Moderate Anxiety	
2 Mild Anxiety	
1 Minimum Anxiety	

From *Managing Your Anxiety* by Christopher J. McCullough and Robert Woods Mann. Published by Jeremy P. Tarcher, Inc. Copyright © 1985 by Christopher J. McCullough and Robert Woods Mann.

Successive-Approximations Training

Date: _____

You can keep a record of your progress in successive-approximations training on this chart.

	Trial																				
GOAL	1	2	3	4	5	6	7	8	9	10	11	12	13	14	15	16	17	18	19	20	21
1																					
2																					
3																					
4																					

5 _____

6 _____

7 _____

8 _____

9 _____

Situation Hierarchy

Date: _____

Use this form to break down an anxiety-arousing place or situation into manageable pieces or smaller situations. Start with the least anxiety-arousing aspect (1) and the most anxiety-arousing aspect (9). Fill in intermediate situations (2–8). These will be successive goals in successive-approximations training.

Describe Location or Situation

9

8

7

6

5

4

3

2

1

From *Managing Your Anxiety* by Christopher J. McCullough and Robert Woods Mann. Published by Jeremy P. Tarcher, Inc. Copyright © 1985 by Christopher J. McCullough and Robert Woods Mann.

Displeasure-Frustration Inventory

Date: _____

Use this form to list your current feelings of displeasure or frustration. Describe and rank your current feelings (1 = slight, 3 = moderate, 5 = extreme). Describe your feelings and response at the time.

Situation:

What feelings do I still have about it?

How strong are those feelings? 1   2   3   4   5

What did I feel at the time?

How did I express my feelings at the time?

Situation:

What feelings do I still have about it?

How strong are those feelings? 1   2   3   4   5

What did I feel at the time?

How did I express my feelings at the time?

Situation:

What feelings do I still have about it?

How strong are those feelings? 1   2   3   4   5

What did I feel at the time?

How did I express my feelings at the time?

Worry Inventory

Date: _____

Use this form to list all of your current worries and the intensity of your feelings about these worries (1 = slight, 3 = moderate, 5 = extreme). Describe your feelings and response at the time.

What am I worried about?

How do I feel when I think about this?

How intense are these feelings? 1   2   3   4   5

If a cherished friend or child had these feelings, how could he or she decrease or eliminate this worry without creating additional problems (for example, guilt)?

What am I worried about?

How do I feel when I think about this?

How intense are these feelings? 1   2   3   4   5

If a cherished friend or child had these feelings, how could he or she decrease or eliminate this worry without creating additional problems (for example, guilt)?

Guilt Inventory

Date: _____

Use this form to list and evaluate your current feelings of guilt, embarrassment, and shame (1 = slight, 3 = moderate, 5 = extreme). Describe your feelings and response at the time.

What do I feel guilty, embarrassed, or ashamed about?

How intense are these feelings? 1   2   3   4   5

What would I say to a cherished friend or child who had these feelings?

What do I feel guilty, embarrassed, or ashamed about?

How intense are these feelings? 1   2   3   4   5

What would I say to a cherished friend or child who had these feelings?

What do I feel guilty, embarrassed, or ashamed about?

How intense are these feelings? 1   2   3   4   5

What would I say to a cherished friend or child who had these feelings?

What do I feel guilty, embarrassed, or ashamed about?

How intense are these feelings? 1   2   3   4   5

What would I say to a cherished friend or child who had these feelings?

Assertiveness Log

Date: _____

Use this form to keep a record of significant interactions with others.

What happened?

How did I feel?

What did I do/say?

Was my behavior:

__ Assertive

__ Passive

__ Aggressive

What happened?

How did I feel?

What did I do/say?

Was my behavior:

__ Assertive

__ Passive

__ Aggressive

Assertiveness Log, (*continued*)

What happened?

How did I feel?

What did I do/say?

Was my behavior:

___ Assertive

___ Passive

___ Aggressive

Negative Fantasies Inventory

Date: _____

Here are a few abbreviations you can use.

Types of negative fantasies: FA = Fantasized argument
LD = Fantasized life-or-death situation

Enjoyment: 0 = Enjoyed not at all, 5 = Enjoyed a great deal

Origin: C = Childhood, O = Other, ? = Not sure

Negative Fantasy	Type	Enjoyed (0–5)	Origin	Substitute Fantasy Resolution

From *Managing Your Anxiety* by Christopher J. McCullough and Robert Woods Mann. Published by Jeremy P. Tarcher, Inc. Copyright © 1985 by Christopher J. McCullough and Robert Woods Mann.

Negative Thoughts Inventory

Date: _____

Here are a few abbreviations you can use.
   Types of thoughts: PP = Pessimistic prediction

   NSD = Negative self-description

   WI = What-if thinking, IO = If-only thinking
   Origin: C = Childhood, O = Other, ? = Not sure

Negative Thought	Type	Origin	Substitute Thought

From *Managing Your Anxiety* by Christopher J. McCullough and Robert Woods Mann. Published by Jeremy P. Tarcher, Inc. Copyright © 1985 by Christopher J. McCullough and Robert Woods Mann.

Relaxation Scripts

INCREASING AWARENESS OF MUSCULAR TENSION AND MUSCULAR RELAXATION

Lie down comfortably on your back and take two or three slow, deep breaths from your abdomen.

The objective of this exercise is to help you increase your awareness of the difference between muscular activity and inactivity. As Dr. Edmund Jacobson—the developer of progressive relaxation—discovered many years ago, the startle reaction occurs very easily in people who habitually and unthinkingly contract their muscles to some degree.

We now understand that this continuous unnecessary muscular work produces the by-product lactate, which—in sufficient quantity—is associated with nervous overreactivity. Indeed, this unnecessary work may be the reason, or at least one reason, why excess lactate is found in the blood of habitually anxious people. As you become more aware of the difference between muscular activity and inactivity, you can learn to refrain from habitually contracting your muscles. By doing this, especially if you improve your nutrition and other self-care practices at the same time, you can reduce the amount of lactate entering your bloodstream; you will reduce the number of startle reactions you experience; and you can increase your overall sense of well-being.

While you are doing this exercise—or any exercise—be careful not to jerk or strain your muscles.

Imagine that you are holding the neck of a heavy sack of gold coins with your left hand. Now lift it up into the air, feeling the weight of the sack in your hand and in your entire left arm. Count slowly to five, using your inhalations and exhalations to pace your counting: one . . . two . . . three . . .

follow the stream up the canyon to its source, an abundant spring surrounded by palm trees. You remove your clothes and bathe in the comfortably cool water, sitting in a niche in a boulder that fits your body.

You feel totally secure and at peace. Everything seems to be in its place. Everything seems to fit together. When you gently paddle the water with your hand, you think, "Is my hand pushing the water or is the water pushing my hand?" You smile at this playful question.

You notice that a large, soft, white towel has been laid out on the sandy bank where you left your hiking boots and worn and dusty clothes, which have been replaced by a soft and beautiful tunic and sandals. Bowls of inviting fruit lie within your reach. You smile in gratitude and eat some delicious berries.

A small bird lands on a rock near you and turns its head quizzically. It seems to ask, "Is everything all right?" You nod and say, "Umm-hmmm, thank you, everything is fine." The bird makes a cheery sound and flies away.

In the clean, clear water of the spring, you can see bubbles rising up from deep within the earth. They rise to the surface and disappear.

A blind man with a full white beard, dressed in a dark robe, comes up the path to the spring. He deftly uses a staff to find his way among the boulders and sits down on one not far from you.

"Do you know what thoughts are like?" he asks.

"Um-hmmm," you reply. "They are like these bubbles."

"Ah yes, the bubbles," he says with a smile. "Do you know what emotional reactions are like?"

"Umm-hmmm. They are the ways we have learned to physically and psychologically respond to thoughts and other events. For example, if the thought 'I am helpless' arises, the muscles in my neck and shoulders may contract, I may clench my teeth and hold my breath. The thought 'I need help' or 'I want to reach safety' may arise."

four . . . five. Observe how your fingers and hand feel. Observe how the muscles in your forearm feel. Observe how the biceps muscle in your upper arm feels. Now drop the sack and let your arm fall to your side. Starting with your fingers, observe the feelings in your left hand and arm all the way up to your shoulder.

Now imagine that your left arm is floating in warm water and that with your right hand you are reaching for the neck of a very heavy sack of diamonds. This sack is just as heavy as the sack of gold coins you just lifted with your left hand. Now, lift it up into the air, feeling the weight of the sack in your hand and in your entire right arm. Your right arm is doing work, while your left arm is floating effortlessly in the warm water. Compare the way the fingers of your right hand feel with the way the fingers of your left hand feel. Compare the way your right hand and forearm feel with the way your left hand and forearm feel. Compare the way the biceps muscle in your right arm feels with the way the biceps in your left arm feels. Observe whether you are inadvertently and unnecessarily contracting the muscles of your left arm. Now count slowly to five, using your inhalations and exhalations to pace your counting: one . . . two . . . three . . . four . . . five. Now drop the sack and let your right arm fall to your side.

Now imagine that both of your arms are passively floating in warm water and are being gently massaged with tender, loving care by skilled nurses. The nurses are massaging your fingers. One of them humorously says, "Let your fingers be as limp as spaghetti." The other says, "Yes, let your hands and arms be as limp as spaghetti. Let them feel warm and heavy as we massage them for a moment."

The muscles in your arms are now not tense or contracted. They are not doing any work at all. They are not producing excess lactate. You are not doing anything with them. Enjoy the pleasant feeling in both your arms. This feeling is given the name "relaxation." Relaxation is not something you *do.*

It is the absence of effort. It is the absence of physical work. It is the absence of muscular contraction.

Imagine that you are a movie actor playing the hero of one of the tales of "A Thousand and One Nights." You have been falsely accused of stealing the largest sapphire in the world from the Caliph of Bagdad. You are to be crushed to death by a huge block of stone (which is really a prop made of styrofoam). As you perform for the camera, you are chained to the spot and the block of stone is being lowered onto your shoulders. You struggle and strain and bring your shoulders up to your ears and try to hold the massive weight with your neck, shoulders, and upper back. You can feel tension in your shoulders as you struggle to support the weight that is slowly being lowered onto them. Now, as the weight becomes heavier and heavier, count slowly to five, using your inhalations and exhalations to pace your counting: one . . . two . . . three . . . four . . . five.

The director yells, "Cut! It's lunchtime!" and you stand up straight, lower your shoulders, shove the big block of styrofoam aside, and step out of the chains. One of your co-workers massages your shoulders and back for you. Again you count slowly to five, using your inhalations and exhalations to pace your counting. This time you release more and more tension from your shoulders each time you count: One . . . two . . . three . . . four . . . five. Your neck and shoulders and upper back feel pleasantly warm and heavy. Many people carry unnecessary tension in their shoulders and neck, as though they were carrying a heavy weight or bracing for a heavy blow. Whenever you remember this exercise, check your neck, shoulders, upper back for unnecessary tension, take a deep breath, and release the tension, allowing your shoulders to settle down.

The muscles in your neck, shoulders, and upper back are now not tense or contracted. They are not doing any work at all. They are not producing excess lactate. You are not doing anything with them. Enjoy the pleasant feeling in them.

This feeling is given the name "relaxation." Relaxation is not something you *do*. It is the absence of effort. It is the absence of physical work. It is the absence of muscular contraction.

Now raise your eyebrows and wrinkle your brow tightly. Count to five as before: one . . . two . . . three . . . four . . . five. Now frown, pushing your eyebrows down as far as you can. Count to five: one . . . two . . . three . . . four . . . five. Now raise your eyebrows again and wrinkle your brow tightly. Now frown, pushing your eyebrows down as far as you can. Now allow your forehead to rest. The muscles in your forehead are now not tense or contracted. They are not doing any work at all. You are not doing anything with them. Enjoy the pleasant feeling in your forehead. This feeling is given the name "relaxation."

Now tense the muscles around your eyes tightly. Count to five as before: one . . . two . . . three . . . four . . . five. Now allow the muscles around your eyes to rest.

Now tighten your jaw and squeeze your lips tightly together. Count to five: one . . . two . . . three . . . four . . . five. Now allow your jaw and lips to rest. Your upper and lower teeth should not be touching.

The muscles of your face are now not tense or contracted. They are not doing any work at all. You are not doing anything with them. Enjoy the pleasant feeling in your face. This feeling is called "relaxation." Relaxation is not something you *do*. It is the absence of effort. It is the absence of physical work. It is the absence of muscular contraction.

Many people carry unnecessary tension in their face and jaw, as though they were warding off a blow. Whenever you remember this exercise, check your face and jaw for muscular tension. Let the muscles around your eyes and mouth relax. Smile inwardly to yourself and feel muscles around your mouth form a smile. They are working for you. You are smiling with them. Enjoy this pleasant feeling. Whenever you remember this exercise, relax and then smile inwardly.

AUTOGENIC TRAINING

Sit or lie down comfortably.

Your eyes can be open or closed, whichever is most comfortable for you. If you keep your eyes open, let your gaze rest easily and comfortably on the ceiling, wall, or floor. Do not stare fixedly at one spot.

Picture someone who is sitting or lying down as you are, someone who is completely relaxed. Repeat each of the following formulas two or three times, at a very leisurely pace:

"I feel mentally alert and physically relaxed."

Now picture the feet of the relaxed person.

"My feet feel heavy, warm, and relaxed."

Now picture the ankles of the relaxed person.

"My ankles feel heavy, warm, and relaxed."

Now picture the knees and calves of the relaxed person.

"My knees and calves feel heavy, warm, and relaxed."

Now picture the thighs of the relaxed person.

"My thighs feel heavy, warm, and relaxed."

Now picture the abdomen, hips, and buttocks of the relaxed person.

"My abdomen, hips, and buttocks feel heavy, warm, and relaxed."

Now picture the lower back of the relaxed person.

"My lower back feels heavy, warm, and relaxed."

Now picture the chest and mid-back of the relaxed person.

"My chest and mid-back feel heavy, warm, and relaxed."

Now picture the shoulders, neck, and upper back of the relaxed person.

"My shoulders, neck, and upper back feel heavy, warm, and relaxed."

Now picture the arms and hands of the relaxed person.

"My arms and hands feel heavy, warm, and relaxed."

Now picture the scalp of the relaxed person.

"My scalp feels heavy, warm, and relaxed."

Now picture the throat of the relaxed person.

"My throat feels heavy, warm, and relaxed."

Now picture the face and jaw of the relaxed person.

"My face and jaw feel heavy, warm, and relaxed."

Picture yourself in a cozy cabin in the snow country, warming your hands before a cheerful fire in the fireplace.

"My hands are warm."
"I can feel the pleasant warmth on my hands."
"Warmth is flowing into my hands. They are pleasantly warm."

"I feel inwardly and outwardly alert and physically relaxed."

Picture your breaths coming in through the soles of your feet and sweeping through your entire body. As you exhale, imagine your fears, worries, and negative thoughts being washed out of your body.

"Pure, cleansing air is sweeping through my body."

"It is washing away fears, worries, and negative thoughts."

"Pure, cleansing air is sweeping through my body."

"It is washing away fears, worries, and negative thoughts."

"I feel life and energy flowing up my legs, through my abdomen, solar plexus, chest, arms and hands, neck, shoulders, head, and face."

"I feel deeply refreshed and full of vibrant energy."

"I feel light, alive, and energetic."

Now, if your eyes are closed, open them. Take a deep breath, stretch your arms out, and twist your body gently from side to side several times to conclude this exercise.

VISUALIZATION

Lie comfortably on your back and yawn once or twice. When you yawn, you automatically breathe deeply, from your abdomen. The object of this exercise is to help you release muscular tension in your body by reminding you of conditions in which you have felt very peaceful and relaxed.

It is a warm morning in the desert. The fragrance of sage and wildflowers is carried in the warm air. You stand at the mouth of a canyon. A stream of crystal-clear water runs past your feet. You are hot and tired, and you kneel down and refresh yourself with a drink of this clean, clear water. You

"Does all of our behavior consist of these emotional reactions?"

"Unfortunately, this seems to be true for most of us most of the time," you reply.

"Is there any escape from emotional reactions?" the man asks.

"No escape is needed if we are able to recognize such thoughts as 'I am helpless,' 'I need help,' or 'I want to reach safety' not as things with the power to govern us or trap us, but as reflections of the past conditions of our lives.

"Every time any thought arises or any event occurs, we are at a point of choice. This choosing point is our freedom. We are always free to choose between reacting emotionally or simply allowing the bubbles—whether they are thoughts or traffic sounds or the sounds of birds singing or dogs barking—to move through our awareness."

"You have much understanding," he tells you.

"My wish is to put this understanding to use in my everyday life. In this, I am just a beginner. I often carry anger, resentment, and worries on my back."

"Even so, your answers are honest and pleasing. As you may have guessed—since this is an imaginary visualization exercise—I have the power to grant you three wishes. What three things would you wish for yourself and for all people?"

Go ahead and make these three wishes. Speak out loud if you wish.

After a moment, the blind man says, "Remember your freedom to choose. You can do small things every day to help make these wishes come true in your life and in the lives of others. Stay with us as long you like and return here whenever you like. Your clothes are being washed and mended. They will be returned to you shortly. For now, I bid you adieu."

When you wish to conclude this visualization, yawn once or twice and clap your hands together three times. You will feel invigorated and refreshed, and your heart will be full of compassion for yourself and others.

QUIET SITTING (A SIMPLE
RELAXED-AWARENESS EXERCISE)

Follow the general guidelines given for relaxation in regard to posture, clothing, and so forth.

Sitting up in a comfortable, very stable, and balanced position, choose one or two breathing exercises to begin your period of quiet sitting. For example, you might take three abdominal breaths while releasing tension from your shoulders as you exhale.

Affirm your right to sit quietly with a phrase that is meaningful to you, such as: "I now take refuge in my own inner nature, which is in harmony with the universe."

Break through any sense of loneliness or isolation by recognizing the universal nature of suffering. Choose a phrase to express this idea, such as: "I sincerely wish for compassion for myself and all others who experience anxiety and pain," or simply, "Compassion for all living creatures."

It is helpful to regard thoughts and stray noises—such as traffic noises, birds singing, dogs barking, or children playing—as bubbles rising to the surface of a liquid. You do not need to try to ignore them. Just recognize them clearly for what they are and return your attention to your breathing.

If you have a lot on your mind, you may wish to keep your notebook at hand so you can write down any thoughts that you wish to give your attention to later.

In regard to breathing, your objective is not to learn to breathe in a special way but simply to learn not to disrupt your breathing by holding your breath, or by overbreathing (hyperventilating). Allow yourself to breathe slowly, deeply, and rhythmically from your abdomen, without tensing your shoulders or chest walls. You will find that you will tend to breathe this way when you sit in a comfortable, very stable, and balanced position.

You are not trying to do anything, to gain anything, or to make something happen. You are just sitting quietly.

You can use a pocket alarm or a clock to remind you when the allotted time has passed. You may wish to begin by sitting for four or five minutes at a time several times a day. (By the way, children may enjoy sitting quietly for four or five minutes once or twice a day—but not for longer periods.)

Several short sessions (as many as 8 or 16 a day) may be more beneficial for beginners than long sessions. If you ride to work on a bus or train, you can practice quiet sitting on the way to and from work, as well as at lunchtime and during breaks. It is good to gradually lengthen your sessions (up to a maximum of around 15 minutes) if time seems to pass slowly while you are sitting; on the other hand, if time seems to pass quickly while you are sitting, you should probably shorten your sessions.

Many people who sit regularly do so for 10 or 15 minutes once or twice a day. The morning is an especially good time to sit, and many people find sitting at bedtime to be beneficial in helping them work through the events of the day and prepare for a good night's sleep.

Suggested Readings

ASSERTIVENESS

Butler, Pamela E. *Self-Assertion for Women*. New York: Harper & Row, 1976. Practical techniques for reconciling the "feminine" value of compassion with the "masculine" value of self-reliance. Instructive for men as well as for women.

Cooper, Morton. *Change Your Voice, Change Your Life: A Quick, Simple Plan for Finding and Using Your Natural Dynamic Voice*. New York: Macmillan, 1984. A simple technique that can be learned in 5 minutes for eliminating stress and strain from your voice and speaking more expressively.

Gordon, Thomas. *Leader Effectiveness Training*. New York: Wyden Books, 1977. Communications skills and problem-solving techniques for managers and leaders. Useful for everyone in everyday life.

Gordon, Thomas. *Parent Effectiveness Training*. New York: Wyden Books, 1970. Practical problem-solving and communications skills for parents.

EXERCISE

Anderson, James L., and Cohen, Martin. *The West Point Fitness and Diet Book*. New York: Rawson Associates, 1977. Good practical advice about exercise and physical fitness.

Cooper, Kenneth H. *The New Aerobics*. New York: Bantam, 1970. Dr. Cooper, of the U.S. Air Force Medical Corps, introduced the concept of aerobic exercise a little over 15 years ago. This book describes the aerobic exercise program adopted by the U.S. Air Force and Navy and by the Royal Canadian Air Force. Especially helpful for people over 30, it can help you determine appropriate levels of exercise for your age, sex, and general condition. The starting point of the program is a medical checkup by a physician.

Hittleman, Richard A. *Yoga for Personal Living.* New York: Warner, 1972. An illustrated guide to simple stretching exercises.

GENERAL HEALTH
The Planetree Health Resource Center publishes an excellent catalog of self-care books, products, and cassette tapes. Copies may be obtained from the Center at 2040 Webster St., San Francisco, CA 94115.

MEDITATION, FREEDOM, AND SELF-CONTROL
Carrington, Patricia. *Freedom in Meditation.* New York: Anchor Press/Doubleday, 1977. An authoritative handbook on meditation from the point of view of Western clinical psychology. Includes much practical advice on meditation techniques.

The 14th Dalai Lama, His Holiness Tenzin Gyatso. *Kindness, Clarity, and Insight.* Edited and translated by Jeffrey Hopkins; coedited by Elizabeth Napper. Ithaca, N.Y.: Snow Lion, 1984. This is a collection of talks given by the Dalai Lama on his recent tour of North America. The Dalai Lama is the head of the Tibetan Buddhist religion, which joins Buddhist philosophy with the older Tibetan religion. Within Tibetan Buddhism, a highly developed meditative tradition has flourished for centuries.

Hirai, Tomio. *Zen and the Mind: Scientific Approach to Zen Practice.* Tokyo: Japan Publications, 1978. Dr. Hirai, a psychiatrist, explains the physiological effects of meditation and offers practical guidance regarding meditative posture, breathing, and concentration.

Suzuki, Shunryu. *Zen Mind, Beginner's Mind.* New York: Weatherhill, 1973. In 1958, at the age of 53, Shunryu Suzuki came to San Francisco, where he headed the Soto Zen mission and founded the San Francisco Zen Center. This book contains transcriptions of his informal talks on meditation and practice. Reading it is like being in the presence of a great teacher. Half the time you are perplexed, and half the time you discover something you had not noticed before. Soto Zen emphasizes cultivating the direct experience of reality and freedom through quiet sitting.

Tarthang, Tulku. *Gesture of Balance: A Guide to Awareness, Self-Healing, and Meditation.* Berkeley: Dharma, 1977. A Tibetan Buddhist teacher discusses basic meditative practices as they relate to present-day America, in clear and simple language. Many people have found this to be a calming and comforting book. There is a passing reference to reincarnation, but the book is not based on religious beliefs so much as on Buddhist philosophy and psychology.

NUTRITION

Abbey, Laraine C. Nutritionist Abbey has worked on diet improvement with many people suffering from agoraphobia. A brochure listing available reprinted newspaper columns by Abbey may be obtained by sending a stamped, self-addressed envelope to Laraine C. Abbey, R.N., M.S., Warren Plaza, West-Route 130, E. Windsor, N.J. 08520.

Bronson Pharmaceuticals. Bronson sells vitamins by mail. They offer free literature on supplemental vitamins and minerals, including the article "On Good Nutrition for the Good Life" by Linus Pauling, which appeared in the *Executive Health* newsletter in January 1981. To request this literature, write to Bronson Pharmaceuticals, 4526 Rinetti Lane, La Cañada, Calif. 91011–0628. (We do not endorse or recommend Bronson products over those of other pharmaceutical companies.)

Mindell, Earl. *Earl Mindell's Vitamin Bible.* New York: Warner Books, 1979. Much helpful information from a nutritionist and pharmacist about vitamins and minerals. Designed to help the reader determine his or her particular needs, in consultation with a physician.

Nutrition Almanac, 2d ed. New York: McGraw-Hill Paperbacks, 1985. This popular handbook is a good reference for the vitamin and mineral contents of foods and the relation of vitamin and mineral deficiencies to health problems.

Ornish, Dean. *Stress, Diet and Your Heart.* New York: Holt, Rinehart & Winston, 1982. Dr. Ornish, of the Harvard Medical School, states the case for a low-fat diet and also covers stress-management techniques. The book includes many recipes for vegetable dishes that utilize the underrated complex-carbohydrate foods plus herbs and spices.

Passwater, Richard A. *Supernutrition: Megavitamin Revolution.* New York: Pocket Books, 1976. Passwater presents the case for megavitamin (orthomolecular) therapy to improve physical and mental well-being. In a preface for physicians, Dr. Raymond F. Chen characterizes the traditional medical approach to nutrition as being based on a "two-state" theory: that one is either sick or is well. As Chen sees it, this theory "runs counter to common sense . . . health has many gradations." He supports Passwater and Pauling's view that nutrition may make the difference between suboptimal health and optimal health and well-being.

Rosenberg, Harold, with Feldzamen, A. N. *The Book of Vitamin Therapy.* New York: Putnam's, 1974. Discusses how to determine optimum amounts of vitamins and minerals to meet individual needs.

Understanding Vitamins and Minerals. The Prevention Total Health System Series. Emmaus, Pa.: 1984. A good reference volume with up-to-date information about vitamin and mineral supplements.

PHOBIAS AND AGORAPHOBIA

The Phobia Society of America publishes a newsletter for its members and publishes helpful booklets about phobias and agoraphobia. For a free list of available publications, write to the Phobia Society of America, Publications Department, 5820 Hubbard Dr., Rockville, Md. 20852.

Weekes, Claire. *Simple, Effective Treatment of Agoraphobia.* New York: Bantam, 1979. Dr. Weekes shares many insights into the problem of agoraphobia and explains her "four concepts" technique for coping with anxiety attacks.

PHILOSOPHY AND PSYCHOLOGY

Dyer, Wayne. *Gifts from Eykis.* New York: Pocket Books, 1983. Under the guise of writing a fantasy novel, popular psychologist Dyer explores the logic (or illogic) of such statements as "Elevators scare me," and, "My father is to blame for the way I am today," in conversations with a being from another planet.

Kalupahana, David J. *Buddhist Philosophy: A Historical Analysis.* Honolulu: University of Hawaii, 1976. A scholarly account of the development of Buddhist thought.

Mayeroff, Milton. *On Caring.* New York: Harper & Row, 1971. Mayeroff writes, "In the sense in which a man can ever be said to be at home in the world, he is at home not through dominating, or explaining, or appreciating, but through caring and being cared for." Mayeroff places the idea of self-care in the context of compassion for oneself and others.

Needleman, Jacob, and Lewis, Dennis, eds. *On the Way to Self-Knowledge.* New York: Knopf, 1976. This book contains chapters on psychiatry and the sacred; the Christian sacred tradition; and Tibetan Buddhism.

Pelletier, Kenneth. *Mind as Healer, Mind as Slayer.* New York: Delacorte, 1977. This important book moves us past the idea of "psychosomatic" illness to the understanding that good health always has physical, psychological, and cognitive dimensions. Pelletier shows how certain unrealistic beliefs and habitual patterns of behavior come to be manifested in psychological stress, anxiety, and physical diseases.

Rahula, Walpola. *What the Buddha Taught.* New York: Grove Press, 1974. Dr. Rahula, a Buddhist monk and scholar, presents an authoritative account of the teachings of the philosopher Siddhattha Gotama, who came to be called "the Buddha" (the enlightened one).

Yalom, Irvin D. *Existential Psychotherapy.* New York: Basic Books, 1980. Examines the beliefs and assumptions that underlie severe and pervasive anxiety. Considers the relation of existential philosophical concepts to the problem of exaggerated anxiety.

PSYCHOLOGY (SELF-HELP)

Ellis, Albert, and Harper, Robert A. *A New Guide to Rational Living.* North Hollywood, California: Wiltshire Book Company, 1975. The "rational-emotive therapy" described addresses the illogical beliefs by which many of us attempt to live our lives.

Fensterheim, Herbert, and Baer, Jean. *Stop Running Scared!* New York: Dell, 1977. Many of Christopher's clients report they have found this book helpful in working on cognitive issues.

Halpern, Howard M. *Cutting Loose: An Adult Guide to Coming to Terms with Your Parents.* New York: Bantam, 1978. Psychotherapist Halpern offers guidance for dealing with your "inner child" as well as for putting the relations between adult children and their parents on an appropriately realistic basis.

Jacobson, Edmund. *Progressive Relaxation*. Chicago: University of Chicago Press, 1929. In his classic book, Dr. Jacobson contends (1) "to be excited and relaxed are physiological opposites" and (2) "The easiest thing in the world is not to be nervous. There's nothing easier because it involves no work."

Rubin, Theodore Isaac. *The Angry Book*. New York: Collier, 1969. In this anecdotal book, Dr. Rubin has a great deal to say about angry feelings and the problems that arise when we fail to confront or recognize them. Some of the points he makes are quite valuable to those who tend to convert their angry feelings into anxiety.

Shealy, C. Norman. *90 Days to Self-Health*. New York: Dial, 1977. Dr. Shealy provides many excellent relaxation exercises in his systematic self-care program.

Stroebel, Charles F. *QR: The Quieting Reflex*. New York: Berkeley, 1982. Dr. Stroebel's book about his excellent stress-reduction technique.

PLANNING AND ORGANIZATION

Lakein, Alan. *How to Get Control of Your Time and Your Life*. New York: Wyden Books, 1973. A practical guide to planning and organizing the use of time in the workplace and at home.

Suggested Cassette Tapes

Ellis, Albert. *He Who Hesitates is Lost.* A cassette tape available from *Psychology Today* magazine (see below).

Hearts of Space. "Hearts of Space" is a music program that is broadcast on public radio stations around the country. A catalog of "new age" music—music for relaxation and reflection—is available for $1 from Hearts of Space, P.O. Box 31321, San Francisco, Calif. 94131. Enclose a stamped, self-addressed envelope with two first-class stamps.

Jacobson, Edmund, and McGuigan, F. J. *Principles and Practice of Progressive Relaxation.* An audio cassette program available from ISHK Book Service, P.O. Box 176, Los Altos, Calif. 94022. Dr. Jacobson is a leading scientist in the field of behavior therapy and the developer of the progressive relaxation technique.

McCullough, Christopher, and Mann, Robert Woods. Several relaxation and other cassette tapes developed for use with our original self-care program are available from the San Francisco Phobia Recovery Center, P.O. Box 40308, San Francisco, Calif. 94110.

New Dimensions Radio. "New Dimensions" is an interview program broadcast on public radio stations. Many of the programs deal with meditation, psychology, and Eastern thought. Cassette tapes of these programs are available from New Dimensions Radio, 267 States St., San Francisco, Calif. 94114.

Planetree Health Resource Center. The Planetree catalog lists relaxation tapes. See the General Health listing in the Suggested Reading section.

Psychology Today. A wide selection of relaxation tapes is available from the cassette tape division of *Psychology Today* magazine. For information, write: Psychology Today Tapes, P.O. Box 770, Pratt Station, Brooklyn, New York 11205.

Stroebel, Charles F. *Quieting Reflex Training for Adults.* Bio-monitoring Audiocassettes. New York: Guilford Publications, 1978. Stroebel, E., and Stroebel, Charles F. *Kiddie QR.* A children's version of the QR techniques. Wethersfield, Conn.: QR Publications, 1980.

Weekes, Claire. *Hope and Help for Your Nerves.* Recordings by Dr. Weekes on long-playing records or cassette tapes are available from Galahad Productions, P.O. Box 5893, Lake Charles, La. 70601.

Bibliography

See the list of Suggested Readings for other books cited in the text.

"Agoraphobia Update." *The Harvard Medical School Health Letter*, January 1985.

Beck, Alan, and Katcher, Aaron. *Between Pets and People: The Importance of Animal Companionship.* New York: Putnam's, 1983.

Benson, Herbert. *The Relaxation Response.* New York: Morrow, 1975.

Berelson, Bernard, and Steiner, Gary A. *Human Behavior: An Inventory of Scientific Findings.* New York: Harcourt, Brace, & World, 1964.

Bowlby, John. *Separation: Anxiety and Anger.* Attachment and Loss, vol. 2. New York: Basic Books, 1973.

Brown, Barbara B. *Stress and the Art of Biofeedback.* New York: Bantam, 1978.

Cotler, Sherwin B. "Assertion Training." In *Modern Therapies,* edited by Virginia Binder, Arnold Binder, and Bernard Rimland. Englewood Cliffs, N.J.: Spectrum, 1976.

Cousins, Norman. *Anatomy of an Illness as Perceived by the Patient: Reflections on Healing and Regeneration.* New York: Norton, 1979.

Ellis, Albert. *Humanistic Psychotherapy: The Rational Emotive Approach.* New York: McGraw-Hill, 1973.

"Exercises for Relaxed Travel." *American Way,* August 1984.

Goleman, Daniel. "Psychology of East Gaining Attention in Western World." *The New York Times,* 9 October 1984.

Gray, Jeffrey. *The Psychology of Fear and Stress.* New York: McGraw-Hill, 1978.

Hawkins, David, and Pauling, Linus, eds. *Orthomolecular Psychiatry: Treatment of Schizophrenia.* New York: W. H. Freeman & Company, 1973.

Horney, Karen. *Self-Analysis.* New York: Norton, 1942.

Jacobson, Edmund. *Anxiety and Tension Control: A Physiologic Approach.* Philadelphia: Lippincott, 1964.

Jacobson, Edmund. *Progressive Relaxation.* 2d ed. reprint. Chicago: University of Chicago, 1974.

James, William. *The Principles of Psychology*. New York: Henry Holt & Co., 1980.

Kapleau, Philip, ed. and trans. *The Three Pillars of Zen: Teaching, Practice, and Enlightenment*. New York: Harper & Row, 1969.

Koestenbaum, Peter. *Managing Anxiety: The Power of Knowing Who You Are*. Englewood Cliffs, N.J.: Spectrum, 1974.

Koestenbaum, Peter. *The New Image of the Person: The Theory and Practice of Clinical Philosophy*. Westport, Conn.: Greenwood Press, 1978.

Longo, Vincenzo G. *Neuropharmacology and Behavior*. New York: W. H. Freeman & Company, 1972.

Mahler, Margaret S. *On Human Symbiosis and the Vicissitudes of Individuation*. New York: International Universities Press, 1968.

Mahler, Margaret S.; Pine, Fred; and Bergman, Anni. *The Psychological Birth of the Human Infant: Symbiosis and Individuation*. New York: Basic Books, 1975.

Malcolm, Janet. "The Patient is Always Right." *The New York Review of Books*, 20 December 1984, pp. 13–18.

May, Rollo. *The Meaning of Anxiety*. Rev. ed. New York: Norton, 1977.

Pauling, Linus. *Vitamin C, the Common Cold, and the Flu*. New York: W. H. Freeman & Company, 1976.

Pitts, Ferris N., Jr. "The Biochemistry of Anxiety." *Scientific American*, February 1969, pp. 69–75.

Rachlin, Howard. *Introduction to Modern Behaviorism*. 2d ed. New York: W. H. Freeman & Company, 1976.

Robins, Lee N., *et al.* "Lifetime Prevalence of Specific Psychiatric Disorders in Three Sites." *Archives of General Psychiatry*, vol. 41, October 1984. (This is the study cited in Chapter 1 that was sponsored by the National Institute of Mental Health.)

Sheehan, David V. *The Anxiety Disease*. New York: Scribners, 1983.

Stern, Barbara Lang. "Calm Down in Six Seconds: How to Handle Stress with Fast Method." *Vogue*, October 1981.

Name Index

Subject Index